# ECONOMIC DEVELOPMENT AND UN REFORM

## TOWARDS A COMMON AGENDA FOR ACTION

# ECONOMIC DEVELOPMENT AND UN REFORM

TOWARDS A COMMON AGENDA FOR ACTION

## A PROPOSAL IN THE CONTEXT OF THE MILLENNIUM DEVELOPMENT GOALS

by Carlos A. Magariños

UNITED NATIONS INDUSTRIAL DEVELOPMENT ORGANIZATION

Vienna, 2005

The views expressed in this publication are those of the authors and do not necessarily reflect the views of the Secretariat of the United Nations Industrial Development Organization. The description and classification of countries and territories used, and the arrangements of the material, do not imply the expression of any opinion whatsoever on the part of the Secretariat concerning the legal status of any country, territory, city or area, or of its authorities, or concerning the delimitation of its frontiers or boundaries, or regarding its economic system or degree of development. Designations such as "developed", "industrialized" and "developing" are intended for statistical convenience and do not necessarily express a judgment about the state reached by a particular country or area in the development process. Mention of firm names and commercial products does not imply the endorsement of the United Nations Industrial Development Organization.

ID/423

UNIDO Publication
Sales No.: E.05.II.B24
ISBN 92-1-106431-7

*This book and the proposal contained in it are intended to pay homage to the many lives risked and lost and the generous energies invested by those men and women who still believe — in spite of the injustice and oppression that prevails in many quarters — that a better world is possible and that we all have a role to play in building it, to achieve the ideals of freedom, equity, peace and development for the generations to come.*

*On a more personal note I would like to dedicate this work to my wife Belén, who supports me, and gives me the strength to continue believing and dedicating my best thoughts to those ideals while, at the same time, allowing me to recall the extraordinary importance of the simple miracle of every day life. Finally, my gratitude goes to the newcomer, Tomás, for bringing a new perspective to my life and my work.*

# CONTENTS

# ACRONYMS

| | |
|---|---|
| ACC | Administrative Committee on Coordination |
| ADM | Division of Administration |
| ATS | Austrian schilling |
| AWPB | Annual Work Plan/Budget |
| BWIs | Bretton Woods Institutions |
| CCAs | common country assessments |
| CEB | Chief Executives Board for Coordination |
| CEOs | Chief Executive Officers |
| CFCs | Chlorofluorocarbons |
| CPAP | Country Programme Action Plan |
| CPC | Committee for Programme and Coordination |
| CSOs | Civil Society Organizations |
| CSR | Corporate Social Responsibility |
| CTCs | UN Centre for Transnational Corporations |
| DAC | Development Assistance Committee |
| DDSMS | Department for Development Support and Management Services |
| DESA | Department of Economic and Social Affairs |
| DESIPA | Department of Economic and Social Information and Policy Analysis |
| DFID | Department for International Development |
| DPCSD | Department of Policy Coordination and Sustainable Development |
| ECHA | Executive Committee on Humanitarian Affairs |
| ECOSOC | United Nations Economic and Social Council |
| EPTA | Expanded Programme of Technical Assistance |
| EU | European Union |
| FAO | Food and Agriculture Organization |
| FDI | foreign direct investment |
| G-18 | Group of 18 |
| G-77 | Group of 77 |
| GA | General Assembly |
| GDP | gross domestic product |
| GEF | Global Environment Facility |
| GNI | gross national income |
| HIV/AIDS | Human Immuno-Deficiency Virus/Acquired Immuno-Deficiency Syndrome |

| | |
|---|---|
| HLCP | High Level Committee on Programmes |
| IAEA | International Atomic Energy Agency |
| IBRD | International Bank for Reconstruction and Development |
| ICT | information and communication technologies |
| IDA | International Development Association |
| IDB | Industrial Development Board |
| IDDA | Industrial Development Decade for Africa |
| IDF | Industrial Development Fund |
| IFC | International Finance Corporation |
| ILO | International Labour Organization |
| IMF | International Monetary Fund |
| IPF | Indicative Planning Figure |
| IPRs | Intellectual Property Rights |
| IPs | Integrated Programmes |
| ITCs | International Trade Centre |
| JIU | Joint Inspection Unit |
| JPOs | Junior Professional Officers |
| LDCs | least developed countries |
| MDGs | Millennium Development Goals |
| MNCs | multinational corporations |
| MOU | Memorandum of Understanding |
| MP | Montreal Protocol |
| MYFF | multi-year funding frameworks |
| NCPCs | National Cleaner Production Centres |
| NIEO | New International Economic Order |
| OCG | Office of the Comptroller General |
| ODA | Official Development Assistance |
| OECD | Organization for Economic Cooperation and Development |
| OPEC | Organization of the Petroleum Exporting Countries |
| PACs | Programme and Project Approval Committees |
| PBC | Programme and Budget Committee |
| PCF | Programme Coordination and Field Operations Division |
| POPs | Persistent Organic Pollutants |
| PRGF | Poverty Reduction and Growth Facility |
| PRSPs | Poverty Reduction Strategy Papers |
| PSD | private sector development |
| PTC | Programme Development and Technical Cooperation Division |
| R&D | research and development |
| RBM | results-based management |
| RCS | Resident Coordinator System |
| RCs | Resident Coordinators |
| SF | Special Fund |
| SMEs | small and medium-sized enterprises |

| | |
|---|---|
| SUNFED | Special UN Fund for Economic Development |
| SSA | Sub-Saharan Africa |
| TFP | total factor productivity |
| TNCs | transnational corporations |
| UK | United Kingdom |
| UN | United Nations |
| UNCED | United Nations Conference on Environment and Development |
| UNCTAD | United Nations Conference on Trade and Development |
| UNCTs | United Nations Country Teams |
| UNDA | United Nations Development Agency |
| UNDAF | United Nations Development Assistance Framework |
| UNDG | United Nations Development Group |
| UNDP | United Nations Development Programme |
| UNEP | United Nations Environment Programme |
| UNESCO | United Nations Educational, Scientific and Cultural Organization |
| UNFIP | United Nations Fund for International Partnership |
| UNFPA | United Nations Population Fund |
| UNHCR | United Nations High Commissioner for Refugees |
| UNICEF | United Nations Children's Fund |
| UNIDO | United Nations Industrial Development Organization |
| UNO | United Nations Organization |
| UNOID | United Nations Organization for Industrial Development |
| UNOPS | United Nations Office for Project Services |
| UNU | United Nations University |
| USG | Under-Secretary-General |
| USSR | Union of Soviet Socialist Republics |
| WFP | World Food Programme |
| WHO | World Health Organization |
| WTO | World Trade Organization |
| WWII | World War II |

# ACKNOWLEDGEMENTS

This book would have not been written without the collaboration of three persons: Francisco Sercovich, Sajjad Ajmal and Doris Hribernigg.

Francisco Sercovich helped me to develop many of the ideas contained in these pages and took the pain of reading the many manuscripts and supervising the publication of the book. Anything I can write here would fall short of expressing the enormous gratitude I feel for him and his tireless work.

Sajjad Ajmal wrote almost the complete second part of the present book, reorganizing the information contained in a previous work on UN reform, adding a lot of new information and actualizing developments related with UNIDO's reform process. He managed to do so in addition to his already very heavy schedule of work and I am very grateful to him for documenting the Agency's record.

Readers may notice the use of two quite different writing styles for the two parts of the book; this is deliberate. Precisely because the proposal contained in the first part reflects my own views, and not necessarily those of UNIDO, I have written it in the first person singular. The second part of the book is written in a more traditional manner as it represents a factual account of the history of reform of UNIDO, albeit including the last seven years under my leadership.

Doris Hribernigg organized the information required for chapters two and three and produced a very complete version of chapter three. Her rigorous analysis helped me to give form to many of the central arguments of the book. I am most grateful to her.

Fernando Riquelme Lidon, Adrie De Groot, Octavio Maizza Netto and Nilmadhab Mohanty revised the manuscript and gave relevant opinions. My gratitude goes to all of them. My special thanks go to Paul Makin for his dedicated work of editorial supervision and for securing the publication deadlines. A very special note of gratitude goes to Julio Camarena-Villasenor for his valuable contributions.

Professor John Ruggie of the John F. Kennedy School of Government of the Harvard University gave me inspirational support and his work in the UN was particularly relevant to shape aspects of my proposal related with the concept of issue-leadership. Professor Jeffrey Sachs, Director of the Earth Institute at Columbia University, provided comments on the first versions of the proposal that were also very useful, as was his participation at the last UNIDO General Conference and his support for the ideas I exposed there.

My gratitude goes also to Louis Frechette, Deputy Secretary-General of the United Nations, and José Antonio Ocampo, Under-Secretary-General for Economic and Social Affairs, for their support and inspiration. I am also most grateful to Klaus Topfer, Executive Director of the United Nations Environmental Programme, and to Lennart Bage, President of the International Fund for Agricultural Development, for their comments and support. I am also most grateful for the encouragement received from Yevgeny Primakov, Former Russian Prime Minister.

My dear colleagues Juan Somavia, Director-General of the International Labour Organization, Jacques Diouf, Director-General of the Food and Agriculture Organization, and Koichiro Matsuura, Director-General of the United Nations Educational, Scientific and Cultural Organization, were also a source of encouragement.

Finally, my deep and sincere gratitude goes to the staff of UNIDO and its Member States for their terrific support and encouragement. I have learnt a great deal from them.

# INTRODUCTION

CARLOS ALFREDO MAGARIÑOS
Director-General of UNIDO

This book is a practical proposal to increase the policy coherence and operational effectiveness of the UN system in the field of economic development. The proposal is based on the experience gained during my seven years of work at the helm of one of the specialized agencies of the United Nations (UN). Its core aim is to reorganize the economic development functions of the system by agreeing on a common business plan structured around shared programmatic priorities.

There are many reasons for embarking upon such an endeavor. They range from the need to modernize institutions set up about half a century ago to the need to address the acute disparities afflicting most of the developing world and to meet the challenges imposed by an increasingly regulated global trade and financial system.

I believe that the overriding motive to revise the multilateral architecture for economic development is the need to improve its contribution to the fight against poverty and the quest for global security. Nonetheless, I consider throughout the book many of the other arguments. For that purpose I have organized the discussion around two major axes: that of the 'institutional' aspects covered by most of the UN reform proposals (chapters 2 and 3) and that of the 'programmatic' challenges to be addressed by the system to improve its effectiveness (chapters 4 and 5). This is, of course, an arbitrary distinction introduced to facilitate the analysis and to simplify the key message of the book: that more attention should be given to the programmatic aspects of the reform efforts undertaken at the UN system.

The 'institutional' aspects revolve mainly around bureaucratic, administrative and financial arrangements to improve coherence at the system level, including operations in the field. The 'programmatic' challenges relate to the need to align and harmonize the normative and operational functions of the system in the field of economic development so as to maximize its contribution to the collective goals of the UN established by its Member States at the major UN conferences and summits.

Within this 'programmatic' dimension of UN reform I will address (particularly in chapter 5) a number of issues related to how the theory and practice of development economics have evolved since World War II. The knowledge and information available half a century ago, which laid the foundations for the system's current economic development architecture, remains relevant and valid to categorize the problems confronted by developing countries. However, the evolution of economic thinking, the availability of new tools of economic analysis and the new global trade and financial agreements have considerably influenced the *practice* of development economics, demanding the adaptation of the UN's economic development functions to these new realities.

One way or another, all reform proposals, although focused on managerial changes, administrative measures or institutional arrangements, contained elements of a programmatic nature. Moreover, these programmatic elements gradually grew in importance over the years, particularly from the mid-1990s onwards — not surprisingly, after the fall of the Berlin wall and the easing of the East–West tensions.

Now the time has come for this gradual and slow shift in accent from 'institutional' to 'programmatic' arguments in UN reform proposals to be carried forward and sped up, placing a number of substantive issues at the core of the reform process with a view to strengthening the link between development, peace and security and ensuring a positive reciprocal interaction between them.

This book argues that thanks to the early efforts devoted to the so-called 'institutional' arguments, circumstances are now ripe to place the 'programmatic' issues at the core of the reform efforts of the multilateral system, in particular with regard to the revitalization of the UN's economic development functions.

Let me be explicit from the outset. This is a very humble proposal, which does not intend to rediscover fire or reinvent the wheel. Quite the contrary, it attempts to devise a practical approach that takes due note of the constraints affecting a process of change in a context as complex as that of the UN.

For this reason the book takes stock of previous reform initiatives at the UN related to economic development. Chapter 3 is entirely devoted to reviewing a number of such proposals. I consider this exercise very important to understand the dynamics of change at the UN and to identify the roots of success or failure in attempts to transform the system.

Some of the reform proposals presented since the inception of the UN marked special moments or left a visible trace, even if their recommendations were not accepted or implemented. Such was the case with the Jackson study (1969), the Gardener Report (1975), the Bertrand report (1985), the Childers-Urquhart Proposal (1985), the South Commission (1990), the Nordic Project (1991), the Commission of Global Governance (1994), the Independent Working Group (1995), the Nordic Project II and the European Union (EU) proposals (1997). Additionally the last two Secretaries-General, Boutros-Ghali (1992) and Kofi Annan (1997 and 2002) felt the need to outline their own reform programmes. As one can see by just looking at the dates, the process of change at the UN has been accelerating over the last decade.

Almost all these reform proposals (that of the South Commission being a notable exception) paid prominent attention to administrative, financial and bureaucratic arrangements seeking to increase the coherence, efficiency and effectiveness of the UN economic development functions. This they did by advocating:

1    A single development authority (Jackson report 1969, Gardener report 1975, Bertrand report 1985),
2    An Economic Security Council, basically by reforming the Economic and Social Council, ECOSOC (Bertrand report 1985, Nordic Project 1991, Independent Working Group 1995), or
3    A single department for economic and social issues (the Nordic Project 1991, later implemented by Secretary-General Annan). Most of these proposals looked at the system either from the outside in or, inside, from the top down.

The reform proposal put forward here can claim originality in at least two aspects. In the first place it gives less weight to bureaucratic arrangements and more to organizing the system's activities around a set of substantive economic development topics or issues in the search for coherence, efficiency and effectiveness. Examples of those topics are capacity-building for private-sector development (PSD), policies for the rural and informal sectors of developing-country economies; technology transfer and diffusion; trade capacity building; and energy and the environment — each and all of which topics call for more policy coherence and operational effectiveness of the UN's economic development functions. In the second it adopts a bottom-up approach, drawing from the actual experience of reform of a particular piece of the UN's economic development machinery.

From the perspective of the present proposal, there is no doubt that renewed administrative, financial and bureaucratic arrangements are needed to achieve a proper management of resources. Nevertheless, their effectiveness in accomplishing better coordination, more coherence and improved efficiency will always be a function of the relevance and the quality of the substantive contributions these new arrangements are able to deliver — for example, in the field of economic development.

Without pretending to offer a definitive answer, the proposal contained here seeks to promote a slight but significant conceptual shift by emphasizing that neither the establishment of a new body nor the creation of a new coordinating mechanism will suffice to enhance the relevance of the UN's contribution to economic development unless and until a relevant set of substantive issues — selected through the proper political process, approached with a modern outlook and clustered around a clearly defined agenda — gives renewed focus and better guidance to the system's normative and operational activities.

The inclusion of the United Nations Industrial Development Organization's (UNIDO) experience as a case study in the second part of this book illustrates the sense and relevance of the bottom-up approach. UNIDO's reform process has been successful and its results very encouraging. However, as we shall see, to maintain its pace and consolidate its achievements over the long run, the agency will have to address and overcome constraints on two fronts: its relationships with the other UN programmes, funds and agencies acting in the economic development field; and its field coverage and reach.

On both fronts, UNIDO can only advance if it can count on a blueprint of the way forward for the system as a whole. Such a thing exists with regard to field coverage: the agency is integrating at an accelerated pace into the Resident Coordinator system. However, no clear roadmap exists for the most relevant front: that of the substantive interventions in the fields mentioned above for UN programmes, funds and agencies.

The relevance of the bottom-up approach emerges from verifying that efficiency gains achieved through a successful reform process in a particular UN body can only go as far as system-wide efficiency allows. In the case study in the second part of the book, the ceiling for improvements in a particular agency is set by the system's productivity in the field of economic development.

It is from this standpoint that I have developed the proposal presented in chapter 1. My interest in the subject — the way forward for multilateralism in the economic arena — does not come from a desire to perform a duty to which I was not called, such as revisiting the architecture of multilateral development. On the contrary, I felt almost compelled to get involved in it due to the stage reached by UNIDO's own continuing reform process.

I sincerely hope that the ideas contained in this book will help to spark some interest and, above all, some additional actions to reorganize and reinvigorate the UN's economic development functions. I do believe that this is a pivotal need of the development community in general and the developing countries in particular.

To conclude, I must confess that I had serious doubts about releasing a new book on UN reform. It is always difficult to produce a new work in an already overpopulated field. I did it only when I was able to convince myself that there was something new to say and some originality in the approach proposed, supported by an actual experience of success in reforming one of the UN bodies, which I wanted to share.

I have tried to explain in this introduction the reasons that convinced me. Whether my arguments are persuasive will certainly be judged by the readers. But what I believe undeniable in a system that counts more reform proposals than years of existence is that its Member States have certain unsatisfied expectations on how the system works or what it delivers. It is my desire to make a contribution to addressing those concerns.

# PART I

# A PROPOSAL TO REINVIGORATE THE ECONOMIC DEVELOPMENT FUNCTIONS OF THE UNITED NATIONS SYSTEM IN THE CONTEXT OF THE MILLENNIUM DEVELOPMENT GOALS

CHAPTER 1

# TOWARDS A BUSINESS PLAN
# FOR JOINT ACTION

## INTRODUCTION

There is a compelling case for giving renewed emphasis to the work of the UN system in the field of economic development, particularly in the context of the fight against poverty and the implementation of the Millennium Development Goals (MDGs). Sustained economic growth is a powerful force for reducing poverty: the visible success achieved in this area by China and other Asian countries makes it evident. If the world is any better in terms of reducing global poverty levels it is due to the contributions made by the dynamism of those economies.

In the 1990s, for example, East Asia's per capita income grew by 6.4 percent annually, and the number of people living on less than US$ 2 a day fell by 15 percent. Similarly, during the same period South Asia experienced 3.3 percent annual growth in per capita income and a reduction in poverty of 8.4 percent. In contrast, negative growth rates in Sub-Saharan Africa (SSA) led to increased levels of poverty. According to United Nations Industrial Development Organization (UNIDO) estimates, the average rate of annual per capita GDP growth required for 30 SSA countries to reach the MDG target of halving poverty by 2015 is about 4 percent (assuming no changes in income distribution) (UNIDO, 2004).

However, it must be recognized that in many cases economic growth alone may not be enough to reduce poverty. For economic growth to translate effectively into poverty reduction it must generate jobs for the poor, raise their income levels, and give them better access to health, education, nutrition, shelter, safe drinking water, sanitation, and other vital services. Equally important is to curb HIV/AIDS, malaria and other pandemic diseases.

As will be shown in chapter 5, most — if not all — of the countries that have succeeded in achieving economic development and translating it into social progress did so by combining sound macroeconomics with market-oriented reforms, good governance with reliable institutions and the proper interaction between incentives and the supply of public goods, so as to balance economic dynamism with social inclusiveness. Most of them, far from adopting one-size-fits-all models, developed their own approaches.

In the last instance, it is progress on the economic front that makes it possible to sustain advances in the social sector. While it is important to make AIDS drugs affordable, it is even more important to ensure that AIDS sufferers have the means to continue affording those drugs and ensuring the nourishment they need. Similarly, the supply of shelter should not just meet current requirements but also keep pace with future demand. In all such cases what is essential is a growing economy to generate the resources needed for social advances.

This is not new. The international community has been working for a long while to address these interconnections and improve its effectiveness in that endeavor. The 1994 Human Development Report, the Independent Working group on the Future of UN in 1995 and the Commission on Global Governance in 1996 proposed the establishment of an Economic Security Council with the objective of addressing concurrently issues of global poverty, unemployment, food security, international migration, potential ecological crises and a new framework for sustainable development.

The Economic and Social Council of the United Nations (ECOSOC) has itself been working on renewing its profile and achieving more relevance. Some time ago it established a high-level 'segment' (forum) with the participation of different UN bodies and the Bretton Woods institutions (BWIs) to analyze global economic issues. More recently renewed attention was given to the interaction between that body and the Security Council, specially with regard to post-conflict reconstruction efforts — that led, for example, to the establishment of ad-hoc advisory groups on Guinea-Bissau (in 2002), Burundi (2003) and Haiti (2004). These recent developments are particularly welcomed and deserve to be strongly supported, on technical grounds, by the UN bodies working in the field of economic development.

Based on resolution 57/270B, the General Assembly will receive in 2005 the outcome of a review by its functional commissions on their working methods. The ultimate goal is to maximize their impact on the implementation of the goals set out by the global conferences. A multi-year programme for its coordination segment on the follow-up to global conferences is also expected. And as recently as in 2003, the Secretary-General proposed to set up 'thematic study groups' or 'expert working groups' that enable adequate participation by a wide range of stakeholders. He suggested that an 'expert group' should carry out research on core policy issues of the Financing For Development Agenda, and report back to ECOSOC with specific recommendations.

In this context, I see the MDGs as an organizing principle for the international system, offering programmatic coherence for the UN's activities, particularly at country level, and constituting the basis for an integrated, multi-sectoral approach to development. Adopting them for this purpose would provide an opportunity to achieve a demonstrable coming together of the system's various organizations around common objectives, wherever possible pooling resources, engaging in collaborative programming, and devising innovative alliances and partnerships to deliver results. The MDGs certainly provide a chance to maximize our collective capacity to develop comprehensive, effective and sustainable approaches to key issues, and increase our collective impact on the ground.

# DIAGNOSIS: DISPERSAL AND DILUTION

Individual approaches and independent initiatives still characterize the UN system's work in the field of economic development. Efforts are dispersed and resources spread thinly over a broad range of often unrelated, and at times overlapping, activities. Additionally there is no mandatory or systemic procedure to compare experiences or benchmark the performance of the technical cooperation projects, their results and cost-effectiveness. This tends to limit the collective impact of the system in promoting economic development and prevents the development of more integrated programmatic approaches.

The consequences of such a structure are certainly many, but three major shortcomings stand out:

a    **Insufficient critical mass.** Not only are resources thinly spread, but command of the knowledge, experience and skills vested in the UN system is also diluted. The same occurs with the outcome of the many initiatives and UN programmes in the abovementioned areas. Articulation of work on a voluntary basis would help overcome this handicap. The complexity of issues such as trade, investment promotion, technology diffusion (including environment and energy applications) and private sector and rural development makes it all the more difficult to achieve progress and increase the relevance of our contributions in these areas, particularly when information about what others are doing and the intended outcome of their programmes and experiences are shared only partially or not at all.

b    **Absence of a common approach.** Many bodies of the UN system do have elaborated views on a great variety of issues pertaining to economic development. However, this does not amount today to a clearly identifiable, consistent and well-articulated system-wide view.

c    **Inability to price.** A lack of focus, insufficient analytical depth and the ensuing dispersion and overlap, weaken our capacity to price technical cooperation programmes and related investment needs in the area of economic development (such as technology transfer, trade capacity building and private sector development, PSD) in order to assess more rigorously their cost-effectiveness in pursuing the desired outputs (say, in income per capita terms). Granted, this is not an easy field and many scholars feel rather uneasy at having to confront it. But it needs to be addressed.

These problems have emerged from the vicissitudes of many years of evolution of the economic development functions, as I will try to explain in the following chapters. They constitute serious limitations and sometimes even a disincentive to reform the UN bodies operating in this field. What I have seen at first hand working in the system, however, is that the assets accumulated during an average of four decades by these institutions are worth restructuring and that their brands are powerful tools to provide leadership, confidence and ownership in developing countries struggling to implement effective policies to fight poverty.

It is clear that the UN system can (and certainly needs to) do more to concert and coordinate its work in this field. Consider these facts and figures: the UN Department of Economic and Social Affairs (UN-DESA), UNIDO, UNCTAD, ITC, the Regional Commissions and the UN University jointly employ about 4,300 people, of whom about 2,000 are professionals. Together, their financial resources amount to some US$ 1.3 billion[1]. The potential collective impact of these combined assets, if deployed in common or in a complementary manner, is clearly enormous. While individual organizations can claim that their activities are achieving the intended results, it is difficult to make the same assertion for the system as a whole, or even for the group of organizations mentioned.

A renewed system-wide, strategic focus on economic development would help enhance the UN system's collective contribution to the achievement of the MDGs. This would, in turn, help close the gap and reinforce the links between sustainable economic development on the one hand, and human development on the other. In addition it would provide a stronger link between the UN's economic development functions and post-conflict recovery programmes. Both relationships are called for in the Millennium Declaration.

# THE CHALLENGE OF COORDINATION

Many mechanisms have been tested in attempts to reorganize the UN machinery, and the economic development functions have been no exception (indeed, they are a special case). Institutional arrangements, managerial strategies and bureaucratic adjustments have all been proposed, and some of them even put in place. However, the malaise that gave rise to the problems outlined above proved very resilient and still persists.

My assumption, as I will elaborate below, is that institutional arrangements are necessary, but do not suffice. They will only deliver better integration of efforts and collective responses by the system if articulated around a strong programmatic core and in the presence of the right set of incentives. Apt leadership is also required. A concrete case study of this hypothesis is presented in the second part of this book, which examines the reform exercise at UNIDO. The MDGs provide an opportunity to test it at the UN system level.

---

1 The figures pertain to regular/operational and extra-budgetary resources for 2004-2005. These figures do not include the relevant components in UNDP, UNEP, ILO, FAO and other organizations working in the area of economic development.

The challenge is to cluster, in a clearly articulated manner, the contributions of the UN's economic development functions to the MDGs, overcoming the three constraints referred to above.

Different approaches were tried in the past, at different times and in various contexts. At the end of the cold war some agencies were considered irrelevant and threatened with withdrawals of donors (some actually materializing) and closure[2]. Poor performers or those with low productivity levels were faced with the threat of reduced funding levels. All these certainly appear as powerful spurs to improve performance and seek greater coordination. However, besides being out of fashion, their impact on mobilizing heavy bureaucracies well experienced in these matters, like those of the UN or the BWIs, has been rather limited.

Another approach was to seek concentration of power in a single authority. This was recommended from many quarters in many reform proposals and in some cases (like that of UN DESA) even implemented. Although this produced important efficiency gains, the final results are far from what is needed in the context of a system-wide strategy to achieve the MDGs.

More recently an innovative approach was developed, very much in line with the need to increase the ownership and leadership of the developing countries in the implementation of their economic and social policies: coordination at field level. Undoubtedly this is a much better approach than the previous two: more modern and closer to the real world's needs. Unfortunately it calls for a high degree of articulation and coordination of donors' policy priorities and practices and it proves hard to implement in the absence of a minimum level of coordination at headquarters level — those of both the donors and the multilateral agencies.

A fourth approach — which can actually complement the previous one and even help to overcome its shortcomings — would be to develop a scheme of issue-leadership (see page 26ff for a definition of this concept). It was tried to some extent under the reform proposals of Secretary-General Kofi Annan and is particularly suitable for the MDGs. It requires agreement on two things: the programmatic focus to be adopted (e.g. the MDGs) and the list of issues that need to be developed in order to achieve the programmatic goal (something attempted with the targets attached to the MDGs).

The problem with applying this approach to the multilateral system with regard to the MDGs is that it cannot be developed exclusively in a 'managerial' fashion (of goals and targets) as in the business milieu. It will require more than that to articulate a set of technical contributions that corresponds to the needs of the clients and whose leadership could be strengthened by a center of excellence from inside the system. In addition, an incentives system has to be developed to support the scheme, and proper technical and managerial leadership must be supplied (which means little leeway for typical multilateral political appointments).

---

2  Closures or mergers are very unlikely in the intricate legal framework of the multilateral system and are certainly politically unpopular.

To sort out these problems and solve the coordination challenge I propose formulating a sort of business plan or common agenda for action. Such an agenda must be drafted and adhered to on a voluntary basis, with proper rewards for the relevant contributions — voluntary adherence in order to avoid disrupting the current budgets and programmes approved by the governing bodies of the different organizations, agencies, funds and programmes and appropriate rewards to break bureaucratic inertia and the lack of incentives to come out of the shell.

The absence of a framework for collaboration and coordination in the field of economic development has hindered the achievement of a critical mass of expertise and experience in the UN system. It has also made more difficult the accumulation of knowledge and experience along common lines of work. And it has made equally hard the measurement of the true value or cost-effectiveness of the system's interventions and its accountability for the results delivered.

A common agenda for coordinated action is required not only to overcome these constraints but also to marshal the full potential of the system towards comprehensive implementation of the MDGs. Such an agenda would facilitate a more rational division of labor on economic development within the UN system, further specialization around the core competencies of the organizations concerned, strengthening of synergies and enhancement of the system's collective impact. It would also create an incentive for donor countries to increase the coherence of their funding policies and raise the likelihood of attracting additional resources to support the UN system's efforts in the field of economic development. It could also facilitate the implementation of an issue-leadership approach.

Efforts to achieve this objective will have to go well beyond simply listing topics on which cooperation is desirable, to a careful selection of subjects on which the resources of the system must be put to work. If we really want to connect the UN's peace and development functions, much more research, analysis and experience-sharing exercises will have to be undertaken in order to allow the system to accumulate knowledge along clearly defined tracks and refine its contributions and interventions, particularly in the economic development field.

It will not be enough at this stage to adopt as a sort of common agenda titles like those suggested by the 1994 Human Development Report or the Commission on Global Governance. To achieve the MDGs it will be necessary to describe the contents of those titles, as we do in an academic or business programme, and organize our work around them — in line with the efforts made to develop the definition of targets in order to measure the progress in achieving MDGs, or by the policy clusters of the Millennium Project. Perhaps, to some extent, that was the idea embodied in the Secretary-General's proposal of 'expert groups' conducting research on core substantive policy issues.

What I am proposing is that a system-wide, MDG-based operational strategy for the UN's economic development functions be elaborated building on key aspects of the current approach to development, with its emphasis on macroeconomic stability, market-oriented reforms and good governance. More specifically, the strategy should aim at:

1    Defining the MDGs as the common policy orientation for the work of the system towards sustainable economic development;

2    Identifying priority areas for coordinated responses by organizations of the system with a mandate in the field of economic development and elaborating a well-defined, results-oriented, work plan built around an agreed economic agenda designed to draw fully on the capacities and comparative advantages of different parts of the system;

3    Developing the appropriate mechanism or modality for coordinated interventions on the basis of the agreed work plan; and

4    Exploring alternative avenues for mobilizing the required resources.

## SETTING UP A COMMON AGENDA FOR ACTION

To be relevant, an agenda of this sort must be limited to a low number of issues, and it will require an intellectual framework to choose the fields on which it will concentrate. I will try here to use one consistent with the rationale that will be presented later, in chapters 4 and 5.

It is difficult to simplify the problem of development to the extent needed to arrive at a common denominator on which most people would agree. Different schools of thought assign different weight to different factors in assessing the roots of underdevelopment. And yet, we need to find some minimum common ground on which to base the formulation of a common agenda for action.

To put the framework I am proposing in a rather stylized way, it can be said that developing countries typically need to go through three different transitions in their search for development: a human development transition; a productivity transition; and an environmental transition:

1    The *human development* transition means moving from a situation in which poor education, nutrition and health services translate into high mortality rates, high fertility rates, and low levels of human assets, to one in which the society manages to reduce mortality and fertility rates and increase its investments in areas like education, health and nutrition so as to build human capital in a sustainable manner.

2    The *productivity* transition entails mobilizing knowledge, skills, information, science and technology throughout the society and the productive system to allow the economy to innovate and incorporate technical change. This process is required to provide increasing and sustainable levels of agricultural and industrial productivity so as to raise income levels and living standards.

3    The *environmental* transition involves improving the productivity of each ton of water, soil or energy the economy borrows from the planet, improving the quality of technologies employed and basically moving from environmental degradation to sustainability. It also implies achieving successful urbanization, managing properly

the migration flows from the rural areas to the cities and addressing the problems posed by slums so as to enhance the quality of life in the cities.

These transitions are neither rigidly sequential nor one-time events. Although there is no single recipe to be followed, they normally need to be transited along parallel tracks and, to make things harder, the approaches to achieving them need to be permanently updated and their results benchmarked.

Nowadays we describe as developed the countries that have managed to go through all three transitions. Beyond some commonalities, they have done so in very different manners, adopting different policies and strategies. In general, these countries have focused on aligning their incentives systems and the strengthening of their institutions to provide public goods. They have been able to make such a process sustainable by adapting continuously to the evolutionary forces of a dynamic global society.

For the poorest economies of the world, achieving any of the three transitions is extremely difficult. They are not in a position to afford the human and financial costs involved in overcoming their current predicament. And although they are offered policy prescriptions seeking to align their incentives and price systems, these prescriptions appear to neglect the supply of public goods, both in amount and quality, required by their societies to trigger economic development.

The international community has long been aware of this problem and has approached it through the adoption of a number of international goals and targets agreed upon in various international conferences. The most complete and ambitious set of such goals was embodied in the Millennium Declaration supported by some 160 heads of state and government in September 2000 in the framework of the annual session of the UN General Assembly.

If we really want to succeed in achieving these goals and targets we must admit that we will have to address the current undersupply of public goods by the global society and in particular the capacity of the less developed countries to supply them locally, at their national level. I believe this is the area where we in the UN must focus most of our efforts.

Rather than focusing on the minute details of policy recommendations pursuing sound macroeconomics, market-oriented economies and good governance, we may want to try harder to sharpen the focus and deepen the analysis of the developmental implications of these policies, in terms of the institutional requirements and the supply of public goods that are needed to make them work properly. This is the basic rationale behind the menu of topics suggested below for a joint UN business plan or common agenda for action in the economic development field.[3]

---

3  Such an undertaking is certainly not meant to neglect or overrule the set of activities and programmes currently carried out by development-oriented funds, agencies and programmes. It is only intended to provide a point of convergence to align such contributions on a voluntary basis, rewarding them accordingly.

# SUGGESTED MENU OF TOPICS

Following the rationale introduced above, I will attempt here a preliminary identification of areas of work. This exercise focuses on the need to strengthen the supply of three specific public goods: 1, market efficiency and integration; 2, knowledge; and 3, environment; with an additional area of endeavor that requires special attention: 4, benchmarking and monitoring economic performance.

## 1   MARKET EFFICIENCY AND INTEGRATION

Market efficiency requires *commercial markets integration* and the *development of the private sector.*

### A   COMMERCIAL MARKETS INTEGRATION

Expanding trade flows are the most powerful growth engine for developed and developing countries alike. Multilateral trade negotiations are a central component in achieving this. Understandably, most multilateral cooperation in this field has been geared towards building negotiating capabilities in the developing countries to enable them to look after their interests and participate effectively in trade negotiations. It is barely necessary to underline how important these negotiations can be in the fight against poverty, particularly in the hypothesis of the removal of subsidies and market distortions in agriculture and textiles.

However, trade negotiations have been somewhat oversold as a means to achieve growth and thence reduce poverty. The most trade negotiations can do is create business opportunities for developing economies, but these face serious hurdles that are plant-specific, related to the local business environment and to the physical and technological infrastructures. These problems often offset whatever natural or acquired comparative advantages the countries involved may enjoy. They have to do with the supply-side response to trade opportunities and the compliance with standards and technical regulations.

*i     Supply-side problems.* The many years of experience of the Yaoundé, Lomé and Cotonou conventions, as well as other schemes of tariff concessions and import duty reductions, have conclusively demonstrated the need to move international trade cooperation well beyond its traditional focus on training negotiators. For developing countries, and LDCs in particular, seizing the opportunities opened by multilateral or regional trade agreements means addressing the absence of exportable supply capacity.

Intensive technical and managerial upgrading and other export-related technical assistance services are indispensable to enable them to reap the potential benefits. The productive systems of developing countries and LDCs are often unable to take advantage of economies of scale since they were originally built to serve relatively small domestic markets. Often the production mix, that is, the number of different products and models produced in a single facility, is quite large and diverse, further worsening the scale problem. Substantial distance from the technology frontier, increased cost of transport, insurance and other export-related support services are only a few examples of the problems that need to be considered to evaluate the real capacity of developing economies to profit from the opportunities of multilateral or regional trade pacts.

*ii     Standards and technical regulations.* The ability to meet standards and technical regulations contemplated by the Uruguay Round is crucial to most developing countries, afflicted as they are by technological backwardness affecting product and process specifications, and by the lack of an adequate quality infrastructure, including testing, accreditation and certification facilities and institutions. To add to their difficulties, product and process standards and technical regulations in the advanced industrial countries are becoming ever more stringent as a result of the increasing awareness of consumers and governments about risks posed by current practices to human and animal health as well as to the environment. The provision of the public goods required to address these constraints is essential.

Specialized, expert assistance in these highly technical fields hence becomes a vital component of aid packages. Consolidating cooperation programmes in the trade negotiation and trade policy fields with programmes that support export market development is the right way to go.

## B    PRIVATE SECTOR DEVELOPMENT

Economic development is increasingly driven by the private sector, which makes the development of a strong and dynamic private sector another precondition for achieving market efficiency and integration. Private firms are a means of non-market coordination indispensable for market efficiency. It would be futile, therefore, to seek such efficiency in the absence of the necessary entrepreneurial and organizational capabilities for decentralized decision-making.

However, the policies and institutions required for PSD do not receive adequate attention. A clear example is provided by the minimal role assigned to the private sector in MDG-related poverty reduction strategies, particularly in the poorest countries. Once again, this is at least partly a legacy of received theory, which posits access to capital as nearly the only requisite.

Clearly, ensuring conditions for the supply of risk capital is essential. However, the technical, entrepreneurial and management skills that underlie PSD do not necessarily flow to where they are most needed. In fact, the reverse appears to be the case. Resources allocated to skill formation in developing countries are characteristically lacking, as is the supply of non-financial services for PSD, particularly those relating to entrepreneurial and technological development and foreign market access. Small and medium-sized enterprise (SME) development receives far less than the attention it requires as a bedrock of entrepreneurial talent. Finally, institutional innovations to address the linkages between the rural and urban economies and between the informal and formal economies by tapping into the potential of micro-entrepreneurship are also extremely rare.

The multiple initiatives and activities of the UN system in this field would benefit from system-wide articulation and critical mass formation. Examples include technology diffusion for which private enterprise is the key vehicle, and trade facilitation, whereby private enterprise is supported to cope with emerging technological challenges to reach foreign markets.

*i*      *Investment promotion.* This is an area of paramount concern for developing countries. Private investment flows play an important role in the development of all economies, yet foreign direct investment (FDI) largely bypasses the developing world (with the exception of a few emerging economies). The typical prescription in this field consists in recommending good governance, sound macroeconomic management and the improvement of the business climate through the adoption of investment codes, the establishment of investment promotion agencies, one-stop shops for investors and like measures.

However, an important number of countries have failed to attract FDI even after having earnestly embarked upon the implementation of these prescriptions — or have attracted FDI only to public services or extractive activities with limited capacity to produce spillovers for the rest of the economy.

A consolidated business plan could help sharpen the focus and deepen the contents of UN research and technical cooperation programmes dealing with this matter. It could do so by addressing government and market failures affecting developing countries' capacity to attract FDI, and attempting to work with private investors, global corporations and investment banks in developing new financial instruments and mechanisms (in association, for example, with the World Bank group's International Finance Corporation, IFC) to help reduce the transaction costs and risks associated with investments in developing economies.

Examples of institutions working in developed countries but widely unknown in the developing economies are risk assessment boards or companies, and those specialized in rating risk levels of individual companies for actors in the financial system in order to facilitate rate competition in the supply of commercial loans. Another mechanism to be studied to facilitate equity investment in developing country companies is the organization of investment portfolios with companies from different countries and sectors (so as to diversify risks). These portfolios can be organized through the use of securities to offer a fixed rate of return in financial markets, therefore allowing them to go public. Instruments such as these are designed to generate and disseminate information to allow market agents to assign resources more efficiently.

*ii*      *Global value chains.* The ability to connect with global markets is vital to ensuring the emergence of strong and dynamic private sectors in developing countries. Global markets are served by global value chains. Spread around the world, enterprises in global value chains perform related activities to bring a product (or service) from design and development to production, marketing and sales to consumption, after-sales services and eventually recycling.

The focus of interest of these chains is not just the enterprises; it is also the shifting links and contractual relations among them. Enterprises expand their product lines and expand internationally by forging new links with enterprises already active in the global economy, dominated by criss-crossing global value chains encompassing R&D, production, logistics, marketing and exchange — where all the links are between enterprises rather than between countries.

Global value chains have the power to unfetter enterprises, but they can also constrain them. The impetus for the formation of global value chains comes from enterprises in advanced countries, either as buyers or producers. The conditions for developing country enterprises to participate are not confined to such 'hard' items as price, quality and punctuality, but also include the capacity to learn and absorb advice from the lead enterprises. Particularly in manufacturing, the insertion of local activities in wider networks is a great opportunity for developing countries to upgrade their capabilities.

To enable participation in global value chains most of the advanced economies developed the right set of institutions to support the necessary innovation and learning processes, as well as business advisory services. Similar institutions are needed in the developing world to allow their private sectors to participate in one of the most dynamic fields of the global economy.

*iii* *Corporate social responsibility.* Corporate Social Responsibility (CSR) plays an increasing role in the business environment. Due to the globalization of trade, increased size and influence of companies, the repositioning of governments and the rise in strategic importance of linkages between stakeholders and brand reputation, the past twenty years have seen a radical change in the relationship between business and society. CSR has emerged as a pragmatic response to consumer and civil society pressures. These have mainly been focused on multinational corporations (MNCs) serving advanced markets but often operating in developing countries.

In this context the Secretary-General's 'Global Compact' encourages MNCs to comply with international standards in labor, human rights and environment. MNC compliance poses both challenges and opportunities for developing country SMEs seeking to become members of the global supply chains.

CSR is a field where both the MNCs and the multilateral development community have to seek mutual cooperation, since the understanding of how compliance with international standards can become a source of opportunity for developing economies requires dedicated analysis, research and policy assessment.

*iv* *Informal sector and rural development.* Because most of the poverty in the developing world is concentrated in rural areas, PSD cannot be addressed without regard for rural development. In the poorest countries rural development demands strengthening the supply of public goods targeting non-income poverty and related basic needs, such as those aimed at health, nutrition, water and sanitation, energy and feeder roads. These, by themselves, can have a direct impact on agricultural productivity and, indirectly, on the development of productive non-agricultural rural activities.

Agricultural and non-agricultural rural development, in turn, make it necessary to find ways to integrate the informal and formal sectors of the economy so as to prevent the growth of an increasingly segregated low-productivity informal economy and to tap available entrepreneurial energies.

## 2   KNOWLEDGE

For the proper dissemination of knowledge, a balance needs to be sought between the application of *intellectual property rights* regimes and the management of *competition policies*. The right set of *institutions for the dissemination of knowledge* also needs to be developed.

### A   THE INSTITUTIONAL SETTING

Technology (just as capital) does not flow easily towards the countries and regions where it is most scarce. Yet those countries and regions need to acquire, adapt and absorb technology inflows competitively if they are to develop a strong and dynamic private sector and participate in international trade flows while meeting increasingly stringent commercial, technical, environmental and social standards.

Costly learning processes are involved. The market often fails to persuade rational private decision-makers to incur the cost, so the deficit must be addressed by the provision of public goods and related incentives. Rarely are such public goods and incentives part of the conventional prescriptions.

This shortcoming is all the more puzzling because advanced industrial countries have a rich experience of providing such public goods by means of sophisticated technological infrastructures. These have also been crucial to successful industrialization in countries of East Asia and elsewhere. And yet, the international system has largely failed, as have the markets, to ensure that this institutional experience and expertise flowed as needed to the developing world. Addressing this failing ought to be high on the international agenda.

The UN system is actively involved in this field. However, there is a need to establish system-wide priorities and enhanced operational coordination to ensure effectiveness and impact.

### B   IPRS AND COMPETITION POLICIES

It is widely recognized that one of the factors that strongly influences the ability to foster economic development is the quality of institutions. Ownership rights are prominent among these. Intellectual property rights (IPRs), which protect the ownership of knowledge assets, are crucial for economic development in that they do not only provide an incentive to generate knowledge, but are also expected to help disseminating it. IPRs have become increasingly important since the Uruguay Round due to their ever widening scope, which now covers not just intangible assets held by private enterprises but also much broader social and public assets such as those in the fields of health, education and biodiversity.

For private enterprises, the generation and dissemination of knowledge are often not easily reconciled with one another, which places SMEs at a disadvantage. Therefore antitrust or antimonopoly legislation has been developed to ensure a level playing field in industrialized countries.

LDCs in particular have to pay a high price for introducing IPRs. They have to enhance their scientific and technological capabilities and monitor the market power enticed by IPRs, if they are to avoid that the full enforcement of IPRs impoverishes their potential in this area. Relatively more advanced developing countries also suffer from the lack of ability to deal with the impact of IPRs in their economies. Ultimately, the problem lies in ensuring that domestic enterprises have the right degree of preparedness before they are subjected to cutthroat R&D- and innovation-driven competition.

Although crucial to both the developing and developed worlds, since it decisively affects market entry and the channels of technology flow, the diffusion of competition policies in the developing world is not nearly as significant as that of IPRs. While important progress has been made in the adoption and enforcement of the latter, this has hardly been the case with the former.

If the diffusion of technology is to be given the priority it requires, this problem needs to be tackled head-on, particularly in view of the increasing diffusion of information and communication technologies (ICTs), biotechnologies and other advanced technologies.

## 3    ENVIRONMENT

Promoting economic development in a modern society implies articulating output growth with the incorporation of environmentally sound technologies and new materials in order to protect the environment from further deterioration and, whenever possible, to rehabilitate previously polluted areas.

The same logic, applied to the implementation of multilateral protocols such as that of Montreal regarding chlorofluorocarbons (CFCs) and the Stockholm convention regarding persistent organic pollutants (POPs), should be extended to several industrial sectors to achieve regenerative approaches to productive development, fostering environmentally sound technology transfer to developing countries and boosting their business opportunities.

## 4    BENCHMARKING AND MONITORING ECONOMIC PERFORMANCE

Productivity growth results from improvements in economic governance, including the definition of standards relating to the functioning of markets, the diffusion of knowledge and the impact of economic activity on society and the environment. These are sought through a large number of microeconomic interventions such as those in the fields of competition, IPRs and environmental and social conduct. In turn, the gauging of productivity growth provides guidance on the directions to be pursued for technology diffusion and PSD.

Placing the emphasis on productivity performance certainly does not override other considerations, such as those relating to employment, fair labor relations and good pay for labor services. Actually, the very fact that this dichotomy is most likely to be raised every time that reference is made to productivity is an eloquent indication of the failure to articulate adequately the economic and social agendas.

Catching up in terms of productivity is of decisive importance to the narrowing down of the egregious growth disparities in the world economy I mentioned at the outset. It is also a precondition for sustainable social improvement. Conversely, enhancing human capital is a precondition to succeed in productivity catch-up. Private-sector-led productivity growth may provide developing economies with the opportunity not just to increase market efficiency but also to dovetail it with other objectives such as equity and social justice. For this to occur, in addition to drawing on a wide variety of policies and actions, it will be also necessary to ensure that *technology diffusion* and PSD are nurtured so that developing countries can effectively and competitively connect with, and draw from, global trade, financial and technological flows to foster economic growth.

There is little doubt that the international community and, in particular, the developing countries themselves, need better standards to assess the performance of economic reform programmes and make it consistent with good governance. However, the information and research outputs required to do so are not forthcoming. The measurement and monitoring of productivity performance at the various levels of aggregation is a vital but neglected area of attention in the developing world. The tools and policies available to developing countries to foster productivity performance are particularly weak. Productivity performance is considered crucial in the advanced industrial economies, which pay it the attention it deserves. This ought to serve as a useful guide for the developing world. Productivity performance is not just a field of intellectual interest for abstract discussions; it is a very practical yardstick of sustainable improvements in income levels and living standards.

A business plan that duly monitors productivity performance in the developing world relying on the consolidated contribution of all the relevant UN agencies, programmes and funds, would enable a quantum leap in the scope, reach and impact of their action in the field of economic development. It would also provide an excellent tool to gauge the impact on economic performance of the efforts aimed at building social capital, as is the case in the advanced countries.

# THE AGENDA AT WORK

Whatever the ultimate choice of topics, making a proposal like this operational entails ensuring that it will fit such an intricate legal system as that of the UN. This poses four key challenges:

1    The first challenge is making a common agenda for action relevant and workable for the multiplicity of UN bodies involved in economic development. In my view there are two main ways of going about this:

☐    One is having the system-wide, MDG-based, common agenda for action formulated through any of the existing mechanisms of coordination within the UN system, namely, the United Nations Development Group (UNDG) and the High Level Committee on Programmes (HLCP) of the Chief Executives Board for Coordination (CEB), without an explicit mandate necessarily emanating from an organ of the UN Secretariat. One possible scenario would be having the HLCP play a leading role in the drafting of the common agenda and doing so in cooperation with the UNDG and DESA.

For some of the agencies involved, the implementation of the voluntary common agenda to better perform their MDG-related economic development functions may not entail policy changes but, rather, managerial accommodations. In other cases, the approval of the respective organizations' governing bodies might be needed.

☐    If such is the case, a second, not necessarily alternative, way may be sought. The General Assembly or the ECOSOC could pass a resolution calling on the UN bodies involved in economic development to formulate a system-wide, MDG-based agenda, requesting the Secretary-General to report on it and inviting the relevant executive heads to follow up. The governing bodies of the relevant specialized agencies, funds, and programmes could later endorse the resolution.

2    The second challenge concerns organizing the work of the various UN bodies once the programme has been formulated. My proposal is to resort to the concept of issue-leadership, a sound and well-developed management principle used both in business and academia, and used in the UN in the past. It basically consists in clustering the various institutions to work jointly on a common issue and pooling their contributions according to their respective mandates and fields of excellence.

Leadership is exercised according to issue, rather than along institutional or bureaucratic lines. A good example of this approach was developed by Professor John Ruggie in the formulation, implementation and management of the Global Compact, with many partners (ILO; UNHCR; UNDP; UNEP and UNIDO), each contributing according to its own mandate and expertise, with a view to foster a responsible participation of SMEs and MNCs.

As can be appreciated, this approach would very well suit the proposed menu of topics outlined above, since the accent is placed on the need to move those topics forward by means of meaningful contributions to their various dimensions, rather than giving any agency the lead on any specific topic. The division of labor would be determined by the quality of the technical contributions to the topic in the various fields of expertise involved. The issue-leadership approach can also be a powerful tool to overcome the limitations of the traditional project-by-project approach to technical cooperation, modernizing it with a more programmatic approach.[4]

**3**    A third issue is that of rewarding the various UN bodies contributing to the common agenda. This is essential to make the whole scheme work. Even if the problems reviewed above were to be properly solved, the development of an incentives system would remain as a key one to be tackled in order to ensure that the relevant UN bodies participate in an effective manner.

In addition, one of the goals of setting up a common business plan for better implementing the MDG-related economic development functions of the UN system is attracting additional funding from donors. The panel presided by former Mexican President Ernesto Zedillo in the run-up to the Monterrey Conference on Financing for Development quoted a figure of some US$ 100 billion as the indicative amount of official development assistance (ODA) needed to achieve the MDGs (including some US$ 20 billion for the supply of global public goods). The report produced by Professor Jeffrey Sachs in the context of the Millennium Project asks for some US$ 150 billion in ODA for 2005 and almost US$ 200 billion in 2015 (still below the 0.7 percent of gross net income (GNI) pledged in Monterrey), while the Chairman of the Development Assistance Committee (DAC) of the Organization for Economic Cooperation and Development (OECD) estimates that ODA flows will reach about US$ 100 billion by 2010.

If only a portion of future ODA flows were applied as a reward mechanism for those UN agencies contributing to a common, MDG-oriented business plan, this plan would count with substantive additional funds to pursue their joint efforts while strengthening the UN's economic development functions. Responsibility for the

---

4   UNIDO has already experimented with different mechanisms for better integrating individual project efforts and joint programming with external partners, which could help with the implementation of the proposal made here. During the 2003 WTO Ministerial meeting in Cancun, a MOU was signed between UNIDO and the WTO. Under this agreement UNIDO and WTO jointly develop programmes to assist nine countries to achieve a measurable increase in their exports by removing supply-side constraints; to develop systems and prove conformity to market technical and regulatory requirements; and to integrate into the multilateral trading system. Joint programmes are being formulated for joint submission to donors in 2005. This approach is being very well received in the countries involved. Another model for joint programming was agreed between UNIDO and UNDP on 23 September 2004, addressing the recommendations of the UN Commission on Private Sector and Development published earlier in 2004 (see text). Under this programme joint country-level integrated packages of activities are being developed, with other UN and non-UN organizations joining as required in individual countries. A third example is that of the MDG-dedicated technical center in Nairobi co-sponsored by UNIDO, the Millennium Project and UNDP, in cooperation with UNESCO and WHO.

administration of these funds could lie with the Secretary-General or with a steering committee similar to that set up for the funds contributed to the UN by the Turner Foundation.

Allocating funds for the implementation of this common agenda for action would overcome, on the one hand, the funding constraints suffered by the UN bodies involved in economic development due to their perceived remoteness with respect to the achievement of the MDGs; and on the other, the operational constraints of the project-by-project approach, which are indeed a problem for all activities of technical cooperation (not just those relating to economic development).

4    A fourth challenge is making sure that the selection of topics is relevant for field-level operations. Even though I have suggested a framework to limit the number of topics to be dealt with, we can only ensure the relevance of the final menu of issues for the implementation of the MDGs on the ground by improving coordination and facilitating the work of the UN Resident Coordinator and the UN Country Team.

Any menu of topics will have to rely on a critical review of the current generation of Poverty Reduction Strategy Papers (PRSPs) and the United Nations Development Assistance Framework (UNDAF). This will ensure that the topics selected are truly linked with the needs of the people, that a demand-driven approach is effectively adopted, and that full advantage is taken of the experience of previous coordination efforts.

## CONCLUSIONS

I have tried to outline the usefulness of thinking anew but with realism in terms of what can be achieved relatively soon in order to contribute to the international community's overriding priority: achieving the MDGs. These are only preliminary thoughts. They certainly need to be fleshed out with contributions from many quarters. I did not try here to outline a detailed proposal; I only sought to show the possible wireframe of a workable mechanism to revitalize the contribution of the UN's economic development functions to achieving the MDGs.

To bring this mechanism to life a fundamental prerequisite must be met: political will. Not much else is needed. One can solve all other problems, but without the powerful cement of a political determination to make better use of the potent machinery embodied in the economic development functions of the UN, not even the smartest devices have a chance of succeeding. Let me suggest that we have the duty to try.

REFERENCES

UNIDO (2004), Industrial Development Report 2004 – Industrialization, Environment and the Millennium Development Goals in Sub-Saharan Africa, UNIDO, Vienna, 2004.

Chapter 2
# THE UN IN A CHANGING GLOBAL LANDSCAPE

The United Nations of the 21st century faces formidable challenges in adjusting to new political, social and economic realities. These are very different times from those that prevailed when the UN was founded six decades ago, in 1945. Although the Organization can claim major achievements in this period, many still feel that the UN system has yet to fulfill the hopes and aspirations of its founders.

Many ideas and proposals for reform, and for reforming the reforms, have been formulated, and actions have been initiated to cope with an always demanding and changing international scenario. But much still remains on the agenda for the new millennium. Indeed, reform is a continuous process of adjusting to changing realities for 'preventing war, protecting fundamental human rights, establishing conditions for justice and respect for international law, and promoting social progress with sustainable standards of living', as stated in the preamble of the UN Charter. And it is a complex process, since actors in the international community have different political perceptions of the UN's role.

It should thus come as no great surprise that calls for reform of the Organization have been raised with increasing stridency over the years as the UN has struggled with steadily increasing demands, a geo-political context radically different from that of 1945, and unsecured political support and resources.

The UN as a system — and UNIDO as a specialized agency was no exception — have undergone in recent years the most intense scrutiny in their history. Fundamental questions are being asked about the role of multilateral cooperation, and indeed of the UN itself. Its principles have been challenged. Its relevance has been doubted.

The BWIs — the World Bank and the International Monetary Fund (IMF) — and the World Trade Organization (WTO) have not escaped this scrutiny; and there have been loud calls to reform them as well, most audibly at the dawn of the 21st century in the form of protests at meetings of the BWIs and WTO in Washington, Seattle and Prague but also through special panels and reports requested by the United States Congress, which recommended their downsizing or even closure.

At the same time, the multilateral system in general and UN entities in particular are being asked to do more with less, and to be responsive to a new set of demands from its clients. UN agencies are increasingly being judged not only in terms of their own performance, but also in terms of how the UN system as a whole performs. Donors now want clear evidence of unity of purpose, coordination and coherence, and harmony of actions, as well as a significant development impact from individual and collective UN efforts.

The calls for reform, and reform itself, within the UN system and the BWIs, arise from profound political, economic and social changes that in recent years have fundamentally altered the international context of multilateral cooperation and development.

For the sake of simplicity and to facilitate the analysis of their interaction with the dynamics of UN reform, I will group these political, social and economic changes in four main (at times overlapping) clusters:

- ☐ The emergence of a bipolar world in 1945, at the end of WWII.
- ☐ The decolonization process of the 1950s and 1960s.
- ☐ The oil shocks of the 1970s.
- ☐ The end of the Cold War and the acceleration of globalization in the 1990s.

After the terrorist attacks of September 2001 in New York and Washington we are probably in the presence of what can be considered a fifth cluster dominated by the campaign against global terrorism.

## EMERGENCE OF A BIPOLAR WORLD

The UN emerged in the midst of an uneasy political consensus that lasted up to the mid-1970s, based on an uncertain balance between the Soviet centrally-planned economy approach, European social democracy, Third-World economic nationalism and Rooseveltian 'New Deal' policy (Paul, 2000). This consensus granted governments an important role in economic development, emphasized minimum social and economic preconditions, and envisaged national economic planning and regulations, as well as national self-reliance. The consensus permitted the UN system to build up considerable influence — without major competition from the BWIs — and to engage in activities both in social fields and in economic development areas such as trade and industrial development.

## DECOLONIZATION

During the 1950s and 1960s, many colonies gained independence and concentrated on nation-building. They gathered increasing influence in the UN system and in global economic matters. Greater attention was placed on international economic cooperation, and the UN gradually emerged as a global political forum for North–South dialogue on the economic and social issues of the South. The first initiative in that direction was the establishment of the UN Conference on Trade and

Development (UNCTAD) in 1964. Subsequently, new development issues were broached in such areas as industrialization, environment, energy and technology transfer. The UN's development activities shifted towards these new issues, but their impact on the economic progress of developing countries remained limited.

This prompted demands for more radical changes in the world economic system, such as fairer terms of trade and more liberal terms for financing development, in the context of UNCTAD negotiations between the developing countries (represented by the Non-Aligned Movement and the Group of 77) and the developed ones. The latter hesitated to support such reforms as the debate shifted towards the General Assembly and the specialized agencies where the South had gained greater influence.

The Non-Aligned Movement of developing countries argued for a declaration of principles for a 'New International Economic Order', calling for global redistribution of wealth. This was adopted by the General Assembly in 1974 and it was followed by a number of UN declarations and strategies such as:

**a**    The adoption of the International Development Strategy for the Second UN Development Decade.
**b**    The Lima Declaration, in which the developing countries stated their aim of becoming responsible for 25 percent of world industrial production by 2000.
**c**    The UN Center for Transnational Corporations (TNCs), which endeavored to establish a 'code of conduct' for TNCs.

## THE OIL CRISES OF THE 1970s

Around those years oil-producing countries started to organize their energy sectors and adopted policies of nationalization of production and international cooperation among themselves. They created the Organization of Petroleum-Exporting Countries (OPEC), and succeeded in raising oil prices, raising expectations that a new economic world order and a new balance of power would follow.

This process led to a series of oil shocks for consumers in developed countries in 1973/74 and 1979, followed by recession in OECD countries.

Similar expectations emerged in discussions about the performance of the markets and international prices for raw materials and the possible repercussions of collective initiatives for the development of the producing countries. The developed countries expressed reservations but avoided open opposition, arguing instead that the proper forum for discussions about economic change was the BWIs, where they held the balance of power.

By the early 1980s, national policies in developing countries had shifted markedly from inward-oriented to outward-oriented policies, mainly because of the realization that the viability of the former was limited, but also because of the growing forces of globalization. The consensus on the so-called global Keynesianism that had prevailed since 1945 started to fall apart around 1980.

The new governments in the United Kingdom and the United States, under Prime Minister Margaret Thatcher (1979–90) and President Ronald Reagan

(1981–88), respectively, adopted new policies geared towards reducing the role of the state in the economy, and emphasizing market-oriented PSD within the framework of privatization, deregulation of markets and fewer government-provided services. Many other governments, first in the North and later in the South, changed their policy priorities in the same direction. A new era of refocusing the role of the state had begun.

These policy changes had implications for the UN system. Although the UN had enjoyed considerable success in a number of areas, such as decolonization, and provided a world forum where conflicts could be resolved, or at least disagreements aired, and countries could be held accountable for their conduct in international affairs, it started coming in for increasing criticism from many quarters.

The South was disenchanted by the lack of progress towards global economic cooperation and greater social and economic equity. While developing countries deplored the 'ignorance of the minority', the developed countries rejected the 'tyranny of the majority' (Mueller, 1997, p. 32). Disillusion with the UN and criticism of multilateral development efforts were quickened by the change of government in the United States; the Reagan administration emphasized unilateral rather than multilateral action.

## END OF THE COLD WAR AND ACCELERATING GLOBALIZATION

The policies adopted by the United States and the United Kingdom in the 1980s, a renewed arms race and the development of space weapons applications, plus a number of internal factors, combined to put increasing pressure on the Soviet economic system. Throughout the whole of the 1980s, the USSR appears to have experienced declining rates of consumption per capita and productivity levels (see, for instance, Paz Báñez, 1998, p. 413).

This eventually brought renewed pressures for modernization and change that ended in the collapse of the Soviet Union and the demise of the command economic system, radically altering international political and economic relations.

It also brought about significant changes in the relationships between individual countries and the multilateral system. The transition from command to competitive market economies in Central and Eastern Europe, the former Soviet Union and Asia, the reintegration of these countries into the world economic system, and their membership, or application for membership, of international organizations such as the World Bank, the IMF and the WTO, presented special problems and opportunities for the international community and for multilateral cooperation.

As the confrontational politics of the Cold War gave way to more cooperative relations between East and West, new considerations rose to prominence. Donor countries and international institutions became more concerned with promoting peace, democracy, human rights, environmental sustainability and good governance. These concerns have come to constitute a new dimension of the development agenda and present the UN system with new responsibilities and challenges.

The end of the Cold War has created new economic difficulties for some developing countries in the shape of the sharp reduction or cessation of economic aid from the former Soviet Union. On the positive side, the end of the Cold War has led (until recently) to a lowering of military expenditures in developed and developing countries as well as in economies in transition — although these expenditures remain high. Unfortunately, only a small proportion of this peace dividend has gone into aid to the countries in transition and poor countries elsewhere.

Following the end of the Cold War, economic globalization has accelerated greatly over the last decade and a half. The liberalization of international and domestic trading environments, the growth in FDI, rapid technological change and the geographic dispersion of production have all contributed to an increasingly interconnected international system of production and trade.

Globalization has brought to developing and transition countries tremendous opportunities for trade, much larger inflows of FDI with its associated new technologies and skills, and improved market access. The industrialized countries — particularly the private sector — also benefit enormously from trade with developing and transition countries.

However, globalization also poses formidable challenges for most developing countries and economies in transition. It has highlighted the importance of a knowledge-based economy. It has introduced competitive pressures that many developing countries are ill-equipped to meet. The uneven distribution of its economic benefits has fostered a growing fear among low-income economies, particularly the LDCs, that instead of being integrated into the world economy, they may be thrust out to the margins.

That fear is not unfounded. African countries and LDCs, in particular, because of various policy and structural weaknesses, have so far been unable to integrate fully — if at all — into the global economy and enjoy its benefits. Indeed, evidence is growing that the global economic and industrial integration process, so vital for joining the mainstream of economic progress, is bypassing them.

## GLOBAL TERRORISM

Conflict has increased as transition economies and developing countries from Bosnia and Herzegovina and Kosovo in the former Yugoslavia to Rwanda, Burundi and the Democratic Republic of the Congo in Africa attempted to establish independent nations or reassert identities. Often brutal hostilities have created a huge need for post-conflict assistance. Furthermore, a spate of natural disasters — such as floods in Mozambique and drought in Ethiopia — has further increased the need for emergency assistance. Of course, hostilities and natural disasters are not new, but their extent and impact has been growing. Fortunately, so has the will to confront these problems and the capability to do so.

After the tragic events of 11 September 2001 the international community confronts an old problem, terrorism, brought to a new, global scale. The debates on how to best confront this challenge are still under development and a number of different approaches are being considered.

Soon after the attacks on New York and Washington, UN endorsement was sought for action by a voluntary coalition of partners to quash support for terrorist activities in Afghanistan, eventually attacking the country and removing its government. Later, the United States approached the case of Iraq in an entirely different manner as regards the involvement of the international community, adopting a doctrine of pre-emptive intervention, calling into question the multilateral mechanisms to address the problems of peace and security.

These emergencies pose tough demands on the UN system: greater speed and scale of response, better coordination and collaboration, and additional funding needs. Coordinated responses are required for emergency humanitarian assistance, rehabilitation and reconstruction, and to address the problems caused by mass migration and the influx of refugees. To this is added a further challenge: to ensure that emergency and long-term assistance are linked so as to achieve sustainable development. The interlinkage between poverty alleviation and conflict prevention needs to be emphasized. The Secretary-General of the UN has put it in a nutshell: 'Without peace, development is not possible; without development, peace is not durable.'[1]

There is a strong argument that growing inequality of incomes and wealth between and within countries seriously threatens future global economic growth, prosperity and peace. Recent economic research argues that there are good theoretical and empirical grounds to believe that inequality is harmful to growth and poverty reduction. Failure to reduce large disparities between and within countries may affect the fabric of our societies, fuel economic and civil unrest, and cause international migration. At the very least, it may force the adoption of harmful or costly quick-fix remedies to ward off such disruptions.

## GLOBALIZATION AND THE ROLE OF THE UN

The process of integration of the financial and commercial markets, known as globalization, has made its influence felt over the last two clusters or periods mentioned above. Globalization ought not be about further accentuating the division of the world into rich and poor, segregating those moving ahead from those left behind. Unless this process benefits all countries, regardless of how powerful its supporters may be, it risks becoming unsustainable, both economically and politically. Were this to happen, we might soon be haunted by the specters of the past — such as protectionism and trade wars — when we should be engaged in materializing the promise of a prosperous future.

To avoid this fate, the development debate should not be about dichotomies, such as peacekeeping *or* development, BWIs *or* the UN system, normative *or* opera-

---

1  Speech delivered to the Security Council, 25 September 1977.

tional activities, government *or* private sector. If development issues in general, and poverty alleviation in particular, are to be better addressed, what is needed is a more constructive approach — one that recognizes the synergies that exist between peace-keeping and development, between the BWIs and the UN system, between normative and operational activities, and between government and private sector. In today's competitive world it is more necessary than ever to acknowledge that the world's inequalities will only be overcome through partnerships based on cooperation and mutual respect.

Even today, after all what we have seen in the postwar period, many still maintain that international agencies such as the UN should have no role in development. Their argument has two basic strands. First, that development is primarily a private matter and should be left to the private sector and market forces. Thus, there would be no effective role for public intervention. Second, that if there is a case for public intervention, it is only for national governments acting alone or in concert on a voluntary basis, not for international agencies. This line of argument implies that international agencies cannot effectively address national development problems.

There is certainly a strong case for recognizing the vital role of market forces and the private sector in development, on the one hand, and the action of national governments, on the other. But important areas of development still require multilateral action through the UN. Globalization, and such of its manifestations as growing poverty, inequality and environmental degradation, increases, not reduces, the need for the provision of 'global public goods'.

By 'global public goods' I mean 'global commons' such as a sustainable environment; peace and safety; the basic infrastructure of international economic relations; the furtherance of human rights; democratization; poverty reduction and humanitarian assistance; and the creation, adaptation and diffusion of knowledge. Equally important, the provision of global public goods means meeting needs that markets, and often even governments, left to their own devices, cannot satisfy.

These are some of the foundations of the rationale for the role of the UN in development. But to say that there is a need for the UN system is also to say that there is a need for its services to be provided efficiently, and with a discernible impact on development and social equity. This line of reasoning is the driving force behind UN reform.

And these reform efforts must be pursued in concert with a set of emerging new partners in development brought about by globalization. The weakening role of the state, policy shifts towards privatization and PSD, the increasing importance of TNCs, and the accelerated pace of crossborder integration of industry, trade, finance and services, have gradually placed new actors on the international development stage.

## THE PRIVATE SECTOR

To be effective in the economic and social fields, the UN system has been faced with the need to work with the private sector, both as clients and advisers. Increasingly, UN agencies have been cooperating with business on a large scale, with mutual benefits, in areas such as promoting investment and private enterprise development. In 1999, for example, the Secretary-General invited business leaders to join an international initiative that would bring companies together with UN agencies, labor and civil society to advance universal social and environmental principles. In 2000, the Global Compact was launched[2]. Through collective action, it seeks to advance ten core principles relating to human rights, labor rights, protection of the environment, and the eradication of corruption. This way, the private sector, in partnership with other social actors, can help realize the vision of a more sustainable and inclusive global economy.

In March 2004, the Commission on the Private Sector and Development published its report *Unleashing Entrepreneurship* (UNDP, 2004). It tries to answer two questions raised by the Secretary-General: How can the potential of the private sector and entrepreneurship be unleashed in developing countries? How can the existing private sector be engaged in meeting the challenge? The report identifies three important areas in which this can be sought. In the public sphere, reform of laws, regulations and other barriers to growth must be promoted in order to create an enabling environment for the private sector. In the public-private sphere, cooperation and partnerships between public and private players must be facilitated to enhance access to such key factors as financing, skills and basic services. In the private sphere, the development must be encouraged of business models that can be scaled up and replicated and are commercially sustainable.

The UN recognizes the power of the private sector to generate employment, investment and economic growth in a globalized world and that the private sector must be a key player in integrating the developing world into the global economy in order to raise living standards and reduce poverty. Also, the enhanced relations between the UN and the private sector reflect the growing recognition in the private sector of the importance of international norms and standards.

## CIVIL SOCIETY ORGANIZATIONS

A parallel change has occurred with the rapid growth of a multitude of civil society organizations (CSOs), institutions and informal movements outside the sphere of governments: chambers of commerce, industry associations, cooperatives, industry branch organizations, women's groups, universities, and groups representing the

---

2   The Global Compact is a network; at its core is the Global Compact office and six UN Agencies: OHCHR, UNEP, ILO, UNDP, UNIDO, and UNODC. The Global Compact Leaders Summit was held in June 2004 at the UN Headquarters. According to *Action 20*, the operational setting and governance of the Compact is currently being reviewed.

interests of different sections of society in the social, developmental, humanitarian and other fields.

Such organizations originally emerged in developed countries, but became increasingly important in developing countries and also in transition economies, partly because of diminished confidence in decision-making at the national level. These organizations have gained increasing legitimacy and significant influence in many areas of development.

They form a reservoir of human knowledge, skills and stamina upon which economic and social development can draw. They are increasingly viewed as an important forum for popular participation in decision-making and as a complement to the resources of governments and official agencies, including the UN system. They are also seen as contributors to empowerment, decentralization, grassroots development and new forms of participatory development, and as embodying the principle of subsidiarity — the lowest possible and most decentralized level of institutional representation and action. They are increasingly important partners in the public–private sector dialogue on development. In short, they have added a new voice and fresh impetus to the development debate.

The UN system has increasingly involved these new partners of development in regional and global forums and in technical cooperation at the national level. While this has increased participation in international and national development efforts, it has also made the process of decision-making more complex. To an extent, these partners have introduced some healthy competition to some of the activities of the UN system.

As can be seen from these reflections, reform of the UN is not just about cost-cutting. It is also about making the system more responsive to new global realities. It is about UN agencies identifying and concentrating on their core competencies. It is about strengthening joint and collaborative action and partnerships to deal with the multifaceted nature of development. It is about clearer delineation of mandates and responsibilities, and for greater collaboration and coordination, particularly in the field. It is about being more responsive to its clients. But, most of all, it is about making a difference to the lives of so many who have so little.

In order to succeed, the arguments for reform of the UN system must be articulated around a clear and agreed definition of the stakeholders' needs, and become part of a single undertaking for world development. Such a process may be driven by a group of reforming member states that coalesce beyond the boundaries of conventional regional or political groupings to bring about effective and efficient reform. In this, member states have a pivotal role to play — expressing clear priorities, limiting political influence and ensuring in UN forums that discussions are substantial and that mandates are compatible. This is not mere wishful thinking: UNIDO's experience with the development of its business plan (examined in the second part of this book) gives a flavor of the rewards that can be drawn from an approach of this kind.

# THE UN'S ROLE: NORMATIVE vs OPERATIONAL

To understand how the UN adapted to a changing global landscape, it is worth reviewing the debate around the evolving relationship between its normative and operational functions. This can also be useful in helping to understand the logic and dynamics of the system itself and those of the various UN reform proposals.

The normative functions are intended to influence the perceptions of actors in the international community within a specified set of international issues, while the implementation is left to these actors. Normative functions include forums for debate on issues of economic and political significance, setting targets and monitoring the performance of member states.

The operational functions, on the other hand, involve the implementation in recipient countries of decisions made by participating governments (Bergesen and Lunde, 1999, p. 3). The operational functions of the UN system have undergone significant changes in the last decade. Key institutions such as UNDP have assumed new roles. Donors have significantly adjusted their technical-cooperation funding patterns. New strategic and planning frameworks have been introduced.

## EVOLUTION OF THE UN'S NORMATIVE FUNCTIONS

From a very early stage in the UN's history it was obvious that the United States and the major European countries did not intend to create a global supranational organization. They never seriously considered endowing the UN with a major normative function such as determining the development agenda, nor even a regulatory function in the field of international trade. The most normative institutions — the IMF and, to a certain extent, the World Bank — were not part of the UN proper.

With the exception of the fields of decolonization and human rights, the requirement of universal participation and equality — one nation, one vote — as the primary decision-making principle in the UN (in the General Assembly and in ECOSOC, for example), constrained from the very start the scope for the UN to assume the major normative function for which it was presumably best equipped.

Still, as we have seen, the developing countries did try along its history to use the UN as a global platform for voicing their concerns about socio-economic development. Having secured a majority in all the main UN bodies for economic and social development, they worked to achieve a common identity to the extent of grouping in a Non-Aligned Movement and the G-77 independently of the UN.

Ever more frequently they used the UN, first, as a means of obtaining greater financial transfers from the developed countries, and second, in new UN institutions such as UNCTAD, to vote in a more concerted, and gradually also more confrontational way. In contrast, their influence in the BWIs — which had a major normative role, especially the IMF – was rather limited.

The reaction of the developed countries to the increasingly confrontational demands for redistribution of global wealth was of hesitation and passive resistance.

Led by the United States they adopted a defensive stance in UN forums, and deliberately transferred any issue that was strategically important and required international coordination to the BWIs, where they enjoyed the balance of power because of the way the voting system was weighted.

The developed countries pursued two strategies. First, they initially resisted demands for the establishment of potentially important UN agencies dominated by developing countries. For example, in 1960 they established the International Development Association (IDA) under the World Bank umbrella instead of a Special UN Fund for Economic Development (SUNFED) sponsored by developing countries. Second, they accommodated the rising demands of the developing countries for increased development assistance principally in order to gain political influence over those countries and build advantages in the context of a fierce ideological dispute between East and West.

Increasingly, meanwhile, the UN found itself looking at a tripolar world made up by the West, the East and the South. In spite of growing aid budgets for operational functions throughout the 1960s, the dispute over the normative functions remained on the UN's agenda. Though some well-established specialized agencies, such as the ILO, WHO and UNESCO, were still seen as quite successful in the area of norm-creating functions, other parts of the UN's normative institutional machinery were not. Furthermore, the expenditures of the normative-function agencies of the UN and the norm-creating parts of WHO and UNESCO accounted for less than 7 percent of the UN system's total expenditure (Bertrand, 1985).

The developing countries' efforts to extend the normative functions of the UN were reinforced by the drive of the G-77 and China for a new development paradigm, as expressed in the New International Economic Order (NIEO) of the 1970s, in a range of UN forums: the Annual Session of the General Assembly and ECOSOC, where the G-77 and China enjoyed a majority; UNCTAD, which had emerged as an effective platform for the developing countries and as a catalyst of the NIEO; and the governing bodies of UN funds, programmes and specialized agencies, where the South endeavored to add substantive arguments for the NIEO. Among the specialized agencies was UNIDO, where the G-77 and China succeeded in getting a resolution adopted — against the votes of the developed countries — calling for a US$ 300 million fund for industrial development to be managed by developing countries. The atmosphere in UN forums in the 1970s became one of polarized confrontation over global economic issues.

The confrontation culminating in the NIEO decade ended in a standoff between North and South, with the North losing confidence in the UN system's ability to handle economic and social issues on its behalf.

The normative functions of the UN system envisaged in the early stages of its existence — such as providing global forums on economic and social issues — had been *de facto* suppressed during the Cold War because of lack of political consensus and the growth of operational activities for development. The end of the Cold War, therefore, raised hopes for a new beginning for the UN's normative functions. An example of this expectation could be seen in the 1992 UN Conference on Environment and Development in Rio de Janeiro, Brazil.

## EVOLUTION OF THE UN'S OPERATIONAL FUNCTIONS

The suppression of the UN's normative functions during the Cold War gave increasing scope for operational activities in support of development. The post-colonial period brought about a proliferation of new development actors. Many new UN organizations and bodies devoted to development assistance were established, especially from the mid-1960s, in line with the rapid growth in aid transfers to developing countries. Operational development functions were assumed by a wide range of UN bodies — specialized agencies, regional commissions, functional commissions, secretariat bodies and financing schemes.

In 1965, the General Assembly decided to merge the Expanded Programme of Technical Assistance (EPTA) and the Special Fund (SF) into the UNDP, which was expected to become the main coordinating body for financing UN operational functions. Many different UN bodies created institutional capabilities for their operational functions, by means of funds made available through UNDP (and its predecessors) and other sources. The big four specialized agencies — FAO, UNESCO, ILO and WHO — expanded their development activities significantly. UNIDO was created in 1967.

The period 1955–92 saw strong and growing support for ODA through the UN system. This happened in spite of the growing confrontation between North and South, criticisms of the UN, and the lack of progress towards reforming the UN system. The growth in resources for development channeled through the UN system, however, did not reflect political convergence between donors and recipients. Rather, it was the result of careful lobbying by the developing countries, the Cold War, whose protagonists were motivated by the desire to secure political influence in the South, and more genuine aid motives, mainly from the Nordic countries.

The UN's operational development functions expanded correspondingly: the number of staff rose from 31,000 in 1974 to 47,000 in 1994, with operational activities in the field accounting for most of the increase.

From the 1970s onwards, an increasing number of UN funds and programmes, such as UNDP, WFP, UNFPA, UNICEF and UNHCR, expanded their institutional cooperation machinery, which was spreading worldwide, inevitably causing overlaps. By 1995, the number of field offices worldwide had reached 1,125.

In spite of the rapid growth in UN development assistance, the total remained modest compared with other development assistance channels. In 1995, the total net flows of financial resources through the UN amounted to US$ 4.2 billion, considerably less than the grants given by the EU (US$ 5.3 billion), Japan (US$ 10.4 billion), and Germany (US$ 4.8 billion). The importance of non-UN multilateral donors increased, primarily because of the growth of the resources of the EU and the multilateral development banks.

From 1980, much of the growth in assistance channeled via the UN was in the form of contributions earmarked for specific purposes, as donors wished to increase their control of UN funding and activities.

UNDP served as the central funding agency for technical cooperation in the UN system. The resources available were allocated to the countries through the UNDP system of indicative planning figures. Projects were executed normally through a UN organizational entity other than UNDP. The normative and specialized entities of the UN looked to UNDP to fund projects that allowed them to implement the programme priorities established by their governing bodies.

In 1995 UNDP assumed new roles, becoming both a substantive and a funding agency. It now delivers most of its projects through either national or direct execution. Therefore (confirming a trend that started in the early 1990s) access to UNDP as the traditional source of financing was reduced or eliminated for most other UN technical cooperation entities, leaving them with two options: to withdraw from technical cooperation altogether or to engage in their own supplementary fundraising activities.

With the loss of UNDP's central funding role, there was no longer a built-in mechanism that allocated funding to priority needs at some central point within the system. Henceforth that process had to be addressed primarily in the field.

As a consequence, most UN entities started to raise a larger portion of their technical cooperation funding requirements directly from donors, which led to competition between them for donor support. The UN system's technical cooperation entities now operate in a more market-like environment. However, it is necessary to recognize that this is a very special market, without proper coordination mechanisms due to the way the major donor countries articulate their contributions.

In sum, better coordination among those UN activities that target economic development seems inevitable as a result of increasing pressure for high-quality, collectively supported and genuinely locally owned strategies in the framework of the MDGs.

# CONCLUSIONS

The political events that prevailed during the different phases of the existence of the UN have had a relevant impact on its performance and development. In particular, political events contributed to preventing the UN from developing a high-profile normative role in the economic and social fields. A secondary effect, probably not clearly foreseen and evaluated beforehand, was the expansion — without a clear programmatic focus — of the UN system's operational functions related to economic development.

Attempts were made to address this problem by means of institutional arrangements and managerial or administrative coordination mechanisms that sought to put a lid on the proliferation of operational activities — a development that had given rise to numerous concerns about overlaps, duplication and the associated potential waste of resources.

The changes associated with the accelerated pace of the process of globalization, the emergence of new partners in the private sector and the rise of the CSOs added new elements of concern about the relevance of the institutional setting of the UN's operational activities.

Additionally, the increasing bilateralization of technical cooperation schemes after the Cold War and the growing trend towards an expansion of the traditional role of the BWIs in those activities (sometimes taking over the agendas of UN bodies and specialized agencies) completes a worrisome picture for the UN's economic development functions.

A programmatically focused business plan could be a practical response to these hurdles since, as we have seen earlier, it can serve as a vehicle to reconnect the normative and operational functions of the UN. In addition, a programmatic emphasis would also help minimize possible controversial aspects, which we will address further on.

## REFERENCES

Maurice Bertrand, Some Reflections on the Reform of the United Nations, Joint Inspection Unit, Geneva (JIU/REP/95/9), 1985

James Paul (2000), *The United Nations and Global, Social-Economic Policy, United Nations and Global Social-Economic Policy: Analysis* (http://www.globalpolicy.org/Soceon/UN/analysis.htm (1/17/00).

Joachim Müller, ed (1997), *Reforming the United Nations: New Initiatives and Past Efforts*, Vol. I-III, published in co-operation with the United Nations, Kluwer Law International, The Hague/London/Boston, 1997.

M.A. de Paz Bañez (1998), Economía Mundial – Tránsito hacia el nuevo milenio, Pirámide, Madrid, 1998.

Chapter 3

# REVIEWING UN REFORM PROPOSALS

Since the late 1960s more than fifty proposals for UN reform, originating from both within and outside the UN system, have been put forward. Some of these have played a part in changing the system, while others have stimulated dialogue and influenced international public opinion without being formally adopted and implemented.

Member states, renowned personalities, diplomats, experts and CSOs generated most of the early reform proposals. Only two sets of proposals in the 1990s came from the UN itself: the Boutros-Ghali agenda of 1992 and the reform proposals of Secretary-General Kofi Annan of 1997 and 2002.

Most of those reforms targeted the developmental role of the UN system — its proliferation of bodies, inadequate coordination between the UN proper and the specialized agencies, lack of focus and inadequate impact. Remedies proposed to overcome those shortcomings mainly took the form of improvements in institutional arrangements and management issues rather than of programmatic reforms.

Discussions on UN reform have often been passionate since they relate to much hope and expectation about people's lives, security and welfare. They have been significantly influenced by the political, economic and social priorities among member states — and these have changed over time. As we shall see, the bids to reform the UN have gone through different phases:

☐   Initial reform efforts in the framework of the Cold War in the early 1960s focused primarily on organizational, financial and budgetary matters and were driven by concerns in the East about what was perceived to be a UN Secretariat dominated by the West.

☐   A new focus on development appeared in the late 1960s and 1970s, with many newly independent states joining the UN, followed by growing North-South strains and the establishment of the Group of 77. Efforts were aimed at creating new bodies, increasing the efficiency of the system for implementing technical cooperation and the emergence of the UN as a forum for global negotiations on development, trade, industry and natural resources (Jackson Report, Gardner Report, Brandt Commission).

☐ New visions and criticisms accentuated the North-South differences during the 1980s, including those that reflected changing United States policies (Heritage Foundation); calls for financial reform (Maurice Bertrand, Brundtland Commission); and emphasis on improving efficiency, streamlining and budget reductions (Group of 18).

☐ The end of the Cold War was accompanied by a rediscovery, even renaissance, of the UN in the late 1980s and early 1990s. This new wave of enthusiasm for the UN led to further reform proposals (the Nordic Project, proposals by Erskine Childers and Brian Urquhart, Boutros Boutros-Ghali's Agenda).

☐ Following the emphasis placed on peace and security matters in the context of developments in Central and Eastern Europe and the demise of the Soviet Union, in the early 1990s the South demanded a reassessment of the UN's role and purpose. Reform proposals by the South Center and negotiations for an Agenda for Development revealed a lack of common ground among member states regarding the organization's future role. Initial expectations in the security area proved unrealistic and a strong need emerged for the UN to focus and prioritize its activities (Independent Working Group: Commission on Global Governance, Nordic project II and EU proposal 1997).

☐ Recent reform proposals have moved towards programmatic reforms such as the proposals of Secretary-General Kofi Annan of 1997 and 2002 for a structured and comprehensive reform effort as well as that of the Utstein Group + of 2004.

All these reform proposals have one element in common: the quest for cohesiveness and clear sense of direction in a highly diverse system. The concern voiced by the stakeholders of the UN system concentrated on three main elements:

a   The balance between the normative and the operational role of the UN;
b   The perceived proliferation of UN bodies and their lack of coordination; and
c   The cost-efficiency and effectiveness of the UN's development functions.

In order to be able to shape adequately the future of the UN it is essential to reflect on past reform efforts and to draw the lessons they offer. A proper assessment of the need for future reforms demands a clear understanding of the intentions of different interest groups in this process.

## THE NEW FOCUS ON DEVELOPMENT (late 1960s and 1970s)

### THE JACKSON STUDY (1969)

The first major reform effort in this area was proposed in Sir Robert Jackson's study, *Capacity of the UN Development System* (Jackson, 1969). It contained a set of recommendations to rationalize the UN's development system, in particular UNDP, ECOSOC, and coordination between agencies. UNDP was to act as the coordinating body of development assistance, while ECOSOC would become a policy center for development and coordinate the activities of the specialized agencies.

The plan to establish UNDP as the UN system's central financing institution for technical assistance had limited success, and its role as the center for funding and coordination declined. Nor was the recommendation to transform ECOSOC into a policy center taken up. The specialized agencies were not too enthusiastic about seeing their independence curtailed. Nor did member states show much interest, and their delegations in various UN governing bodies suffered from a lack of coordinated positions on key issues.

## THE GARDNER REPORT (1975)

In 1975 the developed countries agreed to establish a group of 25 experts to come up with recommendations on how the UN system could be adapted to meet the development needs and aspirations of the developing countries. The result was the Gardner Report (1975), which expressed concern about the fragmentation, proliferation and multiplicity of UN organizations, the need to achieve consensus through new consultative procedures, revision of voting rights in the BWIs to reflect the interests of developing countries, improvement of working methods, decentralization, coordination, and efficiency. The report called for structural changes in the UN General Assembly and ECOSOC, the establishment of a United Nations Development Agency (UNDA), and the adoption of new consultative procedures to help governments implement agreed solutions. It also made suggestions for the replacement of UNCTAD by an international trade organization.

The General Assembly merely took note, in 1975, of the Gardner Report's recommendations, but subsequently the report was considered by a newly created Ad hoc Committee on the Restructuring of the Economic and Social Sectors of the UN. During the period in which this committee was active, significant differences existed among the member states' outlooks. The proposed reforms of the administrative system revealed a conflict of interest between developed and developing countries.

Unlike in earlier discussions of the Jackson Report, the developed countries, particularly the United States, were concerned about the prospect of a strong, consolidated UN development system, and felt that a more fragmented one would increase their influence (Müller, 1997, p. 32). As a result, the Gardner Report's proposal to establish a UNDA was not adopted. The General Assembly, after consultation and debate, adopted the recommendations of the Ad hoc Committee in 1977. By then, however, the original recommendations of the Gardner Report had been substantially diluted. Overall, the political compromise reached in 1977 provided a clear example of a half-hearted attempt at UN reform.

# IMPROVING EFFICIENCY AND SEEKING FINANCIAL REFORM (1980s)

## THE HERITAGE FOUNDATION (1984)

After the quest for a NIEO by the G-77 and China had failed, and the North had lost confidence in the UN system, the political decision-makers in the United States went even further, questioning the very concept of multilateralism and its translation into government policies, largely on the basis of a study published by the Heritage Foundation (1984). The thrust of this study was that the politicization of the UN increasingly prevented it from achieving, even partially, the goals stipulated in its Charter. The report addressed two important issues: economic development and the environment.

☐  *Economic development.* It argued that the NIEO had supplanted the original development mandate of the UN. It decried the fact that nationalizations had taken place and property rights over patents, trademarks and technology had been questioned. It also contended that many UN projects encouraged planning and government policy intervention, rather than private market-oriented activities, and that 'eliminating the UN development activities would make very little aggregate difference to economic development in the developing countries.'

☐  *Environment.* It maintained that international decision-making was inappropriate, that each country individually should deal with national concerns, and that 'regional compacts or conventions, no doubt, would develop to meet larger geographic, transboundary concerns.'

In other areas the study recommended that the technical agencies of the UN should focus exclusively on technical matters and not on the NIEO; that the function of the General Assembly should be reduced and 'not be allowed to pose as a legitimate and impartial global forum.' It went on to propose that, should these recommendations not be adopted, the United States government should consider withdrawing from the UN. This, in the authors' view, would create an opportunity to design a new system of international cooperation. The report concluded 'that a world without the UN would be a better world'.

This stance contrasted sharply with that of the Marc Nerfin Report (1985) which, after evaluating the UN and its specialized agencies, including UNIDO, argued that 'the world as we know it would not have been possible without the UN.'

The recommendations of the Heritage Foundation Report were largely adopted by the Reagan administration, and found echoes elsewhere:

☐  The United States withdrew from UNESCO in 1984; the United Kingdom followed. This was partly because of allegations of mismanagement in that organization, and partly because of a proposal for a New World Information and Communications Order, which was perceived as an attempt to control the free press.

☐  The FAO was criticized for alleged politicization and mismanagement.

☐    Criticism of the UN intensified over its efforts to establish a code of conduct for TNCs, as well as codes for infant food formula, pesticides and toxic chemicals, and transfer of technology.

☐    The United States administration refused to sign the Law of the Sea Convention, which had been agreed earlier.

☐    With regard to the management of the UN, the United States government criticized what it saw as a lack of transparency and accountability in budgetary matters, excessive paperwork, technically deficient and biased management, duplication and questionable financial management practices.

Other areas that raised concern in the United States were the North–South dialogue under the aegis of UNCTAD, and global negotiations beneath the umbrella of the UN. Because of the confrontational attitude it had adopted, the United States often found itself on the defensive and being outvoted even though other developed countries shared some of its concerns. However, the United States was prepared not only to voice concern, but also to push for action.

The main donor countries saw the North–South confrontation as an exercise in futility, and the South felt it could no longer oppose the efforts of the developed countries to reform the UN — even though developing countries considered these efforts to be against their own interests. In the post-NIEO vacuum, a search was initiated for new UN normative functions that would be attractive to the developed countries, such as those seeking sustainable development.

## THE BERTRAND REPORT (1985)

A report prepared by Maurice Bertrand (1985) for the Joint Inspection Unit (JIU) reiterated many of the recommendations of the Jackson and Gardner Reports. The Bertrand report was even more critical than its precursors about waste, overlapping functions, inefficiency and lack of impact in the field. It claimed that coordination efforts since the late 1970s towards joint planning, country programmes, field coordination and an integrated approach to development, had produced no results. It recommended that ECOSOC — which had been enlarged from 27 to 54 members in 1973 — should be replaced with an Economic Security Council of no more than 23 members from the larger developed countries and with limited geographical representation.

To achieve greater coordination of operational functions, the report recommended the establishment of a single, interdisciplinary development agency responsible for agriculture, industry, health and education, and with integrated operations and offices in various regions and sub-regions. This implied a restructuring of all the operational activities of existing bodies, such as UNDP. The Bertrand report was extensively publicized and attracted much attention both within and without the UN system, but the official response was lukewarm. While within the UN system its main recommendations were considered rather utopian, the Bertrand report was to serve as an important input into the later work of the Group of 18 (see below).

## FINANCIAL CRISES (1980s)

Most observers identified the lack of development impact in the developing countries as a compelling reason to reform the UN's development functions. Attempts were made to strengthen coordination in the field through country programmes, integrated programming and coordination at the country level, but little progress was achieved. Moreover, recipient countries began to make it clear that they felt a lack of ownership of schemes ostensibly meant to further their development.

All these developments came to a head in a series of financial crises in the UN system during the 1980s. Apart from political disagreement, the main cause was the United States' criticism of the UN, which led the United States Congress to call for a reduction of the United States' contribution from 25 percent to 20 percent of the annual budget of the UN or of any specialized agency that did not adopt a voting system on budgetary matters weighted according to each member state's contribution.

However, the introduction of a system of weighted voting would have required an amendment to the UN Charter, which could only be adopted if the smaller member countries forfeited their influence on the budget. Such a change would also have reduced the influence of larger countries, such as the Soviet Union and China. The so-called Kassenbaum legislation led to part of the United States contribution to the UN budget being withheld, and to other countries withholding their assessed contributions for peacekeeping, thus precipitating a financial crisis. As the UN was statutorily barred from borrowing on the commercial market, it tried to cope through organizational reforms, administrative measures, staff reductions and programme and budget reforms.

The developing countries criticized the withholding of funds by the United States — which became strategically stronger through accumulated arrears — and argued against weighted voting, which they considered to be against the very principles of the Charter, based on the sovereign equality of all member states. While the United States defended the withholding as a policy practiced by other countries, the Soviet Union and European countries joined in the criticism — but supported the budgetary cuts, emphasizing the need for improvements in cost efficiency.

## THE GROUP OF 18 (1986)

The financial crisis and the widespread demand for change resulted in the establishment of the Group of 18, charged with taking a long-term view of economy measures and new decision-making mechanisms for budgetary matters that would satisfy both the few large-scale contributors and the majority of member states.

The report presented by the Group of 18 in 1986 (Group of 18, 1986) made a number of recommendations on the intergovernmental machinery, the structure of the Secretariat, personnel policies, monitoring and evaluation, and budgetary procedures. Emphasis was placed on a leaner Secretariat — less top-heavy, less complex and less fragmented, more productive and more efficient. The main breakthrough it contributed was a new budgeting process, which gave more influence to the Committee for Programme and Coordination (CPC) in budgetary issues and broadened its representation; this did not entail weighted voting but it did give *de facto* veto rights to each member of the CPC.

Other recommendations were, to a large extent, restatements of previous proposals for administrative reform. The report was approved by the General Assembly in 1986 by consensus, which was seen as a major achievement. The negotiations on reform towards improved efficiency, through a reduced budget, revealed a striking convergence of interest between East and West in many areas.

However, the developing countries considered the new budgeting process a threat to the principles embodied in the Charter about the adoption of General Assembly resolutions, sovereign equality and majority decision-making. While many developing countries saw the consensus as unconstitutional inasmuch as it granted *de facto* veto rights in budgetary matters to major contributors, the South finally agreed on the proposal in the expectation that the United States would pay up its assessed contributions in full. Implementation of the reforms was swift; it was largely completed by the end of 1989. The United States resumed payment of part of its assessed contributions, and paid part of its arrears. The reforms had reduced the scale of the confrontation, especially between East and West, and led to a greater convergence of views on administrative matters. The United States' representative described the 1989 General Assembly as 'one of the most constructive and realistic within memory', and even went so far as to describe the UN as 'a useful place'.

## THE BRUNDTLAND COMMISSION: SUSTAINABLE DEVELOPMENT (1987)

New approaches to reform were introduced by the 1987 report of the World Commission on Environment and Development (Brundtland Commission, 1987). It addressed issues 'on our common future', and underlined the need to ensure that new approaches to sustainable development had a chance of succeeding.

The commission argued that environmental and development issues should be considered jointly on a global scale. It said that sustainable development, to be achieved in both the North and the South, meant 'ensuring that development meets the needs of the present without compromising the ability of future generations to meet their own needs.' First, population growth should be in harmony with the changing productive potential of the ecosystem (ensuring economic and environmental sustainability). Second, the poor should be guaranteed a reasonable share of resources, and new economic growth patterns should be promoted to alleviate poverty (ensuring social sustainability). The commission specifically recommended that international bodies and agencies should ensure that their operational activities encouraged sustainable development.

Altogether, the Brundtland Commission report was timely and contributed to an increase in the attention given to environmental issues in international forums. Many governments, particularly in the developed countries, had already introduced environmental programmes and policies. The ensuing international interest in environmental issues led to the United Nations Conference on Environment and Development (UNCED) in Rio de Janeiro in 1992. This conference approved Agenda 21 and three conventions, on climate change, biodiversity and desertification. Of overwhelming importance was the fact that the concept of sustainable development was now accepted and assumed a central role in the activities of the United Nations. This entailed new alliances within the UN system – between UNIDO, UNDP and UNEP – and a new momentum for environmental issues, which led to important new normative functions, in the shape of the Montreal and Kyoto protocols.

# REASSESSMENT OF THE UN'S ROLE (1990s)

The case for reform was incomplete. As concerns grew about the insufficient coordination and impact of the UN system, the issue of its governance came to the fore. In the early 1990s, proposals for reforming the system multiplied and related political negotiations — above all within the General Assembly — intensified. The debate, still under way, has been driven by a complex set of determinants and objectives, including:

☐    The desire of some of the major donor countries (led by the United States) to improve the UN system's effectiveness and efficiency by streamlining its operations — which, in turn, would reduce their financial contributions to multilateral development.
☐    Countervailing attempts by the developing countries (expressed through the Group of 77 and China) to safeguard a strong UN system with sufficient capacity to support economic and social development in the South amidst the challenges of globalization.
☐    Efforts to improve the coherence, complementarities and coordination of the UN system's development activities, particularly at the country level, and to define the balance between the normative and operational activities of UN organizations (primarily a concern of the Nordic countries).

The following are some of the more noteworthy current proposals for UN reform that, in various ways, dominated the intellectual and policy debates in the 1990s and are likely to influence the UN reform agenda in the years to come. Only their most important action-oriented recommendations are summarized here.

## THE SOUTH COMMISSION: POVERTY & HUMAN NEEDS

The developing countries have recognized that though they share many problems and experiences, there was a lack of initiative from the South itself to examine these issues, draw lessons from them and take action.[1] The South Commission (South

---

1    The lack of initiative from the South should be viewed in the context of the summit meetings of the non-aligned countries after 1961 where there were repeated proposals for UN reform. The Non-Aligned Movement, however, has always spoken in favour of a reinforcement of the UN and has consequently agreed to forgo an institutionalization of the movement, so that the UN should be and remain the field of activity and platform of the non-aligned countries.

Commission, 1990) underlined that the aspirations of developing countries to advance their development efforts had not materialized. Widening disparities between North and South had been compounded by intensified globalization, while the easing of East–West tensions had led to fears that resources would be shifted from the North to the East, further marginalizing the South. The commission presented a vision of an economically and politically undivided world, in which the primary concerns were overcoming poverty and satisfying basic human needs. It emphasized that prospects for the development of the South hinged on its improving its relationship with the North — while noting that international economic relations were unfavorable to the South in view of the existing world distribution of wealth.

These problems were compounded by the North's new demand to attach priority to environmental protection in relation to development objectives. This aim was complicated by two facts. First, that poverty itself was a major cause of environmental damage in the South — a problem that could only be overcome by economic development. Second, that environmental effects were transmitted from the North to the South through trade in raw materials intended for the affluent consumer lifestyle of the North. The South Commission therefore called for a renewal of the North–South dialogue and negotiations on restructuring world economic relations. Priority, it said, should be given to reform of the international financial and trade system, based on multilateralism and non-discrimination and with the object of promoting sustainable development in the Third World. A programme was formulated to revive economic growth in the South and to move towards a restructuring of the international system in the fields of science and technology, the environment, global commons, development and the UN.

The following were among the South Commission's main recommendations:

☐   A link should be established between total international aid and aid for science and technology.

☐   A regime should be established to provide for the transfer of relevant technology from the North on terms consistent with the development interests of the South.

☐   UNIDO, UNESCO, IAEA and the United Nations University (UNU) should build up a scientific infrastructure with a view to contributing to scientific and technological progress in the South.

☐   International regimes for the exploitation of global commons such as Antarctica and outer space should be established.

☐   An international regime for energy should be established, minimizing disruptive fluctuations in supply and prices, and providing for a fair allocation to developing countries of exhaustible energy resources.

☐   The South should be assisted to develop substitutes for fossil fuels and to adopt techniques for conserving energy.

The commission envisaged the emergence in the post-Cold War period of a new system that would entail the 'radical transformation of the existing arrangements consistent with the goals of democracy, equality and equity in international relations'. In the absence of such a transformation, the South feared that the existing multilateral system would be adapted to new requirements of the North with limited or no significance for the South. However, in spite of all these efforts, the hopes and aspirations of the South, so forcefully advocated in the South Commission's report, were not heeded. Development issues of the South were accorded low priority in the North because of the importance attached to security and reconstruction efforts in the economies in transition as a result of the new spirit of cooperation in the Security Council.

## THE NORDIC PROJECT (1991)

Launched at the end of the 1980s, the Nordic UN Reform Project (referred to henceforth as the Nordic Project) published its conclusions and recommendations in 1991 (Nordic Project, 1991). Presented jointly by the governments of Denmark, Finland, Norway and Sweden, it provided the foundation for a series of reform initiatives by the Nordic countries (both collectively and individually).[2]

One of its key conclusions was that 'a stronger sense of partnership and willingness to reform needs to be fostered among the UN's members'. The report focused on issues of governance of UN operations on the one hand, and on improved system-wide coordination, on the other. The ultimate goals were to reduce duplication of effort and to enhance transparency and accountability within the UN system.

In another document (Nordic Memorandum, 1992) it was pointed out that 'the Charter of the UN did not foresee an operational role for the UN in the economic and social fields, and it provides little guidance on distribution of powers and responsibilities.'

*Governance.* In the area of governance, the report recommended:

☐   Creating an International Development Council as a high-level forum to provide policy guidance and discuss system-wide development issues in the broader context of a rationalized and more effective ECOSOC.
☐   Putting a single senior official in charge of economic and social matters in the UN Secretariat.
☐   Limiting membership in the governing bodies of operational UN funds and programmes to around twenty countries (elected by different regions) in order to improve decision-making.
☐   Extending UNDP's analytical capacities beyond its core mandate to act as a central funding mechanism. The object was not to enlarge the role of the UNDP in project execution but to improve the conceptual underpinning of key development issues (for example through the Human Development Report).

---

2   The Project was taken up again in 1996 in the context of General Assembly negotiations on strengthening the UN system; see further below.

*Operations.* As regards better coordination of operational activities, the proposals advanced by the Nordic Project set the agenda for many years to come, particularly where they concerned the UN's specialized agencies (Nordic Project, 1990). Their traditional analytical and normative roles were seen as having been eroded by an unfocused expansion of their operational activities — driven primarily by the availability of project funding. The specialized agencies were thus called upon to strengthen their analytical and normative roles, define their core competencies and areas of focus, and place more emphasis on 'upstream' activities such as policy advice and sectoral analyses. The specialized agencies were identified as being the best placed to deal with the emerging environmental agenda in terms of negotiating, monitoring and supporting the implementation of international conventions and treaties. In a nutshell, the most appropriate role of the UN specialized agencies was that of centers of excellence rather than merely as executors of projects.

The Nordic Project also strongly argued for the establishment of a unified structure for UN system operations at the field level. As we shall see, this issue resurfaced in the mid-1990s and led to the streamlining and harmonizing of the UN system's operational activities.

## BOUTROS-GHALI'S AGENDA (1992)

In December 1992 Secretary-General Boutros Boutros-Ghali (Boutros Ghali, 1992) emphasized the lack of coordination between the specialized agencies and the UN and also stressed the link between peace and development. He argued that growing peacekeeping activities should not be accommodated at the expense of development. He further suggested that the Administrative Committee on Coordination (ACC) should act more decisively to guide the work of specialized agencies and that ECOSOC should be strengthened. Enthusiasm for a stronger UN system, however, was ambiguous and there was little room for implementing drastic proposals.

In response to the concern that had been expressed at the downgrading of development issues in favor of peace and security concerns, and as a complement to the UN Agenda for Peace, an Agenda for Development was prepared and issued by the Secretary-General in May 1994 (Secretary-General, 1994). The Agenda considered five dimensions of development: peace as the precondition for development; the economy as an engine of progress; the environment as the basis for sustainability; justice as a foundation of society; and democracy as good governance. It assigned an indispensable role to the UN in implementing a new collective development vision, which gave cause for optimism that the main actors for development would be integrated.

In essence, the Agenda, which was normative in character, was about the reform efforts in the UN. However, in contrast to the very concrete proposals contained in the Agenda for Peace, the Agenda for Development focused narrowly on principles and contained little resembling a practical implementation strategy.

In discussions at ECOSOC in 1994, the developing countries expressed disenchantment at the absence of an action-oriented blueprint in the Agenda. In their view, two things were missing: a focus on economic growth, and commitment on the part of developed countries to provide resources for development. The developed countries, on the other hand, emphasized the role of market orientation, human rights, environmental sustainability and democratic systems for development. While it was acknowledged that the UN controlled only a fraction of the resources available for development, it was also noted that the organization had a unique advantage in normative global consensus building.

## THE COMMISSION ON GLOBAL GOVERNANCE (1994)

The Commission on Global Governance was established to contribute towards improving global governance in an emerging 'global neighborhood' (CGG, 1995).[3] Governance was seen as going beyond purely governmental actors to encompass interaction among the institutions, processes and people that together constitute society and through which public and private bodies and individuals manage their common affairs. The commission's point of departure was an increasingly complex world in which the private sector and civil society were becoming more and more powerful as agents of development within the context of economic globalization.

Adopting the common values of democratic principles, the rule of law, human rights, liberty and integrity, the commission endeavored to reconcile global institutions with a more inclusive and democratic framework for global governance. Its recommendations included an integrated framework for governance functions based on the principle of subsidiarity at the global, regional, national and local levels — that is, action is to be taken always at the lowest and most decentralized level possible.

A summary of the commission's report was submitted to the 50th session of the General Assembly, but its main recommendations were not translated into action. The most far-reaching ones, such as the reform of the Security Council and the creation of an Economic Security Council, did not immediately command a consensus and would have required lengthy negotiations.

Others, such as the convening of an annual Civil Society Forum, were found too cumbersome and were eventually rendered irrelevant by a progressive integration of CSOs into the work of individual UN organizations. Finally, the call to review the case for dismantling a number of UN organizations and bodies (such as ECOSOC, the Regional Commissions, UNCTAD and UNIDO) was not based on a solid analysis of their functions and was therefore considered unacceptable by most countries. It did help, however, to trigger reform efforts in the UN organizations affected. In UNIDO, early reform efforts gathered momentum around 1995 and led in 1997-99 to the transformation of the organization, which will be analyzed in detail further on.

---

3  The summary of action proposals of the Report was also issued in 1995 as General Assembly document A/50/79. The commission was co-chaired by Ingvar Carlsson and Shridath Ramphal.

# THE CHILDERS–URQUHART PROPOSALS (1995)

The renewal of the UN system was increasingly being viewed within the context of the organization's economic and social functions and their relationship to the root causes of instability and conflict. In response to a request by a representative group of ambassadors to the UN and in preparation for discussions envisaged for the 50th anniversary of the UN in 1995, two former senior staff members of the UN — Erskine Childers and Brian Urquhart — prepared a study on renewing the UN system (Childers and Urquhart, 1994). Rather than proposing radical reforms, they adopted a pragmatic approach, concentrating on transformations that could be introduced within the framework of the Charter and within the constitutions of the specialized agencies.

Their study drew attention to limitations of past reforms, which were due to such factors as the appointment of government nominees with inadequate skills to top positions, reshuffling of the organizational chart without greater coordination, lack of guidance from legislative bodies and the absence of programmes for staff training. Moreover, it emphasized that earlier efforts at reorganization had not adequately discharged responsibility for the right organizational unit to the right post. The report recommended a consolidated budget for the UN, which should be adopted by the General Assembly.

The authors had endeavored to prepare a practical proposal for gradual reforms, which would be politically feasible, but the governing bodies largely ignored their recommendations.

Overall, administrative reforms succeeded in reducing staff and introducing economy measures in various parts of the organization. However, progress in a number of important areas was limited:

☐    Organizational reforms were undertaken primarily by reshuffling boxes in the organizational charts, which was a zero-sum game and did not lead to greater coordination or effectiveness (Childers and Urquhart, op. cit). A conceptual framework for the organizational restructuring of a multilateral body appeared to be lacking.

☐    The programmes and budgets of the various bodies were originally presented separately, but later combined in consolidated programmes and budgets for each one of them. However, the combined programme budget lacked transparency and accountability. Recommendations for a consolidated programme budget for the whole UN Development System in the mid-1990s were not approved.

☐    In its early decades, the UN had succeeded in mobilizing and associating world-renowned intellectuals in the economics and social fields. Later, however, it became evident that many member states viewed the UN Secretariat as an area where they could gain political influence and control activities by installing their own nationals in senior positions. This reduced the effectiveness of the system and the organizational capability of various of its units. The absence of programmes for staff training only compounded the problem.

## THE INDEPENDENT WORKING GROUP (1995)

As the Commission on Global Governance had done earlier, the Independent Working Group on the Future of the United Nations (IWG, 1995)[4] focused on issues of political and global governance, and on the complex interplay of economic, social, cultural and political factors in conflict prevention and peace building. The group saw national sovereignty being weakened by globalization and attributed to the UN an important role in supporting developing countries in their efforts to adapt to this process.

In the field of economic development, it recommended the establishment of an Economic Council as a principal organ of the UN system. This Economic Council — as a counterpart to an expanded Security Council and a proposed Social Council — would integrate the work of all UN agencies and international institutions engaged in economic issues and, supported by an advisory committee drawn from academia and the private sector, was to promote the global harmonization of macroeconomic policies.

Ultimately, the group's report, submitted to the General Assembly in 1995, received little attention and has not had any significant impact on the UN reform debate.

## THE SOUTH CENTER (1996)

While acknowledging the imperative of increasing the UN system's efficiency and effectiveness, the South Center's report of 1996 (South Center, 1996)[5] expressed concern over the erosion of the system's pluralist and democratic character. It also asserted that underfunding and understaffing were progressively weakening some of its key functions. In particular, the report identified a diminution of the UN organizations' role in supporting economic development. Large industrialized countries were portrayed as aiming to divest the UN of its policy and research capabilities in the economic sphere — as an integral element of a strategy to strengthen the BWIs and the WTO as the lead agencies in matters of economic development. The report criticized the shift of UN resources towards humanitarian and peacekeeping activities as undermining its capacity to contribute towards economic development. It perceived a danger that the UN system would turn away from long-term development issues towards short-term issues of political instability and humanitarian crises.

Among the main recommendations of the South Center Report are:

☐   Strengthening the financing of the UN through a revised system of assessed contributions (with a 12.5 percent ceiling for single country contributions as a percentage of total contributions), a gradual reduction of voluntary contributions, and the introduction of international levies and taxation

---

4   The Independent Working Group was co-chaired by Moeen Qureshi and Richard von Weizsäcker, former presidents of Pakistan and Germany, respectively. The project was sponsored by the Ford Foundation, with its secretariat located at Yale University.

5   The South Center, which in 1995 became a permanent intergovernmental organization of developing countries, prepared a contribution to the economic agenda of the Non-Aligned Movement (NAM) that was submitted to the 11th NAM Summit in Cartagena, Colombia, October 1995.

☐　A more representative Security Council without veto rights and with no permanent seats.

☐　Enhancing the research and policy-making roles of the UN allowing better policy coordination at the global level.

☐　Democratizing the governance and improving the transparency of the BWIs.

## NORDIC PROJECT II AND THE EUROPEAN UNION PROPOSALS (1997)

The first phase of the Nordic Project (reviewed above) was followed up in 1996. This second phase culminated in a new report (Nordic Project, 1996).[6] In parallel, the EU submitted reform proposals at the beginning of 1997 as an input to the debates of the General Assembly Working Group on the Strengthening of the UN System. The EU proposals reflected many of the concerns of the Nordic countries and, taken together, the two sets of proposals greatly influenced those put forward later by the Secretary-General (see below).

The EU reform proposals (European Union, 1997) explicitly recognized that the UN remains the central framework for multilateral cooperation aimed at credibly addressing global issues. The key challenge they identified was that of ensuring sustainable development and poverty reduction amidst an increasingly competitive global economy, with special emphasis on the needs of the LDCs. The report explicitly stated that 'reform of the UN is not about cost-cutting: it is about strengthening and revitalizing the organization to effectively meet the challenges of the future.'

The double role of the UN system was considered to require: first, agenda setting and the establishment of globally agreeable norms (which demanded strengthening intergovernmental processes) and, second, operational activities in the field (which called for more coherence among the activities of UN funds and programmes).

The following reforms were proposed:

☐　Appointment of an Under-Secretary-General (USG) for economic and social cooperation and development issues.

☐　Merger and reorganization of three UN Departments: the Department of Economics and Social Information and Policy Analysis (DESIPA), the Department for Policy Coordination and Sustainable Development (DPCSD) and the Department for Development Support and Management Services (DDSMS).

☐　Unified representation of the UN at country level, with clear authority given to the UN Resident Coordinator; stronger emphasis on joint priority-setting, programming and implementation of activities; and the establishment of common UN premises.

☐　ECOSOC to exercise fully its envisaged role as the coordinating body of all UN funds and programmes, and to be convened in a more flexible manner.

☐　Better cooperation between the UN agencies, the BWIs and the WTO.

---

6　The report was also issued as a UN General Assembly document under the symbol A/51/785 of 27 January 1997.

☐    New and innovative sources of funding to be identified, and the savings made as a result of UN reform to be reallocated to strengthening UN development activities.

☐    UN specialized agencies to concentrate on their normative and guideline roles, with operational activities to rest on comparative advantage criteria.

While fully supporting these reform proposals, the Nordic Group, in its own recommendations, put a stronger accent on integration within the UN system. This related, first of all, to the country level, where it not only urged the definition of a common policy framework and the identification of a limited number of joint priorities but also advocated in the long term a 'unified UN development system'. This was to be backed up by 'functional consolidation' at the level of UN funds and programmes headquarters.[7] The UN specialized agencies would cooperate closely with the funds and programmes and, again, would serve as centers of excellence focusing primarily on their normative tasks.

## MOVES TOWARDS PROGRAMMATIC REFORM

### THE ANNAN PROPOSALS (1997–2002)[8]

In July 1997, UN Secretary-General Kofi Annan presented his own reform proposals to the General Assembly. They acknowledge the persisting gap between the huge action agenda in front of the UN system and the limited resources available. They also underscore the need for a political consensus among member states if the UN is to be effective and to make a difference.

Reiterating the concerns of many earlier reform proposals, the Secretary-General identified rigid, fragmented and sometimes duplicative organizational structures as sources of institutional weakness and ineffectiveness. His reform proposals were broken down into two types of measures (often referred to as two 'tracks'):

☐    Those under the direct jurisdiction and authority of the Secretary-General.

☐    Those within the jurisdiction of member states and thus requiring their approval (e.g. the structure and functioning of intergovernmental bodies).

The most salient reform proposals directly related to the UN system's developmental activities in economic and social fields are selectively summarized below.

---

7  An 'eventual consolidated structure' of all operational funds and programmes is considered the ultimate goal.

8  Cf.: UN Reform dossier: 1997 – 2002, http://www.un.org/reform/dossier.htm. Cf.: Report of the Secretary-General: Strengthening of the United Nations – an agenda for further change. General Assembly, 57th session.

**1**    In areas within his direct authority, the Secretary-General proposed, *inter alia*, the following changes, which have since been implemented:

☐    Reconfiguration of the UN Secretariat's management structure into four main sectors with an executive committee for each: peace and security; humanitarian affairs; economic and social affairs; and development operations. The executive committee on development operations is convened by the UNDP Administrator and has come to be known as the UN Development Group (UNDG). Its membership comprises the main funds and programmes: UNDP, UNFPA, UNICEF and WFP.

☐    Consolidation of three economic and social departments of the UN Secretariat itself (DPCSD, DESIPA and DDSMS) into a single Department (DESA).

☐    At country level, a gradual move toward single UN offices under the Resident Coordinator with a view to facilitating greater cooperation and coherence (the 'UN House' approach, as piloted in South Africa).

☐    Establishment of frameworks (UNDAF), in close consultation with governments, with common objectives and priorities for development support from UN organizations. UNDAF, which was initially intended to operate only at the level of UN funds and programmes, has also become a vehicle for the integration of the work of the UN specialized agencies, thus gradually creating a UN system 'voice' for better coordination with the BWIs.

The Common Country Assessment and UNDAF have helped to shape the analysis of national needs and priorities and translate broad objectives into mission-oriented tasks. These tools have been implemented in most developing countries with the collaboration of the host governments.

Action taken by the Secretary-General in these areas was endorsed by the General Assembly in a resolution passed on 12 November 1997 and reviewed in 2001 by the Triennial Comprehensive Policy Review of Operational Activities to ascertain the political support of member states for UN reforms.

**2**    The following more far-reaching proposals were put forward for the approval of member states:

☐    Creation of a post of Deputy Secretary-General with primary responsibility for overseeing the coordination of multi-sector activities and programmes. The Deputy Secretary-General has also become responsible for coordinating UN reform efforts.

☐    Strengthening the role of the General Assembly by giving it the task of providing more focused strategic guidance to the work of the UN.

☐    Consolidating and streamlining ECOSOC's subsidiary machinery, and strengthening ECOSOC's capacity to engage in discussion of macroeconomic coordination issues.

☐    Improving the governance of UN funds and programmes through joint committees and through joint meetings of their governing bodies.

☐    Creation of a Development Account to be funded from administrative savings.

☐    Review of the Regional Commissions' role within a reformed UN.

☐    Launch of a Special Commission, at ministerial level, to examine the possibility of changes in the UN Charter and in the treaties from which the specialized agencies derive their mandates.

While the last proposal in particular — to launch a fundamental review of the role of the specialized agencies — remains a controversial and unresolved issue, other more specific proposals — such as the new Deputy Secretary-General post and the Development Account — were approved by the General Assembly in a resolution passed on 19 December 1997.

*Programmatic initiatives.* On the programmatic front, the Millennium Summit was held at the UN Headquarters, and 147 heads of state and government and 191 nations in total, adopted the UN Millennium Declaration, which contains a clear set of priorities, including precise, time-bound development goals. These now serve as a common policy framework for the entire UN system. In 2001 a 'road map' towards the implementation of the UN Millennium Declaration (A/56/326) was issued, delineating what must be done and who must do it. One year later, the first annual progress report on the MDGs was issued. It showed trend lines towards targets in eight development areas, producing a profile of progress — or sometimes lack of it — worldwide and within regions. Such progress reports will be issued each year up to 2015.

In 1999, the Secretary-General initiated the Global Compact (mentioned earlier). He launched it the following year, together with more than 50 chief executive officers at the UN Headquarters.

In September 2002, Annan presented his second set of reform proposals to the General Assembly, centered on the need for the UN to align its activities with the priorities defined by the Millennium Declaration and by the global conferences of the past, and to deliver better services. These proposals included reference to the need to change intergovernmental organs such as the General Assembly and the ECOSOC so that they may realize their full potential.

In the economic and social sphere new development goals have been set by the United Nations Millennium Declaration, through which member states have provided the world with a common vision for the new century. This vision is linked to measurable targets for the first 15 years of the century: the MDGs.

*Implementation.* In response to the Secretary-General's 2002 proposal *Action 14,* which deals with field-level coordination of operational activities, UNDG has put in place several mechanisms to enhance coherence. Based on the 1997 reforms' CCA and UNDAF, the joint effort to adopt system-wide mechanisms strengthened the system's capacity for coordinated and mutually amplifying activities. Also, the Resident Coordinator System (RCS) has since been strengthened and the emphasis on the role of the Resident Coordinators (RCs) has changed from a rather individual one to a more collegial responsibility.

The joint UNDG programme and management task force on simplification and harmonization (S&H), established in 1992, has developed programmes in consultation with the UN country teams (UNCT) and national and international partners, for instance the Country Programme Action Plan (CPAP) and Annual Work Plan/Budget (AWPB).

Since the introduction of results-based management (RBM) evaluation between 1997 and 2000, a number of specialized agencies with limited or no country-level structures have recognized the problem of measuring their country-level results. They are now considering ways to increase their participation in system-wide field-level activities and instruments, linking their activities to national strategies.

The introduction of the Poverty Reduction Strategy (PRS) process has made considerable strides, but its links with the CCA and UNDAF process remain unstable. The need to integrate all frameworks and programming tools adopted by the UN system and its individual organizations with national development strategies makes this linkage, however, almost inevitable. A major obstacle for their harmonization is the synchronization of their respective programming cycles. In order to solve this problem, other approaches, such as flexible and decentralized management systems, should be pursued in addition to aligning cycles as much as possible.

There are now over 50 common 'UN Houses' in the developing countries, each occupied by three or more agencies. In addition, more than 30 'Virtual UN Houses', sharing Internet connectivity as well as common service providers, are now in operation. Individual country teams have reported five- and six-digit dollar cost savings as a result of these consolidations.

Coordination mechanisms, such as the UNDG and the Office for the Coordination of Humanitarian Affairs, have helped enhance the collective impact of the separate operational entities, including the specialized agencies. Agencies, funds and programmes have begun to simplify and harmonize procedures.

One area in which clarification is especially needed is in the delivery of technical cooperation. The Secretary-General advocated, to avoid duplicating efforts, that the lead responsibility for a given issue or activity should rest with the entity best equipped to assume it, in collaboration with the rest of the UN. Technical cooperation should be delivered, to the maximum extent possible, by the entities that have an established field presence and experience. Secretariat entities should provide policy guidance and expertise, as appropriate. As stated in his report 'Strengthening the United Nations' (2002) in *Action 15*, the Secretary-General issued the 'Review of Technical Cooperation in the UN', clarifying the relevant roles and responsibilities.

As indicated in *Action 19* the Secretary-General appointed in February 2003 a panel of eminent persons to review the relationship between the UN and civil society and offer practical recommendations for improved modalities of interaction. The panel was chaired by the former President of Brazil, Fernando H. Cardoso, and took stock of existing practice, consulting widely with interested parties and proposing better ways of managing UN–civil society relations. The panel's report was issued on 21 June 2004; it contained 30 specific proposals for reform and improvement. One important theme is the need for the UN to 'connect the global with the local'. The achievement of the MDGs will depend on a collaborative approach made possible through partnerships with governments and NGOs on the ground. Focusing attention on the MDGs also provides an opportunity for local country-level realities to impact on global deliberations.

*Institutional changes.* As mentioned earlier, further institutional changes have resulted from joining three economic and social departments of the UN Secretariat itself (DPCSD, DESIPA, DDSMS) into DESA. The goal of this consolidation was to produce a more coherent and substantive response to the needs of the General Assembly and ECOSOC. This has been largely achieved. But because of the great complexity of DESA's work in policy analysis and technical cooperation, the growing demands placed on it for servicing ECOSOC, the functional commissions and global conference follow-up activities, and many emerging issues falling within the Department's responsibilities, there is an urgent need to reinforce its capacity. Therefore the Secretary-General proposed Actions 16 and 17 in his report:

☐    Creation of an additional position of Assistant Secretary-General to support policy coherence and management in DESA.
☐    Establishment of a policy planning unit in DESA.

A key move to reinvigorate the functioning of the UN family of organizations was the upgrading of relations with the institutions founded in Bretton Woods in 1944. Cooperation between the UN and the World Bank and IMF had never achieved the level envisioned by the founders of post-Second World War multilateralism. Beginning in 1998, ECOSOC hosted a series of annual meetings with Bretton Woods finance ministers. This ground-breaking engagement helped to make possible the successes achieved in 2002 in Monterrey, Mexico, at the International Conference on Financing for Development — organized by the UN with the active participation of the Bank and the Fund, as well as the WTO.

## THE UTSTEIN GROUP[9] + DENMARK, SWEDEN & SWITZERLAND (2004)

In May 2004 the enlarged Utstein group submitted their paper 'The United Nations Development System: Issues for Strengthening and Change' with proposals that seek to support the Secretary-General's agenda through strengthening the UN develop-

---

9   The ministers of international development from Germany, the Netherlands, Norway and United Kingdom first got together as a group at the Utstein Abbey in Norway in 1999. The Utstein Group has a general agreement to coordinate its development assistance policies. Strategies and actions have been regularly coordinated at meetings on ministerial level as well as between senior civil servants.

ment system. Their starting-point is the need for a strong UN development system at country level. The seven countries put emphasis on management reform proposals and recommend corresponding institutional changes.

They aim at improving coordination between agencies and of operational activities on the country level, and furthering the decentralization process by strengthening the RCs in the context of more harmonized UN Country Teams. This includes authority to ensure alignment of individual UN organizations with the UNDAF Results Matrix. Stress is laid on gender mainstreaming as an element of the RC's appraisal. Additionally, they suggest making maximum use of shared administrative services, infrastructure and ICT and, where feasible, having larger UN organizations (e.g. UNDP) represent or 'host' smaller ones.

Regarding governance and policymaking in the UN development system, the group places much importance on three issues:

1    *Policy coherence.* On the grounds that ECOSOC and DESA are not well-enough equipped to provide increased policy coherence, the group recommends that the Joint Meeting of the Boards[10] should receive greater authority and influence and act as the central forum within the UN where important policy issues can be discussed in order to improve joint policy planning.

2    *High caliber leadership of UN organizations.* In their view this could be guaranteed by ensuring rigor and transparency in the selection process for all senior UN appointments.

3    *Relations with the BWIs.* Regarding the relationship between the BWIs and the UN, they support the process of clarifying the division of labor to build a more effective partnership, and the enhancement of the UN partnership with the BWIs and WTO on the Financing for Development agenda.

Improving the stability, adequacy and predictability of the regular budget of UN funds and programmes is another long-term goal of the seven countries, which they want to achieve by supporting multi-year funding frameworks (MYFFs), and installing an informal joint donor/UN funding forum, to replace the current system of individual bilateral consultation with funds and programmes, in order to reduce transaction costs.

Moreover, they advocate improving the linkage between effectiveness and funding of UN organizations, e.g. by Organizations' Evaluation Units reporting directly to their Boards. Additionally, they suggest that impartial mechanisms could be introduced, e.g. strengthening the role of the JIU or introducing a system of independent reviews of UN agencies.

---

10   Through Kofi Annan's first wave of reforms the system-wide Senior Management Group and the cross-institutional Executive Committees have been established to oversee the work of the four main areas of policy. The Executive Boards of the Funds and Programs have begun holding joint meetings — "Joint Boards".

# CONCLUSIONS

As we have seen, the many proposals for UN reform vary greatly in aim and scope. They can be clustered into two main categories: institutional reforms, aimed at improving efficiency and effectiveness through enhanced management and institutional arrangements, and programmatic reforms, seeking a reorientation on a substantive basis.

The former were at center-stage in most of the early reform proposals in the economic development field, while the latter gradually started to play a more important role in the reform proposals of the 1990s.

Institutional reforms have focused on an array of management-related measures to improve efficiency and effectiveness. They are centered on the need for enhanced coherence, coordination and cooperation within the UN system. This has been one of the main themes sounding through reform proposals addressing the UN's support programmes for developing countries, customarily referred to as 'operational activities for development'. The discussion has gravitated from issues of structural reorganization to issues of functional harmonization.

Several proposals have been made for the establishment of a principal organ of the UN system to coordinate economic and social issues. One of the latest envisages the establishment of an Economic Security Council, with the same standing in relation to international economic matters as that of the Security Council in peace and security matters. This new council would be a deliberative, policymaking body rather than an executive agency and would work by consensus without any member wielding veto power.

It can be said that efforts to revitalize the General Assembly's working methods are just at the beginning, while the challenge remains to enhance the Assembly's voice and authority in development matters. Advances have been made by ECOSOC, notably through its high-level meetings with the BWIs and WTO and the creation of an ad hoc advisory group on countries emerging from conflict.

It is the country or field level of UN operations that has attracted most attention. Since the second half of the 1990s more changes have been made to the operational modalities of UN development support than in the preceding several decades. The notion of organizing and harmonizing UN development programmes around jointly identified objectives and priorities (the so-called programme approach) received a strong boost with the establishment of UNDG, the strengthened RC system, and UNDAF/CAA and PRSPs as new instruments.

Programmatic reform proposals in the economic development field only started to show up around the 1990s and have concentrated on a few issues.

The South Commission called in 1990 for a revival of economic growth in the South and a move towards a restructuring of the international system in the fields of science and technology, environment, global commons and development.

One of the most important ideas in this field was the link between peace and development as included in the Boutros-Ghali Agenda in 1992. This agenda for development was prepared as a response to the downgrading of attention to development issues as a result of heightened concerns about peace and security. It included, inter alia, the notions that peace is a precondition for development; that the economy is an engine of progress; and that protecting the environment provides the basis for sustainability.

None of the many proposals in these fields have met with universal approval by member states. Only in the year 2000 did member states collectively adopt the UN Millennium Declaration, which contains a clear set of priorities, including precise, time-bound development goals. These now serve as a common policy framework for the entire UN system.

It is worth asking: why did reform proposals of an institutional nature prevail during most of the UN system's history and the programmatic elements only start to appear as late as the 1990s, and gather pace only towards the end of that decade?

One answer could lie in the political nature of most of the reform proposals in the economic development field.

As seen when we discussed the evolution of the UN's normative functions, there was no intention whatsoever by the developed countries, and particularly the United States, to allow the UN to play a normative role in the field of economic development. Meanwhile, the operational functions of the UN in the economic and social fields expanded and this can partially explain the vivid enthusiasm showed by them towards restructuring and streamlining such functions to make them more cost-efficient, effective and accountable to member states.

The more revolutionary aim of the developing world was to make the UN more responsive to their aspirations of economic and social development and to improve the institutional mechanism for assistance through operational activities. They favored a dialogue on new development issues in the fields of trade, industry, finance, technology and social development, and felt that progress could be achieved only by stronger global cooperation through the UN (where they felt more equitably empowered) and a new collective vision of development. In a way, this was a more programmatic approach.

Although the concept of sustainable development came to be recognized, and indeed assumed a central role in the activities of the UN, the aspirations of the developing countries have clearly not been fulfilled, and success in restructuring the economic and social activities of the UN system has been limited. On the eve of the end of the Cold War, the developing world somehow feared that the developed countries' new priorities, such as energy and the environment, while essential, would have little impact on the development prospects of their economies. Additionally, a few years later, the political focus given to the reconstruction of post-Soviet societies added to their concern about the importance attached by the donor community to their development problems.

Finally, I would like to highlight two features underlying the reform proposals examined in this chapter: the relationship between the UN Secretariat and the specialized agencies and the interaction between the UN economic development functions and the BWIs.

With regard to the former, it is worth recalling that the original agreements between the UN and the specialized agencies contained provisions for coordinating the promotion of the economic, social and cultural objectives of the Charter, including administrative coordination and coherence (Article 58). Yet large portions of these agreements have never been put into practice. Moreover, the positioning of the specialized agencies, ranging from norm-setting to technical cooperation project implementation, remains problematic. The choice between political- or action-oriented organizations has a number of implications, including those for the structure and functioning of governing bodies: the more action-oriented and operational an organization's mandate is, the more its governing bodies must be geared towards taking 'actable' decisions and adjusting to changing conditions.

The second feature has been a very influential element in the evolution of the UN's economic development functions. And it will certainly continue be so in the future. Closer cooperation between the UN and the BWIs was to a considerable extent frustrated by the preference of the more advanced economies, particularly the United States, to work through the latter because of their system of weighted voting — which also explains the preference of the South for the former.

There has been no lack of ideas on reform. What has been missing is political consensus and a concerted will, between East and West, North and South, donors and recipients. Some proposals have led to reform in some areas of the UN; others have stimulated dialogue and influenced the opinion of the majority against the policy priorities of the few — and yet they failed to be formally adopted and implemented. New reform proposals often restated old ideas and, although not implemented, still linger on.

Undoubtedly the numerous reform efforts reflect the growing number of complicating factors in international development cooperation: globalization, the challenge of PSD, the emergence of new partners in development, declining ODA flows due to aid fatigue (though not universally), and the expanded and more diversified needs of developing countries and economies in transition for multilateral assistance.

I think the striking message of this chapter is clear: in the absence of a strong programmatic dimension, no amount of institutional reform can provide the guidance and leadership needed to make managerial and administrative arrangements work. As seen throughout the chapter, some of the institutional arrangements suggested to improve the coordination of the economic development functions of the system have been implemented (e.g. the single Department for Economic and Social Affairs at the UN Secretariat). But while they have reduced overlaps and improved the value for money of the operations, they have not dramatically improved the performance or the quality of UN programmes in the field. This is precisely the problem that the proposal contained in chapter 1 attempts to tackle.

As I attempt to show later through UNIDO's case study, I'm convinced that successful reform processes necessarily entail a balanced combination of institutional and programmatic elements. Neither the former nor the latter can succeed in achieving the desired performance in isolation. And both are only workable in the context of a strong commitment by the member states with the process.

In my personal view the lessons of so many years of efforts at reforming the multilateral economic development architecture clearly underline the importance of discussing programmatic issues, which is not always necessarily a political discussion. It certainly takes courage from all sides to put aside some aspirations and concentrate on the systemic fundamentals. And it also takes seriousness to fulfill and honor commitments.

As mentioned, the case study presented later on the reform at UNIDO provides an example of the case I am making. However, the one example to offer at a global scale is provided by the adoption of the Millennium Declaration and the MDGs. They provide an opportunity to focus more on substance and on programmatic aspects regarding how to achieve them. I think, this is certainly the way to materialize the potential gains of the many institutional arrangements already suggested.

REFERENCES

M. Bertrand Report, 1985: *Some Reflections on the Reform of the United Nations*, Joint Inspection Unit, Geneva (JIU/REP/95/9), 1985.

Brundtland Commission, 1987: *Our Common Future*, World Commission on Environment and Development (Brundtland Commission), 20 March 1987.

Boutros Boutros-Ghali, 1992: *Empowering the United Nations*, December 1992.

Erskine Childers, with Brian Urquhart, 1994: *Renewing the United Nations System*, 1994.

Commission of Global Governance, 1995: *Our Global Neighbourhood*, 1995.

European Union, 1997: *Proposals of the European Union for Reform of the United Nations System in the Economic and Social Area* (submitted to the UNGA Working Group on the Strengthening of the UN System), January 1997.

Heritage Foundation, 1984: *The World without a United Nations: What would happen if the United Nations shut down?*, Washington, DC, 1984.

Independent Working Group (IWG), 1995: *The United Nations and its Second Half-Century*, 1995.

Marc Nerfin, 1985: *The Future of the United Nations System: Some Questions on the Occasion of an Anniversary*, November 1985.

Joachim Müller, ed., 1997: *Reforming the United Nations: New Initiatives and Past Efforts*, Vol. I-III, published in co-operation with the United Nations, Kluwer Law International, The Hague/London/Boston, 1997.

Nordic Project, 1990: *The Agencies at a Crossroads. The Role of the United Nations Specialized Agencies*, a study commissioned by the Nordic UN project, Report No. 15:1990.

Nordic Project, 1991: *Reform Issues in the Economic and Social Fields. A Nordic Perspective*, 1991.

Nordic Project, 1996: The Nordic UN Reform Project 1996 in the Economic and Social Fields. *The United Nations in Development, strengthening the UN through Change: Fulfilling its Economic and Social Mandate*, 1996.

Nordic Memorandum, 1991: *Memorandum of United Nations Governance and Finance*, 22 June 1992.

Sir Robert Jackson, 1969: *Capacity of the United Nations development system*, 1969.

South Center, 1996: *For a Strong and Democratic United Nations. A South Perspective on UN Reform*, 1996.

South Commission, 1990: *The Challenge to the South*, South Commission, May 1990.

Gardner Report, 1975: *A United Nations structure for global economic cooperation*, 1975.

Group of 18, 1986: *Emphasis on improving efficiency*, 1986.

Secretary-General, 1994: *An Agenda for Development*, United Nations, New York, 6 May 1994.

# Chapter 4

# PROGRAMMATIC ARGUMENTS

There is a need to bring into sharper focus the UN's development functions and to spell out in greater detail their contents. The main purpose of doing so is to facilitate their interaction with the human development programmes and post-conflict interventions in which the international community is engaged. Additionally, it should also facilitate an improved and much-needed interaction with the BWIs by pointing the way towards an appropriate division of labor.

It is often the case that economic development-oriented UN agencies claim competence in areas such as capacity-building for PSD, technology transfer and diffusion, or environment and energy. Many of them say they carry out technical cooperation programmes in those areas. But when it comes to describing the nature of their specific contributions and programmes, definitions become rather vague, and the amounts allocated to those programmes from their regular budgets and by donors' voluntary contributions are either small or undefined.

Capacity-building for entrepreneurship development, for example, is quite a broad area that involves subjects of different nature, ranging from government regulations to micro-finance schemes, policy advice and CSR programmes. None of the UN's economic development functions could claim that any of them are their exclusive province. Overlapping and duplication exist, not by design, but because the process of designing the programmes at the level of the system as a whole is random. To some extent, this is also the consequence of donors' policy priorities.

By attending to programmatic criteria, the reorganization of the UN's economic development functions could help eliminate duplication and improve their contributions to the achievement of the MDGs, offering the donors better value for money and, as importantly, better quality of advice in those fields to the developing countries.

Let us consider three particular needs:

☐    The need to improve the interaction between the UN's social and humanitarian programmes and its economic development efforts.

☐    The need to improve the contributions made by the UN's economic development functions to post-conflict interventions.
☐    The need to improve the interaction between the UN's economic development
bodies and the BWIs.

# INTERACTION WITH SOCIAL & HUMANITARIAN PROGRAMMES

At the beginning of the 1990s the international community was thought to have
reached a new sort of economic consensus for development. Indeed the policies applied
in the United States and the United Kingdom in the early 1980s (under
R. Reagan and M. Thatcher), the demise of the Soviet Union towards the end of the
1980s and the accelerated integration of the financial and commercial markets
during the last two decades prompted a shift in policy priorities and, with it, the emergence of a kind of 'corporate strategy' for economic development organized around the
concepts of macroeconomic stability, market-oriented reforms and good governance.

Regretfully, its results have been, at best, mixed. In particular, among developing countries a great sense of disappointment has arisen from that agenda's
failure to translate initial positive results in terms of enhanced economic growth
rates into sustained social progress. The frustration has been so severe that many
political leaders and scholars have called into question the whole of the prescriptions followed during the 1990s, in some cases arguing the need to produce
unspecified new 'models'.

By the mid-1990s it was sensed that the use of the 'corporate strategy' for economic development would not, by itself, suffice to redress the severe social imbalances
of the world. Advice to that effect flowed from many quarters. For example, UNDP's
1994 annual report already highlighted the problem of growth without equity, trig-
gering a whole new brand of development thought around the concept of human
security, a 'people-centered' approach to achieving 'freedom from want' and 'freedom
from fear'. Some resources were made available to put that concept into practice.
More recently, in the year 2000, the World Bank's annual report was devoted to the
*quality* of growth.

Partly to address the concerns of developing countries struggling to implement
the prescribed economic reform programmes and partly as a result of the normal
process of performance evaluation of social programmes in areas like education,
nutrition and health, the international community felt the need to strengthen the efficiency and effectiveness of their contributions to the multilateral system. This,
coupled with the moves triggered by the global conferences of the 1990s, eventually
helped forge a multilateral consensus on the adoption of the MDGs.

Achieving the MDGs provides the focus for a much-needed system-wide 'corporate strategy' for the international community in social affairs and, in my view, is
contributing to a significant improvement in the coordination and integration of the

multilateral efforts to reverse the world's social imbalances in areas like health, nutrition and education. The centrality of the MDGs in multilateral affairs must be celebrated by all quarters in developing and developed countries alike because it represents a major step towards placing real people at the center of the international community's actions.

However, achieving the MDGs also demands a monumental turnaround of the LDCs' abysmal socio-economic and environmental performance in the recent past. Estimates recently released by the FAO show that the average pace of reduction in the number of malnourished people worldwide observed in the 1990s (2.1 million per year) will have to be accelerated *over 12 times* (to 26 million per year) to meet the goal of halving the total number of people with hunger by 2015. In fact, after falling steadily during the first half of the 1990s, hunger has been *on the rise* again during the second half.

According to UNIDO estimates, the rate of annual per capita GDP growth demanded to achieve the MDGs in 30 sub-Saharan African countries varies between 2 and 6 percent, in the absence of significant changes in income distribution. If one compares these figures with the reality of economic stagnation, if not regression, that the sub-Saharan countries have suffered over the last three decades it is possible to perceive the size of the challenge to be confronted (UNIDO, 2004). The Human Development Report 2004 states that, unless things improve, sub-Saharan Africa will be unable to attain universal primary education, halve extreme poverty and cut child mortality by two-thirds before the years 2129, 2147 and 2165, respectively.

It is essential to understand that, in order for these dramatic but absolutely necessary trend reversals to materialize, major policy departures are needed, along with a massive effort to address health, nutrition, environmental and infrastructure constraints. Unless these things happen, the appalling trends of the past will continue indefinitely, with the grave human costs and perils they entail.

Direct emergency relief is being provided by the World Food Programme, UNICEF, UNHCR, WHO and agencies working in crisis prevention and resolution. Alongside these, we also have actions aimed at more long-term outcomes, such as those that address the development of the capacity to access the goods and services that people need. From this perspective, the problem is not just how many people lack shelter today, but what is the rate at which the supply of shelter should grow in order to meet future demand.

The MDGs help us define our contribution to linking these two avenues of action. We have already seen that, in order to reduce poverty by half by 2015, an average rate of growth in per capita income of around 4 percent is required (UNIDO, 2004). But such a rate may not be feasible if, for example, we do not successfully counteract the advance of HIV or hunger. And the reverse is also true: if we succeed in combating HIV or hunger, but fail to foster technology diffusion so as to attain substantially higher rates of economic growth, our success may be ephemeral since the people whose lives are saved will be unable to obtain gainful employment and continue affording the treatments and nourishment they need.

Installing a new growth dynamics requires approaching the problems in a modern manner. Today we have the financial and technological resources required to tackle successfully the problems of marginalization and poverty and, as importantly, we are learning how to use them better to help the poorest countries solve these problems by themselves.

It is not a matter of choosing between direct emergency relief and capability building, or between the social and economic programmes, but of joining both agendas. Provided that the necessary institutional innovations and strategies are in place, the pursuit of the MDGs will contribute to attain the conditions required for growth; it will do so by removing stubborn structural impediments. Reciprocally, growth, diversification, structural change and industrialization are the means to ensure that the goals are sustainable over time.

For all these reasons it is worth paying attention to an area of major concern for developing countries: how to ensure that the conventional prescriptions for economic development (sound macroeconomic management, market-oriented reforms and good governance) are actually integrated with the social programmes in a manner that makes development sustainable. Nobody wants the social programmes to perform as a sort of late remedy to alleviate the undesired side-effects of the economic reform programmes.

The articulation of the economic development and the social 'corporate strategies' adopted by the international community in recent years remains a challenge not just for economic development practitioners but also for those working in the various fields of social welfare. We can work on both fronts separately for a while, but we cannot afford to do so permanently. Everybody expects that, in the end, aid in the social field will cease when the economic progress of the poor countries allows them to make the necessary investments by themselves.

The interventions and investments made to redress the imbalances in the social fields in the LDCs are conceived as a temporal contribution to building human capital while economic development policies bear fruit in terms of capital accumulation. The articulation between the human and capital-accumulation processes (that is to say the articulation between the implementation of social policies and economic development strategies) is often expected to occur automatically, with poor countries reaching a stage of development where they will 'take off' and sustain the process by themselves.

But the quest for growth and equity seems to be a lot more intricate and elusive than that. The reciprocal interdependence of our economic development policies and social programmes is yet to be fully understood. Thus, for instance, we do know that investment and trade flows are powerful tools to connect poor economies with globalized markets and to foster wealth creation, but we don't quite know yet how to use them to fight poverty effectively. And we do know that higher enrollment rates in primary and secondary school are necessary to build human capital, but we know little about how to actually translate that into economic growth.

These links lie at the heart of growth with equity. But they do not seem to materialize automatically. Deliberate efforts are needed to understand how FDI and trade flows may actually work to reduce poverty in the countries in most need, and how to make it happen in a sustainable way by drawing on investments to enhance education, nutrition and health.

I do not claim that the interaction between the social and human development programmes and those aimed at economic development is non-existent or minimal. There are certainly many examples of successful interaction between them. The point here is that, in any case, those interactions do not seem to occur as the result of a deliberate effort of experience-sharing or joint evaluation of technical cooperation programmes implemented by the UN bodies engaged in both the social and economic development camps. They are the result of occasional interactions designed on ad-hoc bases rather than the outcome of an articulated policy.

In order to enhance the relevance of the UN's economic development functions, it is necessary to define more precisely and in greater detail their various contributions. This is also necessary to address the multiple interconnections between diseases, poverty, violence, absence of human rights and lack of development that confine a growing number of the world's population to the margins of the global society we are so eagerly trying to build.

In such a society, driven by the powerful forces of technological change and market integration, there is scarcely any room to keep our political and our economic agendas dissociated. Our actions and contributions must be designed to influence both agendas. In our modern society, peace and progress depend more and more on our capacity to win the hearts and minds of the peoples. And unless we win that battle, the poorer countries will remain ever more vulnerable to the consequences of social unrest and economic deprivation.

I do not claim either that there is a direct link between poverty and terrorism. However, it is hard to dismiss the notion that the presence of abject poverty reduces, if it does not actually sterilize, the capacity of governments to control internal and crossborder trafficking of weapons, persons and illegal substances. In my personal opinion, future national security policies will have to include a strong development component from their very formulation if they are to succeed in addressing the modern challenges posed by global terrorism.

The world's workforce will have increased by 40 percent between 1990 and 2010. About 95 percent of that growth will take place in developing economies, which are expected, during that period, to receive 15 percent or less of the total FDI flows. This group of countries will soon account for 90 percent of the world's youth and will hence have to create the bulk of the new jobs required, without much participation in global trade or financial markets. This prospect calls for adequate policies for rural areas (where most of the poor live), for the informal sector of the economy and for social objectives; that is to say, a good blend of economic and social policies (Meier and Stiglitz, 2001).

Growth with equity has been a priority for quite some time now. But the international community has yet to articulate an integrated approach to facilitate the interaction of the 'corporate strategies' in social affairs and the economic development field. As far as the UN is concerned, the process leading to the issuing and subsequent approval of the MDGs has significantly contributed to an improved understanding and articulation of experience, knowledge and technical cooperation programmes in the social areas. Unfortunately, the same cannot be claimed for the UN programmes in the economic development field.

Addressing this deficit can be viewed as part of the broader effort to enhance, perhaps redefine and reorganize, the role of the UN and its contributions in the field of economic development. To achieve this we probably need to make progress towards a common agenda for action, as proposed earlier. Although this has been attempted in the past, achieving real progress this time entails spelling out such an agenda with an appropriate degree of detail and definition. This will enable us to gauge and match the experience and results from the technical cooperation programmes carried out by the UN bodies operating in the economic development field and, above all, start a joint process of accumulation of knowledge along clearly defined tracks.

I certainly understand that it is easy to gather consensus around a number of topics like global poverty, environmental crises, migration flows, unemployment or food security, or even to make some strides towards a new framework for sustainable development. However, I think that the time has definitely come to invest multilateral diplomatic and political efforts in deepening the degree of definition of the multilateral actions in those fields. Years of experience of the multilateral development community (not exempt from frustration) have yielded the maturity required to attempt such a task. And I think the task is both a technical and a moral imperative of our times.

It is necessary to clarify, for example, which dimensions of global poverty (extreme, moderate, rural, etc.) we will attempt to address and which are the tools we are going to use (rural policies, programmes for the informal economy, micro-finance schemes, etc.) systematically assessing and comparing results. The same is valid for the other fields mentioned above. Although this sort of exercise is taking place throughout the system to some extent, this is not happening on the scale or with the frequency needed to draw system-wide conclusions and accordingly adjust the process of programme formulation and development. Heeding this lesson will also help adjust the estimates of the cost of the programmes by improving the metrics of the UN's economic development functions.

Only then, I think, the economic development bodies will be in a position to contribute effectively to an appropriate link-up of social and humanitarian programmes with long-term development efforts.

# CONTRIBUTIONS TO POST-CONFLICT INTERVENTIONS

According to UN records, currently 37 countries confront some sort of political conflict, and 30 of them are under either UN conflict prevention and peacemaking missions or peacekeeping and peacebuilding operations. This represents almost one fifth of the countries of the world and affects close to a billion people.

Peace and security are the main focus of the UN's attention and the bulk of its energies. This leading purpose arises directly from the UN Charter. The peacekeeping and peacebuilding efforts of the UN Secretariat consume many of its resources. In the last decade or so, the UN budget for peacekeeping operations increased 10-fold from $270 million to $2,700 million (Goulding, 2002). The centrality of that mandate is very much acknowledged by all members of the UN family, particularly for those working in humanitarian relief and human development. And yet, this is an area where the contributions of the UN's economic development bodies, funds and programmes have a long way to go, individually and collectively, to improve their contributions.

Individually, this is so because most of the UN bodies dealing with economic development tend to replicate in countries emerging from humanitarian crises or political conflicts the same sort of programmes they apply to non-crisis situations. That is to say, they adapt programmes originally designed to promote development in an economic environment completely different to the post-crisis or post-conflict context, where the countries involved have dissimilar urgencies and primarily need to create all possible kinds of income-generating activity and rehabilitate their productive infrastructure.

During the reconstruction phase those countries do not necessarily have to focus their efforts on activities or sectors that could generate economic development in the long run, however desirable that might be. They tend to grant preeminence to whatever programme helps them resolve their immediate needs. And they should be allowed to design and be in command of their own programmes, setting their own priorities.

Collectively, the UN's economic development functions often suffer from a low level of coordination of their interventions (in part due to the limitations by design explained earlier), a lack of regular exchange of experiences and knowledge-sharing, or the absence of periodical evaluation and comparison of the results of its technical cooperation programmes in countries emerging from crises or conflict situations.

Additionally the economic development bodies face the challenge of choosing the right moment to intervene in those countries, running the risk of turning up either too early — when basic security and service infrastructure are not yet available — or too late, when the need to bridge the gap between humanitarian assistance and long-term reconstruction becomes more acute.

The UN has accumulated a lot of experience in rebuilding the basic functioning of societies emerging from humanitarian crises or political conflicts. This applies, particularly, to areas such as the organization of a democratic political system — for example, through the organization and supervision of elections or the organization of the basic institutions of the judiciary system, the development of the basic social services in health, nutrition and education and the reconstruction of public utilities and basic infrastructure. However, as compared with these fields, it is often perceived that the UN's store of knowledge scores much lower when it comes to the reorganization of the basic economic institutions and the supply of public goods to contribute to the rehabilitation of countries emerging from crisis or conflict.

At this point, I think it is necessary to clarify one point. The economic development functions of the UN, as we have seen, were established and developed in a particular historical context and were not necessarily designed for multilateral interventions in the fields of peace and security. They cannot be blamed for not having adjusted to performing these tasks or for not having specialized in those fields. I doubt that there ever was any political request or even indication to them as a group to develop such an expertise.

But it is undeniable that such specialization is currently much needed by the system and, above all, by the affected countries. The international community lacks an effective tool to address problems such as the creation of job opportunities in societies emerging from crisis or conflict, since market mechanisms have proven to be, at best, very slow.

In a country emerging from a political or military conflict, the UN has to meet a number of demands. First, troops must be fielded to perform the peacekeeping function as well as provide immediate humanitarian relief to basic human needs like shelter, sanitation or food. Soon after, there is the need to repair the damage to infrastructure, at least in terms of roads, energy supply and communications, that may have been caused by the conflict. In this context, the demobilization of former combatants and the rehabilitation of productive facilities could be seen as priorities of second order, and rightly so. However, some of those second-order priorities, like the demobilization of former combatants, could prove crucial to emergence from the conflict, even for the very implementation of the peace agreements.

It goes without saying that the UN has learnt how to deal with all this even in the absence of an articulated plan to produce an integrated response from its economic development bodies — but I do not think that this fact diminishes the importance of such a shortcoming. Undoubtedly the UN system as a whole could gain a lot from its economic development bodies paying more attention to the specific requirements imposed by these operations, and even more important, the societies emerging from crisis and conflict situations could gain a new tool to build their progress.

The bodies in charge of the UN's economic development functions, if organized around a common agenda, could make very relevant use of their years of accumulated experience. A simple process of information and experience-sharing could boost the value of individual agency efforts if they are brought to bear on relevant problems in post-conflict situations, guided by the recipient country's government and the UN Country Team.

By 'relevant problems' I mean important problems to be resolved by a country emerging from a humanitarian crisis or a political conflict, like the examples already mentioned of demobilizing former combatants or rehabilitating productive facilities. These broad topics call for more detailed analysis, benchmarking and evaluation of the effectiveness of the technical cooperation programmes chosen to address them. The same problems would need to be approached in very different manners according with the particular conflict or crisis under resolution. I think this very fact makes it all the more important to compare experiences, benchmark performance and evaluate results.

Such an exercise would have to contribute to a sharper and fuller definition of the technical programmes delivered by the economic development agencies in the context of UN peacekeeping missions and could help in due course to offset, at least partially, the gradual phase-out of the military presence. This presence very often constitutes the very source of economic activity of society and its withdrawal usually entails a serious impact on the economic performance of a given country. Indeed, by the time a UN military or humanitarian intervention is successfully completed, the host country could have developed such a dependency pattern that its ODA requirements would mushroom, placing an additional pressure in the already considerable budgets to be covered by donors and other contributors.

Technical cooperation programmes and related financial contributions tailored to help job creation for the former combatants and others, rehabilitate productive facilities and formalize the emerging economic operations would not by themselves solve these problems, but if properly organized could attenuate them significantly.

## DISTINGUISHING BETWEEN CRISES

Crises vary across a broad spectrum. Each crisis situation has unique characteristics stemming from unique root causes that determine their course. Stylizing crises and conflicts can be misleading because solutions have to be tailored according to their respective local circumstances. Keeping this in mind, for our immediate purposes we can group the underlying causes and the dynamics of crises in four main categories that are specifically relevant to planning for post-crisis situations.

a    *Natural disasters.* In the last decade 4,777 natural disasters claimed more than 880,000 lives, affecting the homes, health and livelihoods of 1.88 billion people and inflicting economic losses worth about US$ 685 billion on the world's economy (UN 2002). Natural disasters such as droughts, earthquakes, floods, hurricanes, landslides, volcanic eruptions, wildfires, wildlife disease, tornadoes and storms, have a devastating effect on societies. It should be noted, however, that many of today's disasters are man-made. The balance of nature is disrupted when human beings try to control or interfere with the atmosphere, oceans, polar ice caps, forest covers, etc. thereby disturbing the equilibrium of local ecosystems. Reports on natural disasters indicate that in many instances the underlying causes for the devastation were poverty, social exclusion and other structural vulnerabilities long ignored by development efforts.

**b**    *Economic and financial crises.* The quick succession of financial crises since the early 1990s, from that of Mexico to those of East Asia, the Russian Federation, Brazil and Argentina entailed a high degree of volatility, with sharp falls in real output every twenty months or so on average and with varying degrees of contagion. These swings with a modal length of two to four years entail unrecoverable loss of wealth and significant retreats in social progress in the affected countries. Based on a sample of thirty-one developing countries the IMF found that it typically took almost three years for output growth to return to previous trends after the outbreak of a financial crisis, and that the cumulative output loss averaged 12 percent (IMF, 1998). In addition these events have long-lasting repercussions on the domestic economy since they entail, in addition to declines in economic activity, a disruption in the flow of savings to their most productive uses and of the incentive system as a whole, as well as severe constraints in the conduct of domestic monetary and financial policy.

**c**    *Political and social unrest.* Political and social unrest constitutes a possible prelude of full-fledged armed conflicts between communities. Social tensions can become a source of instability and trigger deeper crises. The impact of transition from centrally planned economies to market-oriented ones, for example, generated high expectations among people waiting for a swift improvement in their economic situation, parallel to their gains in democratic rights. Unfortunately, economic developments tend to lag behind because of recession, inefficiency and difficulties in adapting to the new market-oriented situation. The bankruptcy of large state-owned enterprises combines to push unemployment and underemployment to high levels, further contributing to the economic degradation of individuals. This trend can threaten democratic gains by generating political instability — which in turn discourages new foreign investments from creating new employment opportunities.

**d**    *Armed conflicts.* This sort of conflict can occur at two levels: the inter-state, crossborder one; and the intra-state one, within a country's borders. Most armed conflicts are caused by social and political unrest in a country or region. Intra-country conflicts (as opposed to international ones) have been by far the more virulent form of conflict over the past two or three decades.

## UNDERSTANDING TIMING AND TYPE OF ASSISTANCE REQUIRED

It has become apparent that post-crisis international assistance needs to be provided in an integrated manner, incorporating multi-sectoral and multi-dimensional approaches to rehabilitation and recovery efforts. While emergency and humanitarian assistance is usually geared to respond to the urgent and immediate needs of the affected population and its basic social infrastructure, it is equally important to develop a long-term vision for economic recovery and sustainable development. The evolving stages of response cannot be linear, which makes it difficult to draw a clear demarcation between each phase of post-crisis assistance.

This is why many relief agencies extend their programmes into rehabilitation and reconstruction work, sometimes expanding their original mandates and going well beyond their spheres of expertise. At the same time, development agencies also realize that interventions at the early phase of emergency relief need to be carefully linked with complementary elements of post-crisis assistance, in order to ensure a coherent transition from the initial emergency assistance to rehabilitation and development of local productive capacities.

Development agencies traditionally enter post-crisis situations at later stages. However, they increasingly recognize the importance of heeding, at an early stage of crisis situations, the demands of the countries affected, so that the development agenda can be implemented more efficiently and effectively.

Post-crisis development assistance can largely be broken down into three phases: (1) emergency relief and humanitarian assistance, (2) rehabilitation and reconstruction, and (3) sustainable development.

## PHASE I: EMERGENCY RELIEF AND HUMANITARIAN ASSISTANCE

In this first phase, the main focus is on restoring the security of the area, and on satisfying basic human needs. International organizations get involved in providing emergency and relief assistance because local institutions are usually weak and destabilized, so strengthening them in order to provide local ownership is a strong need. Most efforts at this stage concentrate on the logistics of providing relief supplies — food, shelter, basic healthcare, etc. The international community takes up the organizational and distribution tasks to ensure that the assistance reaches the most vulnerable groups in the affected society.

Towards the end of this first phase, an assessment should be undertaken to identify the needs and capabilities of the crisis-stricken economy. Based on the results of the initial needs assessment, a diagnosis should be undertaken of domestic capacities for the sourcing and production of relief supplies and essential commodities. This diagnosis should identify the capacities on the ground that have survived the crisis and are still functioning, existing capacities that have been damaged and need to be rehabilitated, and capacities that have been destroyed and need to be rebuilt.

## PHASE II: REHABILITATION AND RECONSTRUCTION

After a minimum degree of stability is restored, assistance should shift focus from the provision of rehabilitation assistance to enhancing domestic productive capacities, expanding economic opportunities, and generating employment. This includes special attention to the services essential to rebuilding local facilities and building capacity, through:

☐ Reconstruction and repair of important physical infrastructure including roads, transportation systems, communication networks and utilities;

☐   Rehabilitation of key productive sectors in order to provide urgently needed goods and services;

☐   Rebuilding of key social infrastructure, such as the education system, to create a pool of qualified and skilled human resources;

☐   Rehabilitation of hospitals and clinics to improve healthcare;

☐   Reintegration of those segments of the population particularly affected by the crisis, such as internally displaced persons, refugees, and demobilized ex-combatants; and

☐   Mobilization for community involvement, particularly of women.

This second phase is geared towards bridging the gap between emergency assistance and providing for long-term, sustainable development. Assistance programmes should focus on reestablishing the framework of governance by strengthening government institutions, restoring law and order, and enabling the organizations of civil society to work effectively. Measures must be put in place to promote macroeconomic stabilization, rehabilitation of financial institutions, and restoration of appropriate legal and regulatory frameworks. It is also necessary to jump-start the economy through investments in key productive sectors, and by creating conditions for the resumption of trade, savings, and domestic and foreign investment.

## PHASE III: TOWARDS SUSTAINABLE DEVELOPMENT

Completion of the second-phase activities paves the way for the next phase, namely, initiating the march towards sustainable development. The UN and the international community can help countries in their efforts to achieve sustainable development by assisting them to build their capacity to design and carry out development programmes that seek to eradicate poverty through the creation of sustainable livelihoods, empowerment of women, and protection and regeneration of the environment. Policies and concrete actions in the social, economic and environmental areas are needed at this stage, so that long-term growth with equity, sustained peace, and human security can be achieved.

## A NEW FOCUS FOR THE UN'S ECONOMIC DEVELOPMENT FUNCTIONS

The UN economic development bodies should develop a specifically tailored approach towards system-wide reconstruction efforts in post-crisis contexts. The 1990s have witnessed a major shift in international assistance towards responding to crisis situations, many of which resulted from the end of the Cold War. Due to the increasing emergence of aspirations to sovereignty among nations and regions previously subsumed in larger national units, and the resultant civil conflicts, the number of multilateral, regional, and bilateral humanitarian and peacekeeping operations multiplied. Civil wars and conflicts resulted in the destruction of economic assets and the reversal of years of development effort, which demanded that international policy discussions should increasingly address the need to combine peacekeeping with economic reconstruction and rehabilitation.

Realizing the limitations of the mechanisms in place to cope with countries emerging from crisis situations, in May 1997 the High-Level Meeting of the OECD's Development Assistance Committee (DAC) provided a set of general guidelines for post-conflict interventions (DAC 1997). These were further elaborated in 2001, reaffirming the need for effective conflict prevention to reduce poverty, promote economic growth and achieve sustainable development (DAC 2001). As a result, donor governments supported the creation of new units and the expansion of mandates of existing bureaux in government agencies dealing with conflict. The primary emphasis was on operational improvements in aid delivery, better coordination among donors and better targeted and context-specific conditionality.

While the DAC Guidelines provided a platform for more effective intervention in post-conflict situations, the Millennium Summit echoed the calls for more integrated and effective response mechanisms in post-crisis situations. However, the donors did not translate these calls into immediate changes in the substance and modalities of implementation of aid programmes. There were many cases of failure to prevent conflict, some attributed to inequitable and inadequate ways of handling them, which arose from the strategic interests of major powers (UN, 2000).

International organizations recognized a 'transition dilemma [in the] funding and strategic planning gap between relief and development activities in the context of natural disasters and complex emergencies' and stated their resolve 'to continue to strengthen the consolidated appeals process as a coordination and strategic planning tool for the provision of humanitarian assistance and transition from relief to development' (UN, op. cit).

In response to these challenges, the UN established working groups on transition issues in the form of the UNDG and the Executive Committee on Humanitarian Affairs (ECHA) in 2002. Their purpose was to examine more fully the emergence of 'hybrid' or *ad hoc* approaches and appeals processes when coordinating UN responses to transition matters, so as to provide clear and consolidated guidance to UN Country Teams (UNCTs). This initiative had the objective of integrating the efforts of UN agencies into framing a common needs assessment and creating synergies among the different initiatives.

However, still another challenge remains for the international community: bridging the gap created when humanitarian assistance begins to taper off and longer-term reconstruction assistance is still in the planning stage. Achieving a 'seamless transition' from emergency and humanitarian assistance to reconstruction and development has increasingly become an essential factor for ensuring that the international response to whatever disaster a country faces — war, natural calamity, social and political unrest — is effective and efficient. A shared conception of post-crisis assistance and clear modalities of joint collaboration among donors and agencies are therefore needed in order to ensure successful interventions in countries emerging from crises, and to avoid unnecessary overlap and competition in the assistance provided by different sources.

The recently issued report of the High-level Panel on Threats, Challenges and Change, appointed by the Secretary-General, recommended to ECOSOC the establishment of a Committee on the Social and Economic Aspects of Security Threats[1].

Obviously, to be able to make its own contributions better able to address post-crisis situations, the UN economic development bodies need to undertake additional research and systematization of experiences and improve their capacity for programme formulation and pricing, activities that would certainly require reorganizing around common core issues such as those proposed in chapter 1.

Again, as said at the end of the previous section, efforts to improve contributions to rehabilitation programmes in post-crisis and post-conflict situations, or to formulate a development component in national security policies, provide a good opportunity to reorganize and revitalize the UN's economic development functions.

## INTERACTION WITH THE BRETTON WOODS INSTITUTIONS

As we have seen, the origin and evolution of the BWIs differ from those of the UN economic development functions, and these differences have certainly conditioned their relationships, including the way the institutions cooperate with one another.

The IMF and the International Bank for Reconstruction and Development, better known as the World Bank, were given birth in Bretton Woods in 1944 with the objective of rebuilding the international system of exchanges and payments and to facilitate and supply financial resources for the post-war reconstruction efforts. One of the important power brokers of the times, the USSR, did not endorse the establishment of these institutions. However, it did co-sponsor the foundation of the UN the following April in San Francisco, at the international conference where the UN Charter was drafted and approved.

The UN was created in the midst of an uncertain economic consensus between the New Deal policies implemented under president F.D. Roosevelt in the United States, the centrally planned Soviet Union and the emerging European social democracy, followed during the 1950s and 1960s by the economic nationalism of the Third World, propelled by the decolonization process.

The Secretary-General was authorized to conduct certain technical cooperation activities through specialized agencies for the first time in 1948, with an annual budget of less than US$ 300,000. In 1950 the Expanded Programme for Technical Assistance (EPTA) was established with an annual budget of U$S 20 million, financed by voluntary contributions outside the regular budget of the UN.

By 1965 decolonization had brought onstage a large number of new member states: they reached 118 in that year, doubling the number of founding members. As

---

1  General Assembly A/59/565, 29 November 2004.

explained earlier, due to this very fact much more attention began to be placed on international economic cooperation, with the UN playing the role of a political forum for North–South dialogue on the economic and social issues of the South.

The big four specialized UN agencies (FAO, ILO, UNESCO and WHO) expanded their development activities significantly, in line with the growing transfer of ODA to the developing countries. That period witnessed the emergence of institutions like UNCTAD (1964), UNDP (1965) and UNIDO (1966).

Since the developing countries' influence on the BWIs was rather limited due to the system of weighted voting rights in the latter, they tried to mobilize more resources from the most advanced countries by using the UN bodies in the economic development field and voting in greater concert, as explained in chapter 2. After the establishment of these UN bodies, the developing countries continued their quest for a 'new development paradigm' through the UN, as manifested in the New International Economic Order (NIEO) adopted by the General Assembly a decade later, in 1974.

The atmosphere of confrontation and lack of political consensus affected the evolution of the UN's economic development functions, as explained in chapter 3. It prevented most of its bodies from achieving a critical mass of human and financial resources, More specifically, it reduced their potential to accumulate knowledge along common, clearly defined tracks. The UN economic development bodies made a great number of technical contributions, but the model of governance of the scarce resources under their command did not facilitate the mutual articulation of their technical contributions (for example through experience-sharing or common under-takings) along common lines of work. This process was exacerbated by competition for donor funding.

The 1987 World Commission on Environment and Development (the so-called Brundtland Commission) that led to a United Nations Conference on Environment and Development in 1992, was probably the first opportunity to mend North–South tensions in a new political context (which had moved, after the demise of the Soviet Union, from East–West–South trilateralism to North–South bilateralism). This allowed the refocusing of discussions on global economic issues by identifying points of common interest such as the protection of the environ-ment, a global common that must be protected for all nations. The adoption of Agenda 21 led to programmatic adjustments in a number of organizations and helped to sharpen the focus of some of the system's economic development func-tions.

Changes also took place in the BWIs. They evolved considerably from their orig-inal mandates to become a kind of lender of last resort for nations in financial crises (IMF) or a 'knowledge bank' (WB). Both confronted serious criticisms, the most extreme (suggested by a special panel appointed by the US Senate) going as far as to advocate their outright closure. In fact, with the dawn of the new century the IMF abandoned its role as lender of last resort. However, both agencies managed to main-tain a consistent line of thinking and to accumulate knowledge and enrich their experience on the importance of macroeconomic stability and free trade for economic growth — ideas that later, coupled with political developments, gave rise to the bulk of today's conventional policy prescriptions.

Although often failing to bring prosperity for many reasons, macroeconomic stability and market-oriented reforms contributed to most of the economic success stories of the last decades, including notably the case of China, where those recommendations were applied in a very idiosyncratic manner. However, the imbalances brought about by the integration of financial and commercial markets and the political unrest they generated in the political systems of some countries called into question the universality of these recommendations and prompted demands to give globalization a 'human face'.

I submit that we face a new opportunity, as we did in 1992, to meld different political views around common global concerns and needs. The opportunity this time is given by the strong multilateral consensus around the MDGs. The specificity of the targets and their timeframe does not allow for political debate only. Technical contributions are in high demand and the collective wealth of knowledge of the multilateral system can be put fully at their service, overcoming historical constraints of critical mass and lack of accumulation of knowledge along common and clearly defined tracks.

Strengthening a common technical focus is, in my view, the right way to improve the history of low interactions between the BWIs and the UN bodies. Early in 2004 UNIDO undertook a revision of the conditions for achieving the MDGs in sub-Saharan Africa by examining some 30 PRSPs. One finding was a neglect of PSD in poverty reduction. We shared with the IMF our conclusions and our recommendations for strengthening the private sector's contribution to the PRSPs during a meeting with the Poverty Reduction and Growth Facility (PRGF) mission chiefs and senior professional staff of the Departments for Policy Development and Review and Research.

Spelling out more clearly and fully the contents of the UN economic development bodies' contributions would certainly reinvigorate the relationship with the Fund, the Bank and the WTO, making it possible to enhance joint undertakings for the benefit of developing countries. Due to differences in size and trajectories, the UN bodies may attempt this task in an articulated manner, by means of a commonly agreed agenda or 'business plan'. Selecting the topics and providing robust substance to this undertaking will require not just paying due attention to political and institutional considerations, but also taking a closer look at the evolution of thinking and practice in development economics during the last decades (which I will tackle in the following chapter).

# CONCLUSIONS

The topics discussed in this chapter point clearly towards the need to increase the specialization and focus of the UN bodies in the field of economic development by means of analysis, research and better understanding in at least three areas:

☐    Technical cooperation programmes seeking to deepen the multidimensional and often elusive link between investments in human development and economic development.

☐    Adaptation of the UN programmes in the field of economic development to post-conflict and post-crisis contexts.

☐    Clear definition of the UN system's stand on economic development to facilitate the division of labor with the BWIs.

This can certainly be done in a concerted manner by means of a voluntary coordination mechanism in the context of the implementation of the MDGs, as proposed in chapter 1.

## REFERENCES

DAC, 1997: *Guidelines on Conflict, Peace and Development Cooperation on the Threshold of the 21st Century*, OECD, Paris, 1997.

DAC, 2001: *Guidelines in Helping Prevent Violent Conflict*, OECD 2001.

IMF, 1998: World Economic Outlook, Ch. 4, International Monetary Fund, 1998, Washington DC.

Meier and Stiglitz (eds) 2001: *Frontiers of Development Economics*, Oxford University Press, Oxford, 2001.

Goulding, Sir Marrack, *Peacemonger*, John Murray (Publishers) Ltd., London, 2002.

UNIDO, 2004: Industrial Development Report 2004 – Industrialization, Environment and the Millennium Development Goals in Sub-Saharan Africa – The New Frontier in the Fight Against Poverty, UNIDO, Vienna, 2004

United Nations, 2000: *Report of the Panel on United Nations Peace Operations.* A/55/305 - S/2000/809. 55th Session of the General Assembly, August 2000.

United Nations, 2002: *Living with Risk: A global review of disaster reduction initiatives.* Inter-agency effort coordinated by the ISDR Secretariat with special support from the Government of Japan, the World Meteorological Organization and the Asian Disaster Reduction Center (Kobe, Japan), July 2002.

# CHAPTER 5

# INSIGHTS FROM THE EVOLUTION OF THINKING AND PRACTICE IN DEVELOPMENT ECONOMICS

Some six decades have elapsed since the establishment of the BWIs and about four since the inception of a number of UN bodies devoted to the promotion of economic development. The multilateral economic development architecture developed in those foundational years was certainly based on the best available knowledge on economics at the time, and reflected the theories then predominant.

I have already referred to the political changes that shaped the life and evolution of these bodies. I have to add, however, that the passage of time did not affect just the political scene; it also brought about a significant evolution in economic knowledge and thinking. If political and programmatic adjustments in the heavy multilateral machinery normally take time and are adopted with a certain delay, I suppose it will not be difficult to agree that improvements in scientific or academic knowledge in fields like development economics are heeded at an even slower pace and to a more limited extent. There are powerful reasons for this.

To begin with, technical cooperation and other assistance programmes are typically designed or handled by people required to have a measure of expertise and length of experience in given fields. They are not necessarily trained in the difficult task of assimilating the most advanced concepts developed in academia, think-tanks or centres of excellence. The technical cooperation programmes they administrate are logically based in knowledge accumulated through decades of professional experience more than in the adoption of evolutionary thinking or more recent practices. This we can call 'bureaucratic inertia'.

Another reason lies with the decision-making process for the allocation of aid resources. It often entails attaching some conditionalities according to donors' priority subjects and countries. The approval of funds and the disbursement process takes its time, while the adoption of innovations in programme formulation or design normally requires several years, from convincing and mobilizing the interest of potential beneficiaries and donors to securing the necessary administrative approval process. This can be called 'political inertia'.

Both 'bureaucratic inertia' and 'political inertia' have been receiving renewed attention and are currently being better counteracted thanks to a number of coordination mechanisms and newly designed instruments in the context of implementing the MDGs, which opens new hopes for scholars, practitioners and thinkers, providing an enticement to update the design of the programmes being implemented in several fields.

This is not to say that the challenge of achieving economic development changed so drastically that all we knew half a century ago is not relevant anymore to perform our current duties. It is to suggest that the evolution of thinking and practice in development economics is providing powerful elements to rethink the fundamentals on which the logic, structure and dynamics of the multilateral economic development architecture were based. I think our current knowledge and experience justify a new look at the way the system is organized and works in order to make more relevant contributions in the fight against poverty and marginalization.

In a way, with the necessary circumspection, I think that we are at a juncture akin to that in which the founding fathers of the multilateral economic development architecture found themselves half a century ago.

## THE EVOLUTION OF THINKING ABOUT ECONOMIC GROWTH

I will not try to reproduce here what can be found in learned volumes or professional journals on the subject. A proper treatment of this topic would not only be lengthy; it could also prove highly controversial since economists are still far from having reached a consensus about the sources of growth — and indeed still quarrel about them.

Analysis of the sources of growth probably started at the same time as economics itself. Economists and non-economists interested in social sciences will certainly recall Adam Smith's question about the wealth of nations back in 1776, when the discipline was in its infancy. A century later, Alfred Marshall recognized that the search for economic growth was at the centre of economists' interests and provided them powerful motivation. Those were the times when the world was ruled by a relatively small group of independent nations.

My aim here is to concentrate on the evolution of thinking on these matters since the post-war period, during which the multilateral economic development architecture was established and developed and a considerable number of new nations joined the ranks of the developing world. I will attempt to offer here a concise review of the main developments, highlighting only the main lines of thought, without declaring winners and losers in a discussion that is still open.

The Harrod–Domar (1946) model provided the first powerful idea for post-war economists dealing with economic development in poor nations: the level of investment determines growth. For this model the rate of growth in a given year can be predicted on the basis of the ratio of investment to GDP the year before.

A whole brand of development thinking was triggered by this concept. Development economists applied it to predicting the growth prospects of developing countries. I think it is important to note that Domar himself dismissed his theory as a growth model and endorsed Solow's ideas instead. He had just been studying the relationship between short-term recessions and investment in the United States.

The second powerful idea came a decade later from Robert Solow (1957), who discovered that long-term economic growth could be explained by the rate of technological change of a given economy.

Following the logic of the law of diminishing returns, Solow found that he could not explain the long-term growth rate of the United States as the result of capital (plus labour) accumulation, because each additional unit of capital (or labour) should produce a lower return than the previous one, making the economy unable to attain steady growth of about two percent — as it was the case — for the period under study. He concluded that something else accounted for the difference and identified it in technical progress. He thought technical progress, an exogenous factor, was generated by non-economic factors like basic science, unable to be influenced by government policies.

The growth accounting exercises of Edward Denison (1962) demonstrated that the United States growth could be explained by capital accumulation and by Solow's residual, i.e. 'technological progress', in almost equal shares.

It must be noted that both Domar and Solow were analysing the United States economy and by no means thinking about the development problems of the poor countries.

The third idea worth highlighting appeared about three decades after Solow's model (1986/88/90) thanks to Robert Lucas and Paul Romer. This new growth theory can be summarized as follows:

**a**     Technological progress can be influenced by a set of endogenous economic factors and does not respond just to non-economic factors (as thought before); and
**b**     In the presence of technological change, the utilization of additional units of productive factors can be expected to be subject to increasing returns (instead of diminishing returns as assumed until then).

Romer and Lucas considered the residual not to be exogenous (as did Solow) but instead as resulting from endogenous phenomena associated with the working of competition and policies in the fields of education, innovation and technology. For them technological progress generates externalities that raise total factor productivity.

Robert Lucas asked himself in 1990, "Why are investment flows moving away from developing countries when neoclassical models predicted the reverse?" That year the richest 20 percent of the world population received 79 percent of all foreign direct investment (FDI) while the poorest 20 percent received a meagre 0.7 percent. According to the (neoclassical) law of diminishing returns, investments must flow from countries where capital (or whichever other factor) is abundant to countries where it is scarce. What happened was exactly the opposite.

The logical answer was that the returns are not diminishing. The reason for that was to be found in technological progress: technical innovations offset diminishing returns by generating increasing returns.

Economists of all times and different schools of thought could agree about the central role played by capital accumulation in the growth process. What these three major strands of thought showed us is that perceptions of the ways and means to actually achieve accumulation have been enriched over time. Studies concluded that how capital is allocated is more important than capital accumulation itself (Meier and Stiglitz, 2001, chapter 1) to explain cases like that of India, where high savings rates coexisted with sluggish growth.

From the simple formula of domestic savings supplemented by foreign resources (in the form of aid or private investment) in the Domar tradition, to the more elaborate findings of Solow's model where capital accumulation must be coupled with technical change to sustain long-term growth, the role of knowledge and innovation was enhanced over the years. Productivity growth, innovation and technological developments themselves are considered today by many to be the means of attracting and accumulating capital, and achieving economic growth.

Gradually these new approaches gained adepts in many quarters, decisively influencing the policy-making process in important economic spheres like the European Union (as witness the decisions of the European Council in March 2000 in Lisbon regarding the establishment of a European area of research and innovation to achieve a competitive, dynamic and knowledge-based economy).

I suggested in the previous chapter that the multilateral economic development architecture was too busy mediating in the Cold War and the East–West economic and ideological dispute to take due account, properly analyse and fully draw on these developments by translating them into concrete technical cooperation programmes. And after the fall of the Berlin Wall a considerable part of the development system was busy supporting the transition of the former Soviet Union countries from centrally planned to market-oriented economies, as well as the wave of market-oriented reforms in other regions, like Latin America. This left little room for the study and adoption of the increasing levels of sophistication of the new approaches developed by academia.

## LESSONS FROM THE SUCCESSFUL CATCHING-UP PROCESSES

There are quite a few experiences in the world economy (including Africa) that the international community can draw upon to advance the development debate. Since the aftermath of World War II, when the UN programmes and institutions in the economic development field were established, the world economy has registered some successful cases of economic and social catching-up.

The first cases worth noting are those of the European and Japanese reconstruction almost immediately after the war. Prominent features of these processes were:

**a**    A significant amount of resources were effectively channeled for the reconstruction efforts through the Marshal Plan;

**b**    That plan was the fruit of a true bipartisan agreement in the United States Congress and enjoyed full backing of the Administration, and

**c**    The recipient countries, even the smaller ones, were given a genuine opportunity to lead the process of allocation of aid resources, and their institutions were respected and involved in the execution of the plan.

It should not be forgotten that in some cases the reconstruction efforts did not have to start from scratch since even the losers of the conflict did manage to maintain or protect some of their productive facilities and reconvert them after the war (e.g. Nikon moved from the production in wartime of naval optical instruments to its world-famous brand in the photographic industry) and, in spite of terrible human losses, knowledge and capabilities for economic progress were still very much present in those societies.

A different case, starting from very different initial conditions and in a certainly dissimilar context, is that of the two waves of Asian Tigers during the 1970s and 1980s: first, Singapore, Taiwan province of China and the Republic of Korea, and Thailand; later Malaysia, and to a lesser extent, Indonesia and the Philippines.

Additionally, there is the outstanding case of China, whose reforms started in the late 1970s and where impressive strides in poverty reduction and economic growth have been made. In the early 1990s India started a number of economic reforms and, more recently, has managed to add its name to the select list of countries succeeding in a catching-up process. It is obviously necessary to strike a note of caution when one examines these two countries due to their enormous extension and the size of their population; in spite of the tremendous progress made, they both still host large numbers of people in absolute poverty.

Mention must also be made of the more recent examples provided by the successive expansions of the EU. Finland modernized its economy some years ago (in the wake of the demise of most of its foreign trade during the fall of the Soviet Union). This allowed small companies operating in traditional sectors to become global players in high-tech business (e.g. Nokia). Spain, Ireland, Portugal and Greece, in a common drive to join the EU, performed differently in closing the gap with the EU in average income per capita (with the two first scoring better than the others). They received significant amounts of EU cohesion funds to reorganize and modernize their economies — a move reminiscent of the Marshall Plan — with their institutions fully in charge of their administration, keeping in mind that they also received a powerful impulse to modernize their institutions and support systems for the provision of public goods.

In its most recent drive the enlargement of the EU embraced Poland, the Czech Republic, Hungary, Slovenia, Slovakia, Cyprus, Malta and the Baltic States, most of them countries that have worked more than a decade to migrate from centrally planned economic policies to market-oriented ones.

It is important to point out that in almost all the cases of economic progress cited within the process of European enlargement the initial conditions were more similar to those of the post-war period in Europe than those prevailing in Asia in the 1960s.

On a different, lower level are other cases such as those of Mexico, Chile and Brazil in the Americas and Tunisia in Africa, where some degree of economic progress was also achieved along with relative (and still insufficient) social progress and poverty reduction. The case of South Africa is a particularly relevant one, with a very dynamic economy operating in a sort of dual track in a country struggling to integrate its different sectors through an intense democratic exercise.

All these countries share some common features in their general approach to achieving economic progress. They are: sound macroeconomic management, market-oriented policies, open economies, and predictable and legitimate systems of governance (though in some cases fully democratic systems do not yet prevail).

However, the manners in which these countries went about implementing their economic programmes differ considerably. The range includes a large number of ad-hoc interventions in several fields, from financial measures in support of certain sectors or companies to the supply of public goods to enable the dissemination of knowledge, information, skills and technology.

For the sake of brevity, I can summarize the above as follows: the interventions made by these countries were basically aimed at ensuring the right interaction between the incentives system (i.e. the price system resulting from monetary, fiscal and external policies; tariffs; IPR legislation and competition policies) and the supply of public goods, in order to enable the private sector to innovate, incorporate technical change and achieve growth of high quality, creating jobs and providing opportunities for as many economic actors as possible (see Figure 1).

**FIGURE 1**  PRODUCTIVITY FOR QUALITY GROWTH

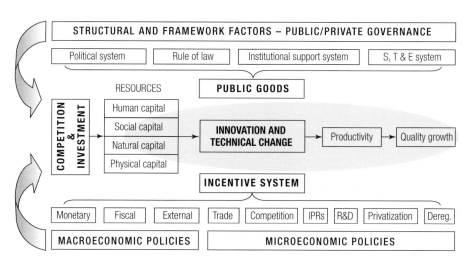

*Source: Magariños and Sercovich, 2003*

Working on just one set of the factors illustrated in the figure is not enough to accumulate capital and translate that into quality growth. Both Nigeria and Hong Kong increased their physical capital per worker by more than 250 percent between 1960 and 1985, yet output per worker increased 12 percent in the former and 328 percent in the latter over the same period. Gambia and Japan increased the stock of capital per worker by over 500 percent over the same period, yet output per worker increased 2 percent in Gambia and 260 percent in Japan. The results hold for the whole sample quoted by Easterly (2002).

The experience of these countries suggests that much needs to be done besides ensuring proper macroeconomic management, market-oriented policies and good governance to accumulate capital and maintain the pace of productivity growth in the economy, allowing it to spill over into the social fabric of a country. Understanding this may well be the key to achieving growth with equity.

The means of accumulating physical capital have changed considerably since economic globalization began to accelerate over the last couple of decades or so as a result of the integration of the world's financial and commercial markets. To cope with this new environment, a new rule-based multilateral trade (and financial) system was introduced during the latter years of the last century, which barred most of the interventions and policies that had been used by the countries referred to above during their process of economic development.

To make relevant contributions in this framework, the UN programmes and institutions involved in economic development will have to continuously strengthen the process already under way of sharpening the focus and deepening the substance of both their research agendas and technical cooperation programmes — and, even more important, the interaction of the different UN agencies, funds, programmes, conferences and commissions will have to be improved.

The Marshall Plan and successive waves of enlargement of the European Union shared some notable common elements. Both processes entailed strong political consensus and determination. Both considered economic development a powerful weapon against the risks of the times — either to contain post-war Soviet expansion or to stabilize the neighborhood (e.g. starting negotiations with Croatia), improve security and the management of migration flows, thus creating and expanding markets. And both processes were led by the recipient country's institutions, which received powerful incentives to upgrade the supply of public goods.

I think those are interesting lessons for the implementation of the MDGs from the perspective of the donor countries and that of the multilateral development architecture.

The current phase of the globalization process and the very evolution of economic thinking, particularly in the field of development economics, in the context of the adoption of the MDGs, provides a unique opportunity to improve the interaction between UN agencies and programmes and, especially, between them and the BWIs, abandoning old intellectual rivalries and focusing on ensuring that the current 'corporate strategy' of prioritizing macroeconomic stability, market-oriented reforms and good governance works for the poor and matches the efforts made by the social programmes to build human capital.

I submit that we can safely say that this endeavor is tantamount to — and updates — the mandate given to the UN for economic development half a century ago. The fact that the UN institutions did not contribute the most to the formulation of the current economic 'corporate strategy' does not in the least belittle its value and the wealth of knowledge and experience accumulated by the system in the field of economic development. This experience and these resources must be put to work for the sake of the progress of the developing countries and the integration of the international community's economic and social agendas.

# IMPLICATIONS FOR THE MULTILATERAL SYSTEM

How can these findings about the evolving economic development thinking and the lessons from successful catch-up processes be drawn upon by the multilateral development architecture? What do they mean for its work?

The multilateral economic development architecture as we know it has been largely devoted to work in topics illustrated in the lower part of Figure 1. Such work consisted basically of shaping the incentives system by recommending detailed policy prescriptions at both the macro- and micro-economic levels. This is normally done by the BWIs in the first case and by the BWIs (on property rights, investment, etc) and the UN bodies (regarding sectoral policies) in the second.

Retaining these focuses might have been appropriate in a policy environment different from the one we have today, but it is not very helpful in the current context, which witnesses new challenges such as those posed by the realization of the need to cope with incomplete markets and demands for sustainable development.

As Meier (2001) argues, economists are most knowledgeable about situations amenable to 'ordinary' economic analysis. But when the policy challenges are discontinuous or unprecedented and, further, when the role of institutions and technical change must be factored in, the usefulness of the economists' conventional policy toolkit becomes severely constrained. From this perspective, big problems demanding innovative development policy responses include, for example, those that are highly country- and time-specific, where institutional change is required or where there are non-market failures.

Whether we assume that the need for public goods constitutes a residual category in a market economy or, rather, that it is central to economic development today, it would appear pretty safe to hold that:

a     By their own nature, markets do not reveal the need for public goods;
b     Revealing and addressing that need requires special analysis, research and appropriate institutional mechanisms;

c      Developing countries do not have access to satisfactory guidance on tackling issues relating to the supply of public goods for economic development; and

d      Developing countries suffer a chronic undersupply of public goods.

In a way, the undersupply of public-good policies for developing countries is only matched by the oversupply of incentives policies.

This brings us back to the MDGs as the organizing framework for the UN system as a whole. At stake is not only achieving the MDGs but, just as fundamentally, sustaining the achievement over time. This necessarily leads to a focus on the underpinnings of long-term growth.

I have made reference in chapter 1 to the three transitions involved in overcoming chronic poverty; that is, those relating to human development, productivity and the environment. I also pointed out that these transitions do not happen at once or in a linear fashion, but that they overlap and recur during the development process. Their dynamics during the passage from pervasive poverty to sustainable development is a far from trivial matter: achieving the MDGs, admittedly an immensely important goal, by no means guarantees endowment with the social capability required to sustain them over time.

Attaining the MDGs in sub-Saharan Africa, for example, means reaching basic thresholds in areas such as health, nutrition, education, gender equality, infrastructure provision and environmental sustainability — all necessary, but not sufficient, to set sustained economic growth in motion. For example, achieving the goals relating to health and basic education can directly contribute as much as 1.6 percentage points to growth per person. Clearly, this falls far short of what is needed to achieve the income poverty MDG.

For income poverty to be halved in most SSA countries by 2015, per capita incomes must grow at an annual average of about 4–5 percent (UNIDO, 2004). Thus, while increased public spending will help create a platform for take-off, prolonged success depends, among other things, on 'crowding in' private enterprise. This requires, among other things, an international economic environment that rewards such steps largely by opening access to developed-country markets. But, in the absence of a buildup of domestic institutional and social capabilities and other conditions required to foster healthy private-sector-led development, developing countries may be unable to take full advantage of world market opportunities. Pivotal among these conditions is that of redressing the undersupply of public goods in areas such as trade capacity building and technology diffusion. Only in this way can the various transitions referred to above have a chance to be completed.

## CONCLUSIONS

For the reasons discussed above, I take the view that a change of emphasis is called for whereby, as far as macro and micro policies are concerned, the UN system ought to assist developing countries principally in acquiring the mastery of benchmarking methodologies. Beyond this, most remaining efforts should be devoted to assisting in redressing the undersupply of public goods for economic development. The latter is the major, still largely unaccomplished, task ahead of us.

The business plan or common agenda for action proposed in chapter 1 is a possible roadmap for the UN system to embark on such a task and thus foster the ability of developing countries, particularly the poorest ones, to go through the three transitions necessary to becoming meaningful partners in world markets.

### REFERENCES

Easterly, 2002: *The Elusive Quest for Growth: Economists' Adventures and Misadventures in the Tropics*, MIT Press, Boston, 2002.

Magariños and Sercovich, 2003: *Updating and Fleshing Out the Development Agenda*, UNIDO, Vienna, 2003.

Meier and Stiglitz (eds) 2001: *Frontiers of Development Economics*, Oxford University Press, Oxford, 2001.

UNIDO, 2004: *Industrial Development Report 2004, Industrialization, Environment and the Millennium Development Goals in Sub-Saharan Africa*, UNIDO, Vienna, 2004.

# PART II

REFORM AT WORK:
THE CASE OF THE
UNITED NATIONS
INDUSTRIAL DEVELOPMENT
ORGANIZATION

# CHAPTER 6

# UNIDO: FROM CONCEPTION THROUGH CRISIS TO SURVIVAL AND THE BUSINESS PLAN

UNIDO presents an interesting case study in UN reform for a number of reasons. First, it was blamed for many of the failures alleged to have affected the UN as a whole. This includes lack of administrative and operational efficiency, ineffectiveness, lack of responsiveness to client needs, and lack of relevance. Second, it was the subject of intense scrutiny by both donor and recipient countries due to the very nature of its activities. Third, its reform programmes since 1993 have been far-reaching. Fourth, both its member states and the UN system acknowledged that its transformation since late 1997 has been one of the most comprehensive and successful.

## INDUSTRIAL DEVELOPMENT, THE UN AND UNIDO 1956–1985

In the early 1950s, at the request of ECOSOC, the UN Secretariat prepared a number of studies on industrial development that led, in 1956, to the establishment of an Industry Section. In 1957, a more systematic programme of studies was approved. Its topics included small-scale industry promotion, environmental planning, industrial management in developing countries, capital intensity in industry, and capital investment and productivity.

In view of the need to pay more attention to economic development issues, including industrial development, in 1960 ECOSOC established a Standing Committee for Industrial Development. During its first meeting, the committee recommended the establishment of a Centre for Industrial Development. This Centre was established in 1961 within DESA (General Assembly Resolution 1712). Its objective was to record, analyze and disseminate the experience gained in technical assistance programmes in support of industrialization. The Centre also aimed to provide the means for a better coordination of all the activities in the industrial field carried out by the UN Secretariat, the regional economic commissions and the specialized agencies.

The role originally envisaged for the Centre involved only *normative* activities. However, even as early as this, the question was raised whether the UN should establish a specialized agency for industrial development with a wider set of tasks. The ECOSOC Standing Committee was asked to prepare a report on the matter. In 1963, it recommended that such an organization be set up; it would report to the General Assembly. The matter was taken up by the General Assembly in 1966 on the back of rapid developments concerning UNCTAD and UNDP.

As mentioned earlier, UNDP was established in 1965 in response to developing country demands. It was charged with providing a framework for coordinating the technical cooperation of the whole UN system. Soon after UNDP came into existence, it was decided, though, to establish UNIDO as a special organ of the UN General Assembly's Resolution 20/89. This was a compromise solution: the developing countries (the Group of 77) had wanted a specialized agency with its own political decision-making governing body (and eventually normative activities, which later came to be called global forum activities), while the industrialized countries preferred a lower-profile organization under the direct control of the General Assembly.

In November 1966, through Resolution 21/52 of the General Assembly's 21st Session, this compromise resulted in the creation of the United Nations Industrial Development Organization[1] (UNIDO) as the organization responsible for coordinating the industrial development activities of the United Nations. Resolution 21/52 is generally regarded as UNIDO's founding document, and in January 1967 the Organization was formally established in Vienna, Austria.

Initially, a large part of UNIDO's activities was continuation of the work of the Centre for Industrial Development, as a global forum for discussions and for normative or analytical functions and the dissemination of information. Technical cooperation activities had still to be developed. Donor member states, however, considered that any such activities carried out by UNIDO should largely be funded outside the budget, mainly by UNDP.

In 1970, based on a capacity study for UNDP by Sir Robert Jackson, UNDP started a new system of country planning and five-year rolling funding for the country programmes, in the form of the Indicative Planning Figure (IPF). IPFs were to be the main mechanisms for coordination of UN technical cooperation. At first, UNIDO was served well by the system of UNDP funding. The value of its technical cooperation increased from US$12.7 million in 1970 to US$40 million in 1976, about 80 percent of which was funded by UNDP. This was a reflection of the high and growing demand from the developing countries for industry-related technical cooperation, which had a direct influence on the allocation of UNDP funds available to them.

While this growth of UNIDO's operational activities was taking place, the political dimension of the development debate between developing and developed countries led to an important milestone for the organization.

---

1  Originally it was called United Nations Organization for Industrial Development (UNOID).

In the context of General Assembly discussions related to the establishment of a New International Economic Order,[2] the Second General Conference of UNIDO, held in 1975 in Lima, Peru, adopted the Lima Declaration on Industrial Development and Cooperation. In it, quantified targets for the industrial development of developing countries were agreed for the first time (they were to have 25 percent of world industrial production by the year 2000; up from a 1974 share of only 7 percent). The 'Plan of Action' drawn up to implement the declaration included a detailed list of general and specific measures aimed at achieving the target.[3] Thirty years later, these ambitious targets have largely not been met.

As part of the 'institutional arrangements' in the plan, it was recommended to the General Assembly that UNIDO should be converted into a specialized agency. It was also recommended that an Industrial Development Fund be established to channel voluntary contributions to UNIDO's technical cooperation activities so that the organization could contribute to the achievement of the Lima Declaration's objectives.

The declaration specified that UNIDO should have both normative and operational responsibilities:

> UNIDO should not only intensify and expand its present operational activities and action-oriented studies and research programme in the field of industrial development but should include among its activities a system of continuing consultations at global, regional and sectoral levels for the purposes set forth in paragraph 61 (d) above. UNIDO should be prepared to serve as a forum for negotiation of agreements in the field of industry between developed and developing countries and among developing countries themselves at the request of the countries concerned. Paragraph 61 (d) specified that these consultations would be in respect of demand and supply, availability of production factors and their costs, the possibilities and conditions of investment and the availability of appropriate equipment and technologies, with a view to facilitating [...] the redeployment of certain productive capacities existing in developed countries and the creation of new industrial facilities in developing countries.[4]

It was not until 1979 that a compromise was reached on the exact nature and responsibilities of UNIDO as a specialized agency. A major bone of contention was the idea, promoted by the Group of 77, that UNIDO should also be a financial organization. This was not acceptable to the developed countries and was left out of the constitution adopted on 8 April 1979 in Vienna, at the second session of the UN Conference on the Establishment of UNIDO as a specialized agency. The constitution did include,

---

2  The New International Economic Order is explained in greater detail in chapter 3.
3  Lima Declaration and Plan of Action on Industrial Development and Cooperation, 1975.
4  Paragraph 66.

however, both the normative and the operational tasks described above.[5] It also stated that the principal objective of the organization was to promote and accelerate industrial development in developing countries with a view to assisting in the establishment of a new international economic order. A subsidiary goal was to promote industrial development and cooperation at the global, regional and national levels. (Countries with economies in transition were added later as targets for UNIDO's assistance through a re-interpretation of UNIDO's constitution.[6])

Even with this compromise, the developed countries were not convinced that a specialized UN agency for industrial development was necessary. Another separate organization would mean another separate assessed contribution, as well as increased demand for voluntary contributions. Other issues weighed too. Some countries had lingering doubts about the desirability of helping to create competitors, especially to their private sectors. There was also concern about duplication and coordination within the system, and the loss of control to a majority that consisted of developing countries. The objections and doubts of developed countries contributed to the delay in the ratification of UNIDO as a specialized agency. They also influenced the degree to which these countries were willing to fund the organization, particularly in the form of voluntary contributions.

## UNIDO AS A SPECIALIZED AGENCY 1986–1992

On 1 January 1986, UNIDO formally became the 16th specialized agency of the UN. Specialized UN agencies are autonomous organizations working with the UN and each other through ECOSOC. Each organization has its own membership, its own governing bodies, Director-General, regular budgets (funded from mandatory assessed contributions), voluntary contributions for extra-budgetary activities and secretariats. UNIDO's governing bodies, which guide the work of the organization, are:

☐   *General Conference:* All member states (now 171) meet once every two years at the General Conference, which approves UNIDO's budget and work programme. The conference also appoints the Director-General, normally at four-year intervals.

☐   *Industrial Development Board:* The Industrial Development Board (53 member states) reviews the implementation of the work programme and the budget and makes recommendations to the General Conference on policy matters, including the appointment of the Director-General, when so required. The board meets once in General Conference years, and twice in other years.

---

5   UNIDO's normative function was added to in 1985 with the establishment of its annual Industry and Development Global Report.

6   *Assessment of UNIDO*, 1997, p. 7.

☐ *Programme and Budget Committee:* The Programme and Budget Committee (27 member states) meets once a year to assist the board in the preparation and examination of the work programme, the budget and other financial matters.

However, the newly independent organization immediately had to deal with a financial crisis — an effective shortfall in the first biennium of almost 30 percent of the regular budget, caused by a rapid decline in the value of the United States dollar, which was the currency for the budget and contributions, whereas most of the organization's expenditures were linked to the Austrian schilling. In addition, several major developed member states paid their assessed contributions late or not at all.

When Mr Domingo L. Siazon (Philippines) took office in 1986 as the first Director-General of the organization as a specialized agency, he planned changes in its orientation to adjust to changes in demand from developing countries and to increase responsiveness, effectiveness and transparency — efforts that were seriously hampered by this financial crisis. He sought to focus more on industrial cooperation with private companies, human resource development, SMEs, industrial rehabilitation and enterprise-to-enterprise cooperation, and to foster a more integrated approach to industrial development. These intentions would be only partially realized as a result of the financial crisis. Important activities under approved programmes and work plans could not be carried out. This situation continued throughout 1988–1989.

On the other hand, voluntary contributions (additional to the regular budget) to UNIDO's technical cooperation activities continued to grow. The annual value of technical cooperation increased from US$ 40 million in 1976, to US$ 120 million in 1988 and to US$ 160 million in 1990. This rapid growth in technical cooperation, in combination with the funding crisis in the regular budget, changed the balance between the organization's global forum/normative and operational functions. Slowly, the volume of studies and analytical work, and of information dissemination, decreased — including work related to technology transfer. As most of UNIDO's extra-budgetary funding was for 'special purposes', where the donor decides which activities they fund, UNIDO's influence on the direction of these activities was limited.

After 1990, UNIDO also had to meet the new challenge of assisting the countries of Central and Eastern Europe and the former Soviet Union to make the difficult transition to competitive market economies. At the same time, Africa's increasingly desperate economic plight could not be ignored. In response, UNIDO tried to use its regular budget to support Africa's development under the Industrial Development Decade for Africa (IDDA) programme and from its IDF.

After peaking at US$ 160 million in 1990, the value of technical cooperation fell rapidly to US$ 118 million in 1993 and to US$ 97 million in 1997. Since then the delivery has been around US$ 69–85 million. [The trend changed in 2003 when delivery rose to US$ 95 million, and then to US$ 98 million in 2004.] Virtually the whole of the decline was caused by the sharp decrease in UNDP-financed activities, which have now dwindled to about US$ 3 million for reasons explained below.

With the start of UNDP's fifth programming cycle in 1992, the funding situation of UNDP changed, due to donors becoming less inclined to support public-sector projects. This contributed to a decline in UNDP funding for UNIDO programmes and projects. This decline was caused by the following: a substantive refocusing of UNDP, in part away from the industry sector; an increasing preference for national execution of projects (in which a UNDP-funded project is carried out by the national authorities), which unfortunately was interpreted by UNDP as largely excluding the specialized agencies; the establishment of UNOPS by UNDP to implement various programmes and projects; and a gradual but consistent decline in member states' contributions to UNDP's core resources.[7]

Figure 2 shows that until 1991–1992 UNIDO's technical cooperation activities were highly dependent on UNDP funding, and that the decline in total volume after 1991 is almost the same as the decline in UNDP funding. The dependence on UNDP funding was helpful as long as UNDP played its original role as a central funding organization that programmed available funds in a sectorally unbiased manner in close consultation with recipient governments and the specialized agencies.

However, from a variety of other sources, direct funding to UNIDO increased gradually until 1990, and stabilized thereafter at about US$ 70–75 million. [The trend changed after 2000 and in 2004 it reached about US$ 103 million]. The IDF, agreed in 1979 with a target annual funding of US$ 50 million, never received more than US$ 30 million, i.e. about 60 percent. In spite of the agreement, several donors actually considered that UNIDO should obtain most of its funding for technical cooperation from UNDP. As a result, UNIDO never received the financial means to set its own course and be more responsive to the needs of developing countries.

**FIGURE 2** UNIDO'S DELIVERY OF TECHNICAL COOPERATION OVER THE YEARS
(US$ MILLIONS)

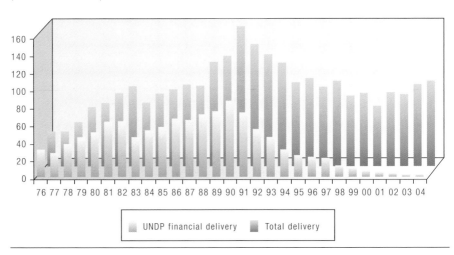

7  'Core resources' mean voluntary contributions programmable by UNDP, which are largely allocated to individual countries and available for the UNDP programmes there.

# BEGINNING OF REFORMS AND
# THE LOOMING CRISIS 1993–1997

UNIDO's Fifth General Conference, held on 6–10 December 1993 in Yaoundé, Cameroon, with Mr Mauricio de María y Campos (Mexico) as the second Director-General (1993–1997), was another milestone in the organization's history. It was the first attempt at a major reform of UNIDO. It sought to address the changes that had been taking place in the world, particularly rapidly spreading globalization with its 'strong trends towards deregulation and restructuring, which require appropriate responses in the field of industrial development'.[8] It did this through a unanimously approved far-reaching reform programme intended to improve the organization's realization of its objectives and to strengthen its role as the central coordinating agency in the UN system for the promotion of the industrialization of developing countries and countries with economies in transition.

The General Conference, the organization's supreme governing body, also recognized a need to improve the direction of UNIDO's work in industrial development towards achieving the socio-economic objectives of increased employment and income in less developed regions — particularly Africa — and for vulnerable sections of the population. Importantly, it was felt that UNIDO's technical cooperation had to refocus, away from its previous concentration on support to governmental institutions and state-owned enterprises, and towards providing policy advisory services for the private sector, particularly SMEs. UNIDO also needed to trim down the fields of assistance and number of industrial sectors it covered, to better reflect its core capabilities, technical expertise and resources. It needed to prioritize activities, regions and sectors.[9]

The Yaoundé Declaration did not specifically address the issue of UNIDO's operational activities versus its global forum function. The declaration reiterated that

> 'the major means of achieving UNIDO's objectives of environmentally sustainable and equitable industrial development remain investment promotion, technology transfer, development of human resources and the creation of an enabling environment, both nationally and internationally, for industrial growth and competitiveness'.

These objectives clearly included elements of both operational and normative activities. The regular budget for 1994–1995 retained all the normative activities that UNIDO had been performing, which came to be called 'global forum' activities after the Global Forum on Industrial Development in India. The System of Consultations, promoted 20 years earlier by the Lima Declaration, and whose aim was to focus inter-

---

8  Maria y Campos, 1995, pp. 74–8.
9  Maria y Campos, 1995, pp. 75–6.

national cooperation and work towards greater equity in the sharing of global wealth — which was not welcomed by the developed countries — became less visible.

However, when implementation of the reform — which was unanimously approved — was getting under way in 1995, the United States, the largest contributor, announced its intention of withdrawing from the organization. The result was a 25 percent cut in UNIDO's regular budget. The withdrawal of the United States was much regretted by many member states, including other major donor countries. The United States decision was seen as premature, as it was taken before the reforms had been given a chance to succeed. Ostensibly, the United States withdrawal was due to 'budgetary reasons', perhaps meant to send some signal to the UN system and other countries, or to meet some domestic agenda.

A common view within the organization, and amongst influential commentators outside it, was that the United States withdrawal had weakened the very logic and objective of reform; it would have been more opportune if the United States had remained a member and worked with the organization to ensure the success of the reform process. This view was supported by an increase in the effective demand for UNIDO's services as measured by what its clients were willing to pay for its services. Between 1993 and 1996, UNIDO not only maintained its technical cooperation delivery levels: the value of projects approved for funding rose by 40 percent.[10]

The disaffection of some other leading donor countries, such as Denmark and the United Kingdom, compounded the problems caused by the withdrawal of the United States. From 1995, when fundamental aspects of the reform had been completed, UNIDO again had to confront doubts about its continued relevance. Two influential development commentators — Ingvar Carlsson, former Prime Minister of Sweden, and Shridath Ramphal, former Secretary-General of the Commonwealth — published in 1995 a report that proposed that serious consideration be given to closing down UNIDO. It also slated UNCTAD for closure.[11]

Other countries — Australia and Canada — did indeed withdraw from the organization, largely on the grounds that they were not getting value for money.[12] Discontent was also expressed by New Zealand. Many developed countries appeared

---

10   An explanation of the terminology used by UNIDO with regard to technical cooperation is called for at this point. Within any given year, the *value* of approved UNIDO formulated programmes/projects refers to the amount of money approved by UNIDO and/or donors for such programmes/projects. *Funding* refers to all funds (freely programmable and programmed) received by UNIDO for implementation of programmes/projects' through various mechanisms such as UNIDO's own funds, trust funds, IDF, international protocols, international organizations, etc. *Technical cooperation delivery* refers to the actual funds spent (from all sources) during the implementation of all programmes/projects and relates to the provision of expertise, equipment, training, subcontracts, etc. to the recipient developing countries in meeting the objectives of the programmes/projects.

11   Commission on Global Governance, *Our Global Neighborhood: The Report of the Commission on Global Governance*, Oxford: 1995.

12   Report of the Joint Standing Committee on Treaties: *Australia's withdrawal from UNIDO*, 1996; Canada left UNIDO on 1 January 1994.

to have lost, or to be rapidly losing, faith in UNIDO, many for reasons that reflected their own domestic political agendas and priorities.[13]

At the same time, Germany, the largest contributor to UNIDO's 'voluntary funds', expressed strong dissatisfaction and suspended its voluntary contributions, including the provision of Junior Professional Officers (JPOs) and Associate Experts, key staff — young and often extremely capable — who serviced UNIDO's field offices.

UNIDO also faced renewed calls for merger with other UN organizations under scrutiny, principally UNCTAD and UNDP. Furthermore, UNDP funds were dwindling rapidly due to UNDP's own difficulties and its move towards national execution of projects, which was particularly detrimental to specialized agencies like UNIDO which, as we have seen, was very dependent on UNDP funds. Arrears caused by non-payment or late payment of assessed contributions amounted to US$ 98.7 million for 1986–1996, and to US$ 44 million for 1997. Almost half of those arrears — US$ 61.3 million — was owed by the United States, which was no longer a member of the organization.

In addition to the financial difficulties caused by the withdrawal of the United States, by arrears in the payment of assessed contributions and by the significantly reduced funding from UNDP for its projects, UNIDO faced the threat of severe budget cuts demanded by some prominent donor countries, notably Germany and Japan. Cuts of as much as 40 percent were discussed. All these events culminated in a crisis for the organization.

While developing countries remained fully convinced of the need for UNIDO and actively defended its mandate, they also took note of the need for the refocusing and reform of the organization as demanded by the developed and donor countries. It was agreed that this was necessary to better meet their requirements and for UNIDO to function more efficiently and effectively in the new global environment.

## THE MOTIVES BEHIND THE 1997 CRISIS

Many reasons underlay the dissatisfaction of member states, especially major donor countries, which reached boiling point in 1997. These reasons fall into two groups:

1    Emerging trends in the external environment affecting wider multilateral cooperation, which conditioned the general attitude of member states towards UNIDO; and

2    Features of UNIDO itself that gave rise to questions about its relevance and the effectiveness of its performance. Many of these questions were not unfamiliar: they

---

13   Australia – and to a lesser extent New Zealand – wanted to concentrate resources on institutions in the region where they had greater interest and responsibilities. Like the United States and the United Kingdom they both questioned the continued relevance in the changed global context of a publicly funded body devoted to promoting industrial development. The United States position was alleged to reflect a 'strong, anti-internationalist ideological trend in the United States Congress'. See Urquhart, 'Blaming the Storm on the Ship', 1996.

had reared their heads in the general case for reform of the UN. Some, however, were new, especially those that concerned the responsiveness of UNIDO to the needs of its clients.

## BROADER TRENDS AFFECTING MULTILATERAL ASSISTANCE

During this critical period, the economies of the more advanced, richer industrialized countries unexpectedly slowed down. This undoubtedly posed a major challenge to multilateral cooperation. Particularly in Europe, industrialized countries beset by high and rising unemployment, especially amongst the young and unskilled, and under severe pressure to cut fiscal deficits, slashed spending, even in such important areas of social domestic need as health, education and social security. As a result, many of these countries gave less priority to funding international cooperation, and ODA fell, particularly aid channelled through multilateral agencies. Such aid as was given was frequently 'tied'.

This cut in aid through multilateral channels was surprising: given the difficulties brought about by globalization — increasing inequality between countries and social income groups, poverty and its manifestations in social problems, mass migrations, environmental problems and severe dislocations caused by rapid reversals in capital flows. All this might have led one to expect more, not less, enthusiasm for multilateral problem-solving.

Many major donors, convinced of the need for overall UN reform, sought out particular specialized agencies to build their case for, or start the process of, reform. UNCTAD and UNIDO were singled out. It will be recalled that the Commission for Global Governance had recommended the closure of both agencies; other influential commentators urged, if not their closure, then their merger.

In their announcements of withdrawal or threatened withdrawal from UNIDO, the governments of the United States and the United Kingdom raised fundamental questions about the rationale for multilateral cooperation, particularly in promoting industrial development. Specifically, some questioned the appropriateness of considering industry as an engine of development, especially in poorer countries. Others, while conceding the importance of industrial development, doubted whether it needed special support. The question was asked repeatedly: could not industrial development be more efficiently and effectively supported by markets and the private sector? Was a publicly funded body still needed to support industrial development in the new global economy, characterized by widespread liberalization, the primacy of market forces, and the leading role of the private sector in development? After all, did not capitalism triumph conclusively over the command economic system when the Berlin Wall fell and the Cold War ceased?

These arguments, though popular, were based on incomplete knowledge. None the less, important donors to UNIDO believed them, and they informed the criticism of the organization and conditioned the generally negative attitude towards it. This view lay behind the Commission of Global Governance's recommendation to close down the organization. Their report seemed to make recommendations without having had all necessary facts available, including those about the reforms undertaken, and ignored UNIDO's potential as a development organization.

It should be borne in mind that industrial development remains a precondition for long-term sustainable economic growth and social advancement. Industry plays a pivotal role in encouraging technological development; increasing productivity; promoting entrepreneurship; generating employment and income; and in creating sectoral linkages, including those with agriculture and the service sector. In relation to the global economy, manufacturing activity and a continuing rise in manufacturing productivity play critical roles by ensuring export earnings[14].

Needs have changed considerably over the last decade. The increased reliance, world-wide, on the private sector, and the associated deregulation and liberalization of trade and investment, imply needs for services and assistance different from those prevailing where and when industrial development was led by the state. But the need for technical cooperation and services on a non-commercial basis, although altered, has not decreased in the large majority of UNIDO's member countries. The role of the state may have changed from that of a regulator to that of a promoter and facilitator, but industrial growth and efficient functioning of the market still require policies and institutional frameworks that only the state can provide.

Consequently, there continues to be a great need for international assistance to strengthen the governmental system, partly with a view to building up an enabling institutional and organizational framework for private-sector growth, but also more generally with a view to enhancing national capabilities for shaping industrial development. International pressure for industrial and technological restructuring in accordance with emerging standards for environment protection and pollution control adds to the needs for international cooperation and services. The growing significance of quality as a determinant of international competitiveness further reinforces these needs, particularly in areas such as international standard setting and institutional capacity building for quality control.

## INTERNAL PROBLEMS OF UNIDO

UNIDO was undoubtedly seen as 'the specialized agency with one of the worse reputations'[15] where the 'slow and sometimes incorrect or nervous responses of the management continued to increase criticism and reduce [the] confidence of a number of member states.'[16]

Many in top management had been appointed on political grounds, with scant attention paid to their technical or professional competence. Most importantly, the organization had spread its limited resources too thinly and thereby reduced its impact. Despite major reform attempts from 1993, UNIDO's activities continued to

---

14   Prof J. Martinssun  Reforming the UN System p144.
15   *Plan of Action for Active Multilateralism*, 1996.
16   Posta, 2000, p. 1.

lack focus and integration. There had been some geographical focusing on Africa, where most of the LDCs were, but it was felt that the organization still needed to cater for the needs of other countries, both developing and with economies in transition.[17] It was also felt that the geographical focus was vague and did not provide sufficient operational guidance for programming or for selecting among the many requests for UNIDO's services.

Despite having gone through a considerable amount of reform effort and several reorganizations, in late 1996 UNIDO faced the worst crisis of its existence, which reached breaking point in 1997 when it faced the risk of being closed. The main reasons for this were:

☐   Differences of opinion between developed and developing countries on the need for such an organization.

☐   Decline in overseas development assistance via multilateral channels.

☐   Misperceptions regarding the need for state intervention to make industry perform effectively.

☐   Domestic political agendas.

☐   Weak internal management.

☐   Over-reach by UNIDO as it tried to tackle too many issues with insufficient resources.

☐   UNIDO's poor public image.


## THE MEMBER STATES RESPOND

The crisis of 1996–1997 threatened UNIDO's very survival. Urgent action was needed if the organization was to be saved and the confidence of member states restored. Several enlightened member states took a number of steps to rectify the situation in the form of the Business Plan and the 'Danish Assessment' of the organization, as described below.

It was obvious that, if UNIDO was to be saved, member states had to play a more active part, particularly through their permanent missions based in Vienna. Their involvement is an interesting phenomenon in itself. It was not based on any ambitious initiative or even on a conscious decision. The involvement of the missions grew gradually until, 'one day, missions discovered to their surprise that they had a lead role in the reform process'.[18]

Having already commissioned a study in 1992 to determine UNIDO's advantages[19], Denmark announced in 1996 that it would carry out an in-depth assessment

---

17   Assessment of UNIDO, 1997, p. vi.

18   Förster, op. cit., p. 1.

19   *A Future UNIDO. A Study of UNIDO's Comparative Advantages, Areas of Concentration, Organization, and Resources*, 1992.

of the relevance of UNIDO to development for consideration by its member states. This study subsequently played an important role in the development of UNIDO's Business Plan, which became the guiding principle for its work. This study independently arrived at conclusions similar to those of an EU missions' assessment of UNIDO and became available at a strategic moment in May 1997.

The Danish Assessment's final conclusion was that UNIDO was relevant: its services were needed and were in high demand. It was an organization with a future, an organization to which at present no viable alternative was available. The Danish Assessment was very well received not only on account of its thorough, unbiased analysis but also because of its professionalism. The respect accorded to the study helped EU and other donor countries to lend their support to the Business Plan.[20]

## DEVELOPING THE BUSINESS PLAN

A special session of the IDB in 1997 produced a 'Common Ground' paper. This contained a very general formulation of the desired future concentration of UNIDO's activities. It outlined the need to continue the reform of the organization and the key functions it should exercise, and formulated the main programme priorities for its future activities. It urged measures to improve efficiency, and new managerial and organizational structures.

Since a number of member states increasingly lacked confidence in UNIDO's senior management, they did not want the direction of UNIDO's future activities to be left entirely in the hands of the Secretariat. Therefore, in order to find solutions together, member states proposed to establish an Inter-Sessional Working Group[21] of member states that could draw on the Secretariat as resource persons.

The debate that ensued during the Special Session of the IDB underscored the urgent need for a document that outlined clearly and definitively the future of UNIDO. Signals were coming thick and fast that decision makers in donor capitals expected as a precondition for future support of the organization an expeditious and meaningful formulation of UNIDO's future priorities and activities, a significant budget cut and a reconfigured management and organizational structure. Without such reassurances the number of withdrawals would increase, and UNIDO would be marginalized or closed.

Against this background, the Inter-Sessional Working Group met frequently to develop a paper on the 'Future Role and Functions of UNIDO', which became known as the 'Business Plan'. The working group laboured under enormous time pressure

---

20  Förster, op. cit.

21  This section is drawn from Posta, op. cit., pp. 2–3. In addition to their formal deliberations during sessions of the policy-making organs, representatives of member states meet in Inter-Sessional Working Groups to examine specific matters as directed by the governing bodies. Since UNIDO became a specialized agency, its policy-making organs have established a number of working groups with mandates that cover a wide range of issues.

requiring regular interaction with various stakeholders and adopting simple and innovative working methods to ensure involvement of all concerned. The end result was that its work was presented, in the form of the Business Plan, to the Seventeenth Session of the IDB in June 1997, and adopted with very few changes.

The elaboration of the Business Plan was not without its problems.[22] One was the lack of any precedent: in no other UN organization had member states worked out their own schedule for reform. Valid legal questions could be raised: should the aim be a resolution or an amendment to the constitution?

Agreeing on a draft Business Plan was far from easy. There were three fundamental problems.

One was *the scope and focus of activities*. All member states agreed that the old-style UNIDO had catered too much to the often diverging wishes of too many member states. Choices had to be made, and activities limited to those fields in which UNIDO could dispose of real added value in comparison with its 'competitor' international organizations. Elaborate discussions took place before a clustering of activities in two main areas was decided: 'strengthening of industrial capacities' and 'cleaner and sustainable industrial development'.

UNIDO had to focus its activities without losing its universal character in industrial development. While it was obvious that fewer, more focused activities would mean the discontinuation of some activities, many member states were worried that the organization might lose its critical mass of knowledge if activities were too narrowly defined. Identifying activities to be discontinued was difficult and painful, and was only done after long and laborious debate.

A second problem was *the future structure of the organization*. Member states had to tread carefully here as personnel management was within the competence of the Director-General. Taking into consideration various elements, member states opted for a structure consisting of two substantive divisions, then called 'investment promotion and institutional capacity building' and 'sectoral support and environmental sustainability'. It soon became clear to member states that the unavoidable consequence of this structural reform, combined with the announced budgetary restrictions, would be some personnel layoffs. This unfortunate development was much discussed and alternatives were sought, but none were found.

A third problem, closely related to the second, was *the budget*. From the outset it was obvious that it would not be possible to maintain the budget at its current level: if the most important donor in the EU, Germany, was to be kept on board, and another important European donor, the United Kingdom, which had already announced its withdrawal, was to be lured back, a budget cut was unavoidable.

---

22  Förster, op. cit., pp. 2–3; Posta, op. cit., p. 4. For details see UNIDO, *Business Plan on the Future Role and Functions of UNIDO*, IDB.17/Dec.2. The Business Plan was formally adopted by UNIDO's Industrial Development Board on 27 June 1997 and by the General Conference on 4 December 1997 through Resolution GC.7/Res.1.

The size of the cut was also the subject of much discussion. The proposed cut had been set at 40 percent, which many believed would spell the end of UNIDO. In the event, it was decided that the Director-General would be invited to present three budget scenarios based on 10 percent, 20 percent and 30 percent cuts. After long and exhausting negotiations, the General Conference of December 1997 accepted a budget reduction of just over 20 percent — a considerable cut indeed, but the only way out of a discussion that many felt was putting the cart before the horse.[23]

## THE BUSINESS PLAN: OBJECTIVES, STRUCTURE AND PRIORITIES

The challenge for the drafters of the Business Plan[24] was to pin down clear comparative advantages for UNIDO, while avoiding overlap and duplication with other multilateral institutions and bilateral technical assistance.[25] The Business Plan is attached as Annex 2 at the end of the book.

The drafters' objective was to develop:

☐　A clear description of UNIDO's future priorities and activities that would provide unambiguous guidance to the Secretariat for the elaboration of programme and budget proposals. The priorities could also help to restructure the organization.

☐　A set of guidelines and measures that would send a clear and convincing message to the capitals of member states that UNIDO was a very different organization from what it had been, reflecting new political and economic realities and development paradigms.

Another objective of the Business Plan was that it should guarantee political and financial support from member states, and thereby ensure the predictable and stable conditions essential for the future success of the organization.

The Business Plan has four major clusters:

☐　Activities to be carried out by UNIDO in the future.
☐　Activities to be discontinued.
☐　Guidance on the future programme and budget, particularly for the next biennium.
☐　A new organizational set-up for the organization, including field representation.

The Plan proposed concentration on the LDCs, especially in Africa, on agro-based industries, and support of small and medium-sized enterprises as the principal means

---

23　Förster, op. cit.
24　This section is based on Posta, op. cit. and Förster, op. cit.
25　Ikeda, op. cit.

of achieving equitable and sustainable industrial development. It emphasised that UNIDO should provide integrated packages of services and support for the integration of women in industrial development.

Cooperation with other UN agencies, particularly in the field, was emphasised, to encourage a unified field presence and integrated activities. Decentralization to the field was necessary to make the organization more demand-oriented, bring its services closer to its clients, ensure effective programming of technical cooperation at the country level, and deliver technical cooperation services in a timely fashion with greater impact. Strengthening of UNIDO's field presence would mean substantive redeployment of qualified staff from headquarters in Vienna. It also implied that the field presence would have greater administrative and financial autonomy, but that a critical number of staff would remain at headquarters, the two groups interacting extensively.

## LESSONS OF THE BUSINESS PLAN

The Business Plan was the product of an intensive process of cooperative, common thinking. Most commentators agreed that it was a success for UNIDO. It achieved a difficult political compromise and an agreed framework and set of priorities for re-launching the organization. Several lessons were learnt from the development of the Business Plan, which may be of value to others undertaking or supporting similar reforms.

1    First and foremost, the Business Plan was only successful because it was *conceived in a cooperative, consensual process involving the key donor and recipient countries*. It was a kind of common denominator of the future role and functions of UNIDO that gave a chance to focus it on the objectives and specific geographies of the greatest importance to donors and recipients alike. This would not have succeeded without the political will, unprecedented efforts and commitment of all parties to come to a common position and to do so quickly.

The ownership felt by all member states, the cooperative spirit in which negotiations took place, and the responsibility assumed by all parties to reach a solution by consensus together ensured the Business Plan's success.

The Business Plan defined for the first time a focus and a set of priorities for the organization. Without clarity of focus and integration of activities, a reform programme is unlikely to be effective: if the multilateral system is to respond to the challenges of the new century, it needs to continue to modernize. And for modernization to succeed, member states need to work in new ways, focused on specific outcomes best achieved through the multilateral system. The modernization of UNIDO is an example of what can be achieved by member states working together. The emphasis on teamwork gave a much-needed new dimension to the organization.

**2** *Leadership* was important in the success of the Business Plan. It was ably exercised by the chairman of the Inter-Sessional Working Group, the chairpersons of regional groups and other stakeholders. An important lesson is that member states must go beyond mistrust and misunderstanding among themselves on the one hand, and of the Secretariat of a UN Agency on the other.[26]

**3** Bureaucratic structures can be made leaner and at the same time become more efficient. This can be achieved in a relatively short period of time if all partners, developing and developed countries, work in concert along with a strong leadership within the Secretariat.

Without the will to get things started and the leadership to ensure the participation of all the major developed and developing countries and countries in transition, as well as of their respective regional groupings — or at least to ensure consultations between these parties — a difficult consensual solution like the Business Plan would not have been possible.

**4** The Business Plan was drawn up by the member states themselves, but key members of the Secretariat were important as resource persons when needed. The confidence placed in those individuals by member states was instrumental in the achievement of a successful conclusion of the process.

**5** For reforms to succeed, it is important that adequate resources are made available by member states.

A Business Plan should not be seen as set in stone. It is a new focus and set of priorities for particular circumstances and a particular time. It must be re-assessed when these circumstances change or are superseded by other events or priorities.

This said, any adjustment in the scope of activities envisaged in a Business Plan must satisfy two conditions:

☐ The management must have demonstrated visible success in the implementation of the current Business Plan. Such a demonstration strengthens the confidence of donor countries and of member states at large that adjusting the Business Plan to the new realities would add to success.
☐ New priorities must respond to changed political or economic circumstances in recipient countries and have the support of major donor countries.

Both these conditions imply that adjustments to a Business Plan in the short term may be counter-productive. However, re-assessment of a Business Plan in the medium to long term may be not only advisable but also essential to ensure its continued usefulness in guiding effective developmental support.

---

26  Tiwari, op. cit.

# THE VITAL IMPORTANCE OF THE DANISH ASSESSMENT

The pivotal importance of the Danish Assessment in the rebirth of the organization and the development of the Business Plan cannot be underestimated. The frequent references to it are a testament to its importance in UNIDO's transformation process.

The Danish Assessment's positive conclusions about UNIDO in May 1997 were critical in persuading major donors, such as the EU, and other member states, of UNIDO's relevance and viability. It also gave initial, but critical, momentum to the development of the Business Plan. However, the Danish Assessment is not only important for its association with the Business Plan. The conclusions reached in the Danish Assessment also had a positive influence on the German and Japanese attitudes towards UNIDO and on the United Kingdom's decision to remain in the organization.

The Danish Assessment powerfully demonstrated that only a careful examination of facts and analyses would lead to proper conclusions about UNIDO's relevance. Its finding was that 'it is difficult to find justification for abolishing UNIDO on the grounds that its services are not needed'.

The Assessment also argued that it would probably not be cost-effective to merge UNIDO with other organizations, unless 'a priori [this] would result in increased effectiveness, efficiency and responsiveness to client countries' needs.' And the organization was undoubtedly needed, since industrial development remains a precondition for sustainable economic growth and social advancement. Although UNIDO did not have the capability to meet all industrial development needs,

> [n]o other international organization has the same comprehensive experience, technical knowledge and multi-disciplinary expertise for continuing and linking industrial technical cooperation services targeted at both the policy and strategy level, the institutional framework level and the enterprise level.

The Assessment recommended the continuation of UNIDO as a specialized agency, but suggested further cuts in administration and support costs, better focusing and integration of activities, and that special attention be paid to UNIDO's normative functions and global forum role. Important as these conclusions of the Danish Assessment undoubtedly were, arguably what was most important for UNIDO's current transformation process was its finding that UNIDO has a comparative advantage in providing 'integrated packages of services', and that it must emphasise cross-organizational coordination and teamwork.

These observations have been the driving force behind the reorientation of the organization and the development of its new service modules and integrated programmes based on organization-wide teamwork.

# CONCLUSION

UNIDO's progression from Centre for Industrial Development in 1960 to autonomous specialized agency of the UN in 1986 and the varying degrees of support it received over the years from developed and developing countries presents an interesting case study. UNIDO is also an organization that experienced many turbulent phases not faced by any other in the UN system. The organization is also unique in that when its survival was at stake, its member states worked together with the senior management, and other staff, tirelessly in an exemplary manner to rescue it and develop a Business Plan to define its future role.

The reform processes the organization underwent — and particularly the lessons to be learned from them — may be especially relevant and useful to other organizations facing similar challenges of relevance and reform, and to their development partners. Along the way, many approaches were tried — some successful and some not. But the end result is that with the commitment of all stakeholders — member states, senior management and staff — the organization was put on a new dynamic path, which would eventually lead to increased efficiency, relevance, impact and stability in all aspects and provide a guiding example for other organizations, particularly those in the UN system, on how best to achieve a meaningful transformation.

## UNIDO MILESTONES 1956–1997

1956    Establishment of Industry Section in UN
1960    Standing Committee for Industrial Development established by ECOSOC
1961    Centre for Industrial Development established by GA Resolution 1712
1965    UNDP established
        Decision taken to establish UNIDO as a special organ of the UN by GA resolution 20/89
1966    Creation of UNIDO through GA Resolution 21/52
1967    UNIDO formerly established in Vienna, Austria
1975    Lima Declaration on Industrial Development and Cooperation. Plan of Action recommends to GA that UNIDO be converted into a specialized agency
1979    UNIDO constitution adopted at the second session of the UN Conference on the Establishment of UNIDO as a specialized agency, Vienna, Austria
1986    UNIDO formally becomes the 16th specialized agency of the UN
        1st Director-General, Mr Domingo L. Siazon (Philippines)
1993    First attempt at major reforms of UNIDO at Yaoundé 5th General Conference with Mr Mauricio de Maria y Campos (Mexico) as 2nd Director-General
1994    Canada withdraws from UNIDO
1995    United States announces its intention to withdraw from UNIDO
        The Global Neighborhood published
        Commission on Global Governance recommends closing UNIDO down

| 1996 | Australia withdraws from UNIDO |
| | Danish in-depth assessment of the relevance of UNIDO |
| 1997 | Paper on Future Role and Functions of UNIDO prepared, which became known as the Business Plan |
| | Mr Carlos Magariños elected as 3rd Director-General |

REFERENCES

Abdel-Rahman, Ibrahim Helmi, 'UNIDO: historical roots and early years', in *United Nations Industrial Development Organization: 30 Years of Industrial Development 1966–1996*, International Systems and Communications Ltd, London, 1995, pp. 48–54.

*Assessment of UNIDO: Capacity Development for Sustainable Industrial Development Under Changed Conditions*, Final Report, Copenhagen, May 1997.

*Lima Declaration and Plan of Action on Industrial Development and Cooperation*, ID/CONF.3/31,1975, chapter IV, 'Note of the Secretary-General' (A/10112).

Maria y Campos, Mauricio de, 'UNIDO: towards the millennium 1993–1995', in *United Nations Industrial Development Organization: 30 Years of Industrial Development 1966–1996*, International Systems and Communications Ltd, London, 1995, pp. 74–8.

Rahman Khane, Abd-El, 'UNIDO: the new economic order 1975–1985', in *United Nations Industrial Development Organization: 30 Years of Industrial Development 1966–1996*, International Systems and Communications Ltd, London, 1995, pp. 55–62.

Siazon, Domingo L., Jr, 'UNIDO: developing private industry 1985–1993', in *United Nations Industrial Development Organization: 30 Years of Industrial Development 1966–1996*, International Systems and Communications Ltd, London, 1995, pp. 66–73.

UNIDO, *Concluding the Reform of UNIDO*, IDB 15/14, 1996a.

UNIDO, *Impact of Reform: An Outline of Improvements at UNIDO 1994–1995*, GC. 6/30/ADD.1, 1996b.

UNIDO, UNIDO 1993 to 1997: New Challenges, New Directions, Vienna, November 1997.

# CHAPTER 7

# ACHIEVING STABILITY: 1998–2000

The survival of UNIDO was not achieved just with the approval of the Business Plan and an associated cut of about 20 percent in the budget. Member states and the organization continued to work together closely in ensuring that the organization not only followed the Business Plan prescription in both programmatic and managerial terms, including appropriate decentralization to the field, but also in adjusting its strategic direction to meet the new challenges it faced.

Achieving stability required a great deal of work and commitment by the new Director-General of UNIDO (Mr Carlos A Magariños, from Argentina, appointed in December 1997) and his team, the organization's staff, permanent missions and member states at large, who have worked tirelessly together since late 1997 to reverse the past trends and enable UNIDO to achieve the status of an eminent development organization and regain the confidence of the international community. The transformation process that took place since late December 1997 has enabled the organization to achieve relevance, efficiency, effectiveness and stability in all aspects. Today, UNIDO is cited as an example of stability, credibility and performance within the UN system and among its specialized agencies.

The Business Plan approved by member states in late 1997 was critical in establishing new priorities and the future direction of the organization. It also re-established the legitimacy of and political support for the organization, particularly from major donor countries. But it only laid the foundation for UNIDO's renaissance. Much work was needed to stabilize its critical financial situation, implement the Business Plan, refine priorities, streamline the organizational structure, improve management and simplify procedures, refocus and integrate UNIDO's services, and instill a new ethos of teamwork to be more responsive to the needs of UNIDO's clients. In short, UNIDO had to be transformed comprehensively; there were those who still had to be convinced that UNIDO 'made a difference'.

# THE PRINCIPLES FOLLOWED

Building upon the Business Plan and following the guidance given in the Secretary-General's reform proposals for improving UN system-wide coherence and effectiveness, the newly appointed Director-General set out five principles for achieving stability and implementing the Business Plan:[1]

**1**    *A clear sense of where industrial development needs to go in the 21st century and UNIDO's role in this process.* This required a more precise definition of UNIDO's services, transformed through continuous review, improvement and innovation, and with a premium on staff creativity and empowerment, and on transparency.

**2**    *A systemic wholesale approach to the transformation of UNIDO's services, instead of a piecemeal one.* Wholesale rather than incremental changes would ensure systemic transformation, not piecemeal reform.

**3**    *A new culture of teamwork emphasizing multi-disciplinary and multinational, cross-organizational teams.* This new working culture should be based on an increase in cross-organizational cooperation, simplified procedures, decentralization and delegation of authority.

**4**    *Elimination of internal and external overlaps and duplication of activities.* Given the resource crisis and the need to re-establish relevance, UNIDO would need to be more productive and only undertake activities in areas in which it has a comparative advantage. UNIDO should therefore strive to become a centre of excellence in only a few selected areas, and withdraw from other areas. It should seek alliances with other development partners to maximize synergies, and hence developmental impact — UN agencies and other multilateral, international and bilateral agencies. It should cooperate more with the private sector and with civil society — NGOs, industry associations, and research institutions and universities.

**5**    Adoption of the Business Plan as the anchor and beacon to guide all actions. The Business Plan should be the basis of UNIDO's structure and focus. First and foremost, attention should be given to the challenges of industrialization facing Africa and LDCs, but without prejudice to UNIDO's universal mandate.

---

1   The Secretary-General, 'Renewing the United Nations', A/51/950, 1997.

# ADDRESSING THE IMMEDIATE CHALLENGES

UNIDO has made tremendous efforts and sacrifices within the constraints under which it had to operate to achieve stability and become relevant, efficient and effective. During the implementation of the Business Plan the organization faced several serious challenges and dilemmas that needed to be resolved to enable UNIDO to play more effectively its important role. The organization has been taking proactive steps to cope with those challenges and meet the demands placed on it by the various stakeholders. The problems faced by the organization can be loosely grouped under the following headings:

☐ *Financial constraints* resulting from a budgetary cut approved in the Programme and Budgets for 1998–1999 of over 20 percent, together with a precarious cash flow situation.

☐ *Administrative demands* such as significant laying off of staff to remain within the reduced budgetary resources, dealing with low staff morale, and improving the decision-making process.

☐ *Adjusting a management structure* that did not correspond to the Business Plan.

☐ *Achieving closeness to clients* through decentralization and field representation to ensure that their needs are properly assessed and addressed.

☐ *Programmatic changes* required to meet the new demands and priorities for UNIDO's future work given in the Business Plan; reviewing a large number of ongoing fragmented activities without sufficient integration to ensure their focus on the core activities prescribed in the Business Plan; defining UNIDO's dual role as a provider of technical cooperation and global forum activities; and defining a clearer role for UNIDO in the UN system.

In the first phase of the transformation, aimed at achieving stability, the following five sets of challenges were addressed. Many of the actions taken were interrelated and sometimes required concurrent execution.

1    Transformation of financial, administrative and management areas.
2    Achieving closeness to clients (decentralization/field representation).
3    Transformation of programmatic areas and meeting clients' needs efficiently and effectively.
4    Addressing UNIDO's dual role, as a provider of integrated technical cooperation services and as a global forum for industry in which UNIDO acquires and disseminates knowledge of the industrial development process.
5    Improving cooperation with other organizations, particularly within the UN system to achieve synergies, and defining a clear purpose and identity for UNIDO.

# FINANCIAL, ADMINISTRATIVE AND MANAGEMENT AREAS

FINANCIAL

In late 1997 the organization faced one of the most acute financial crises in its history, caused mainly by non-payment or late payment of mandatory assessed contributions by its member states[2]. For the first time ever, the organization announced that it might not be able to meet its obligation to pay the salaries of its staff. In addition it had to resort to suspending or delaying payments to its suppliers and subcontractors for essential and critical services. The organization was on the brink of bankruptcy, with very limited cash resources and a wholly depleted working capital fund, which is meant to protect the organization temporarily from such a situation. This predicament had greatly tarnished the organization's reputation and created a high degree of anxiety and uncertainty among the staff, suppliers and subcontractors, member states and other stakeholders.

Therefore, one of the very first measures was to bring the cash flow under control to ensure that the organization could meet all its financial obligations in a timely manner. To achieve this, the Director-General became personally involved on a day-to-day basis in financial matters by temporarily assuming all responsibilities relating to financial and treasury operations of the organization. This unprecedented move by the Director-General had two main objectives: the first, to bring the financial and cash-flow situation under control and introduce strict controls to avoid recurrence of such a situation in the future; the second, to gain, through reviewing the financial transactions and the supporting documents, hands-on experience of all activities and operations of the organization. This would provide a firm grasp of all issues related to UNIDO's staff, programmes and projects, consultants and experts, travel, subcontractors, suppliers, working arrangements, administrative procedures, control mechanisms, and the roles, responsibilities, authority and accountability of various individuals and organizational units.

The financial and cash-flow situation was stabilized by a number of measures, of which, for the sake of brevity, only a short description of the major measures is provided below:

☐ *Introduction of a cash-flow monitoring mechanism.* This entailed periodic reports showing the cash-flow status for the entire year, broken down by month. It detailed the opening cash balances, cash inflows (actual and expected receipts from payments by member states of their assessed contributions and other sources), the cash outflows (actual and projected) for various types of activities and operations, and the closing cash balances. This mechanism allowed the organization to ensure timely matching of cash inflows and outflows to avoid the recurrence of the situation faced in late 1997.

---

2   See Chapter 3.

☐     *Postponing new commitments.* Most new purchases, subcontracts, consultancy contracts and recruitment of experts, staff travel, etc. were suspended for several months to improve the cash flow.

☐     *Review of existing commitments.* All commitments with consultants, experts, suppliers and subcontractors were reviewed to determine whether these were in line with the Business Plan. Action was taken for the mutual termination of those that were not.

☐     *Collection of assessed contributions.* Member states were actively pursued to pay their current assessed contributions and to settle their outstanding obligations.

☐     *Introduction of a new financial authorization system.* This was based on a simplification of procedures, delegation of authority to mid-management levels, as required by the Business Plan, empowerment of staff and strong accountability mechanisms. The Joint Inspection Unit in its report on the 'Delegation of Authority for the Management of Human and Financial Resources in the United Nations Secretariat' stated the following on the measures introduced by UNIDO: 'Their holistic character could be regarded as a best practice'[3].

## ADMINISTRATIVE

An immediate challenge for UNIDO was to find ways to reduce its workforce by about 20 percent, unavoidable given the budgetary cuts of more than 20 percent approved by member states. This reduction needed to be implemented as soon as possible to limit further financial exposure — and also because, due to uncertainty regarding the status of contracts caused by the adoption of the programmatic focus outlined in the Business Plan, staff morale was at its lowest. Some of the main actions taken in this regard were:

☐     *Implementation of an 'agreed staff separation programme'* within the shortest possible time to deal with most of the separations. Through this agreed approach, many staff concerns were alleviated and staff–management relations improved. This programme was implemented in a very efficient and cost-effective manner: initially costed at US$ 15.9 million, the programme actually demanded less than US$ 10 million, saving the organization nearly US$ 6 million of its precious cash. As no provision for redundancies had been made by member states in the organization's Programme and Budgets for 1998–1999, the staff reduction had to be carried out within the prevailing financial constraints, which placed an additional burden on the limited cash availability. The separation programme was therefore budget-driven and resulted in the retention of a number of staff whose skills were not fully in line with UNIDO's new programmatic focus outlined in the Business Plan. Some of these staffers were retrained, others were subsequently separated under mutually agreed conditions.

☐     *Addressing the low staff morale,* which had arisen from uncertainties regarding the future of the organization, the role of the staff under the Business Plan, and the

3   JIU/REP/2000/6 – Delegation of Authority for the Management of Human and Financial Resources in the United Nations Secretariat.

status of contracts — most of which were for terms ranging from a few weeks to a rare maximum of two years. Following the successful implementation of the staff separation programme, a number of measures were introduced to provide necessary stability for the staff and raise their morale. It is worth mentioning that for a service organization like UNIDO, staff are its only major assets. New and clearer job descriptions were prepared for all staff to define their roles, responsibility and authority as well accountability for results; training programmes were introduced to re-skill the redeployed staff; all staff were given employment contracts for a period of three years; and merit promotion and other measures were introduced.

☐ *Rationalizing the number of committees and administrative 'bulletins' and 'instructions'* to increase administrative and operational clarity. In 1998, for example, the number of bulletins and instructions was cut from some 250 to just five and the number of committees from 110 to five. This led to much simpler, quicker and smoother administrative procedures and a system that greatly simplified operational procedures for the organization, resulting in a marked increase in efficiency and accountability for results.

## MANAGEMENT

Weaknesses in managerial structure and style hindered UNIDO's effectiveness for a long time. An early task of the transformation process, therefore, was to install a new management structure and style within the Secretariat with clear terms of reference emphasizing lines of responsibility, authority and accountability. Furthermore, there was a great need to improve the trust and working relationship between the organization and its member states by improving transparency regarding what the organization was doing and involving and soliciting member states' inputs on various important issues. The main innovations in this regard were:

☐ *A new organizational structure*, in line with the Business Plan, consisting of three divisions, was created. Within these divisions, branches and organizational units specifically dealing with the mandate given in the Business Plan were established. Clear terms of reference emphasizing the lines of responsibility and authority were introduced to ensure accountability for results.

☐ *A management team* drawn from the staff on board was established to lead these three newly established divisions and their branches and units. The required staff were also assigned to these divisions, branches and organizational units in order for them to fulfill their new mandate.

☐ *A new internal senior management structure* consisting of an Executive Board and a Board of Directors was established to improve the cohesiveness and effectiveness of UNIDO's decision-making system and ensure the involvement and participation of all senior staff. Together, these two bodies provided essential support and advice to the Director-General to ensure the smoother running, appropriate direction, management and monitoring of the organization's activities.

☐ *A new management framework, with a regional dimension*, was established to develop and monitor the programmes of services UNIDO offers at the regional and country level. The regional dimension was provided by the Regional Bureaux, whereas the functional dimension was represented by the technical branches. Representatives from both areas work in teams to develop and monitor the programme of services UNIDO offers.

☐    *Retreats for senior managers* were held periodically to discuss key policy and programmatic issues. These retreats contributed to providing advice on the reorientation of the organization and redesign of UNIDO's services. They have proven to be very useful, by providing a platform for frank and open discussions leading to decisions that are well-informed and for which ownership by all involved is felt.

☐    *Workshops* were held regularly for headquarters staff, staff brought in from the field (UNIDO Representatives), high-level representation from member states, eminent outside experts and development practitioners, to provide a new dynamic framework for decision-making. These workshops played a major part in clarifying UNIDO's role in industrial development.

☐    *Enhanced information systems* were developed and are being continuously improved to support programmatic decision-making, particularly to monitor programmes, integrate and strengthen financial reporting and improve communication with Field Offices and Investment and Technology Promotion Offices.

☐    *Enhanced transparency and openness within the organization* was achieved with new measures such as: introducing a policy of public access to all documents; management by personal contact, i.e. the Director-General visiting staff for information and discussion, soliciting individual views and concerns and seeking advice and sharing with them his plan of action; encouraging staff to have direct communication with the Director-General by electronic mail; an open office policy in which staff could freely discuss matters of concern with the Director-General; workshops and meetings with staff to keep them informed of developments and to elicit their views in order to increase their understanding and ownership of the transformation process.

☐    *Informing and involving member states regularly to enhance transparency and improve trust and confidence.* This included: early disclosure of all major policies; prompt distribution of all key information to member states; holding informal meetings with them to discuss all major issues (e.g. financial, administrative and programmatic matters); provision of online information on the organization's website on various matters of key importance to member states, such as the status of member states' obligations to the organization; administrative and programmatic issues; utilization of funds entrusted to the organization; and technical cooperation activities.

## CLOSENESS TO CLIENTS

In order for UNIDO to better address the diversified needs and demands at regional and country levels, the Business Plan called for a more decentralized approach that would bring the organization closer to clients, but without asking member states to provide any additional funding and staffing. This was a response to the criticism that

UNIDO's services tended to reflect the expertise and interests of the staff members preparing programmes and projects rather than the requirements of the client countries. This perception may have emanated from the fact that although UNIDO has always maintained an active corps of field staff, throughout its history it has been perceived primarily as a headquarters organization.

The field network aims to keep field staff in touch with UNIDO's clients, in both the government and the non-governmental sectors. It also helps to take advantage of the increasing decentralization of decision-making by donors to their own field offices. Field staff are well placed to assess their host countries' requirements for industrial development. The main purpose of the field offices is to promote and support technical assistance in order to encourage national capacity-building for industrial development at the level of government, public sector, industrial associations and enterprises. This in turn facilitates local ownership of the organization's integrated programmes. The field offices also have a function in advocacy and mobilization of funds, promoting a better awareness of UNIDO's programmes and activities, and providing on-the-spot evaluations of UNIDO's programmes. Their job is to describe UNIDO's services to a client country, suggest the services that would be most appropriate for its needs and relay this information back to headquarters, so that work can begin on the preparation of a tailor-made programme.

For an organization of UNIDO's size, the number of specialists available in many areas is far too limited to permit deployment of technical staff to regional, let alone national, level. Some of the highly specialized technical skills are not tied to specific conditions in various regions and countries. But with the increasing emphasis on policy advice and institutional strengthening, effective programming and service delivery depend critically on regional and country-level knowledge. There is little doubt that strengthened field offices can add to the relevance and quality of UNIDO's services and help make these services dovetail better with those provided by other agencies.

The organization had to find ways to meet this Business Plan requirement without the provision of additional funding and staffing by member states — a demand made all the more pressing because in 1995 UNDP had stopped providing funding for the UNIDO Country Director Programme, which played a very important role in this endeavor. For instance in 1995, UNDP provided funds for 25 out of 43 Country Directors.

Despite these limitations, UNIDO began at an early stage to decentralize responsibilities and delegate activities to the field offices, taking action to empower them, albeit in a gradual and cautious manner, as mandated by the governing bodies.[4] The organization was not, however, able to move forward as far as it would have wished; the difficulties and challenges in this regard were acknowledged by member states.

Still, in testimony to the importance UNIDO attaches to activities in the field, the organization increased by 44 percent the resources allocated to its field programme in

4   This section is drawn from UNIDO, Annual Report 1999.

the biennium 2000–2001. The primary purpose of this was to strengthen UNIDO's field activities and ensure that its services are driven by demand rather than supply.[5]

By the end of 1999, 23 country offices were headed by UNIDO Representatives, the vast majority of whom had been deployed from headquarters, and five regional offices had also been established. In view of the financial constraints, in a few countries the organization established national focal points. With these measures, UNIDO's field officers drew closer to other UN agencies present in the field and started participating in programming meetings for representatives of different organizations and playing a more active role in the preparation of common country assessments (CCAs).

## TRANSFORMATION OF PROGRAMMATIC AREAS

As the organization developed over the years, it steadily lost focus and engaged itself in an ever-expanding range of activities, sacrificing its effectiveness and impact along the way. By the mid-1990s this trend had led to a proliferation of highly divergent programmes and activities (about 250) and a sharp deterioration in UNIDO's international credibility. This prompted the unprecedented direct intervention by member states in the formulation of a new Business Plan for the organization in 1997.

Since one ultimate objective of the Business Plan is to enhance the relevance, effectiveness and impact of UNIDO's technical cooperation activities, actions in this regard required a variety of administrative reforms aimed at smoothing the programme or project management processes while at the same time increasing the project managers' accountability through improved monitoring and evaluation mechanisms. Similarly, supporting measures were taken to enhance the professionalism of UNIDO's human resources within the selected priority services, through appropriate staff training and recruitment policies. Finally, steps were taken to integrate more fully UNIDO's global forum and research functions with its technical cooperation functions in order to enhance the synergies between these two principal components of the organization's mandate.

UNIDO's basic mission is to help countries pursue sustainable industrial development. This is its specialist role in the UN system. But sustainable development is never achieved easily. It means balancing economic, social and environmental concerns. These concerns are central to the organization. They have become the overarching development goals that focus and guide UNIDO's activities, especially in the light of international concerns about the social and environmental consequences of industrialization. A competitive industrial economy is the long-term driving force of economic and social development. Productive employment is a vital means of generating income and accomplishing social goals such as the reduction of income inequality and poverty. A sound environment is required to ensure an adequate supply of renewable and non-renewable resources and to safeguard human health and the quality of life.

---

5   UNIDO, Annual Report 1999, p. 11; see also UNIDO, Annual Report 1998 and below.

To improve programming and better target the needs of recipients, several criteria to guide the process were developed, which required that technical cooperation should be demand-driven instead of supply-driven; overlaps within the organization and with other organizations should be reduced; and UNIDO should specialize in a limited number of fields. This was achieved in the following ways:

☐ *Product redesign.* All existing programmes and projects were reviewed to see whether they met the following criteria: alignment with the Business Plan; availability of in-house technical staff to carry them out; clear need for the activities by the developing countries; and organizational experience of implementing them in the field. The programmes and projects meeting these criteria were grouped into 16 service modules from a total of 250 existing activities

☐ *Process improvement.* To improve delivery, each service module was assigned to an organizational unit of UNIDO as its core competency. Since the requirements of an individual country in most cases required services under more than one service module, UNIDO had to further refine the way in which it offered its services. This was done through the concept of 'integrated packages of services', which the Danish Assessment had identified as UNIDO's comparative advantage. In the terms of the Business Plan, these packages became 'integrated programmes'.

☐ These integrated programmes are packages of mutually supportive services, which combine the collective experience of UNIDO to help overcome the critical industrial development problems of countries, or of particular geographic areas within a country. They embody the organization's comparative advantage, and are comprehensive yet focused since they are based on the view that it is preferable to tackle only one development objective at a time but address it in all of its dimensions. UNIDO's concept gives emphasis to integration and coordination of efforts at three levels: with the strategies and action of the partner country; with the initiatives of the development agencies and donors; and within UNIDO itself. By channeling UNIDO's limited resources to where they are most needed, the integrated approach increases the efficiency of the assistance provided by the organization, produces a multiplier effect and leads to greater impact.

☐ *Production mechanism and cross-organizational teams:* The preparation of an integrated programme for a country required programming missions to those countries by multi-disciplinary teams with in-depth knowledge of the proposed approach and the development problems presented in requests for assistance from a country. In order to respond to complex problems, the successful production of integrated programmes has been extremely difficult due to the time-consuming nature of the exercise and the difficulty of putting together multi-disciplinary approaches and teams — these programmes are a necessary but complex response to complex problems. These mechanisms have contributed to improved analysis of a country's requirements and teamwork among staff from different disciplines.

☐ *Procedures for design and implementation:* UNIDO guided the implementation of its integrated programmes by means of a detailed manual called 'Guidelines for the

Formulation of Integrated Programmes', which was based on a careful analysis of best UNIDO and international practice. The Guidelines enabled teams to prepare viable and fundable integrated programmes that demonstrably met an expressed need and indicate the steps to be followed, by whom and when.

☐ *Performance measurement:* In order to demonstrate visible impact of UNIDO's programmes to recipients, donors and other stakeholders, UNIDO identified three levels of indicators: *milestones*, the results or products delivered by UNIDO; *success indicators* measuring the changes at the level of the direct beneficiaries, i.e. the pilot enterprise; and *impact*, or changes at the target beneficiaries, i.e. the universe of enterprises in a particular sector or geographic location.

## ADDRESSING UNIDO'S DUAL ROLE

UNIDO has a dual role, as a provider of integrated technical cooperation services and as a global forum for industry in which UNIDO acquires and disseminates knowledge of the industrial development process. The Business Plan confirmed these roles.

Global forum activities embrace the organization's agenda-setting, knowledge-sharing, partnership-promoting role. Well performed, they can build UNIDO's image and make it more visible. But before the transformation, UNIDO's global forum activities suffered from inadequate financial and staff resources, and their messages were insufficiently clear. Not surprisingly, their impact was low.

The transformation of UNIDO's programming methods has refocused the organization in both its roles. Despite the budgetary and other constraints, UNIDO has been able to undertake a wide range of activities beyond the confines of specific technical cooperation projects, to support and promote industrial development. These activities have included initiatives to understand the dynamics of the industrial development process and disseminate, through specialized meetings and publications, the lessons learned about a diversity of industry-related issues. In the course of these activities, UNIDO has promoted partnerships and supported global industrial cooperation, both between developed and developing countries and among developing countries. In doing so, it has facilitated the spread of industrial information, knowledge, technology and investment.

A special focus in UNIDO's reorientation of its global forum activities has been to forge partnerships with universities, research institutions and other civil society organizations. The objective is to help UNIDO acquire a stronger analytical base and at the same time to encourage greater international cooperation in the area of sustainable industrial development in developing countries. This approach also enhanced the normative capabilities of UNIDO — an imperative in the context of both UN reform and today's global economy. The research programme is a direct response to the mandate given to UNIDO in its Business Plan to focus its activities on LDCs, particularly in Africa.

As part of the refocusing of its global forum activities, UNIDO developed a partnership of a different kind. This partnership programme seeks to develop a new approach towards capacity-building for small and medium-sized enterprises, and to do so with major players in the business world who have an interest in strengthening their supply chains.

The key to focusing UNIDO's global forum activities has been the development of an umbrella theme to ensure a clear and consistent message, enhance the organization's image, ensure greater visibility, and economize on resources.

## IMPROVING SYSTEM-WIDE COOPERATION

In the reform and refocusing of the multilateral system, a pillar of UNIDO's transformation has been cooperation with other organizations, particularly within the UN system. This has given UNIDO a clear purpose and identity in the UN system. Previously, UNIDO had suffered from isolation from the rest of the system and a lack of focus. Overlap with other agencies was also a problem. To address these shortcomings and promote cooperation between organizations, UNIDO signed agreements with UNCTAD, UNDP, UNEP, and UNFIP. It also initiated cooperation agreements with WTO, ITC, the World Bank and IMF for the implementation of the WTO Integrated Framework of Assistance to LDCs, aimed at improving their trade sectors and trade-related activities.

UNIDO is firmly committed to systemic approaches and to the Secretary-General's reform proposals. The reforms launched by the Secretary-General have given a welcome new momentum to the UN agenda. UNIDO is also actively participating in the United Nations Development Group Office in New York and in the Expert Group and several task forces of the Millennium Project. An important aspect of UNIDO's transformation is to contribute to the renewal and revitalization of the UN system as a whole.

# DIFFICULTIES ENCOUNTERED

In seeking to implement the Business Plan, UNIDO did whatever was possible within the resources and the time available. Many problems were resolved during this process. However, despite the good intentions and support of all those involved, as would be expected from such a major transformation exercise, a number of difficulties were encountered. These have included:

☐ *Retaining universal mandate and relevance.* The Business Plan stipulated a concentration of activities on African and other least developed countries. This was to some extent justifiable on the basis of a needs assessment and considering the limited resources at UNIDO's disposal. But it raised some difficult questions. How could UNIDO retain its universal mandate with a concentration on selected member countries? How could the organization retain its relevance to other member countries?

UNIDO coped with the inherent contradictions by taking a proactive role in some of the least developed countries and at the same time responding to specific requests from other member countries. However, sometimes the process of prioritization or response was heavily influenced by the availability of funding, whether from donors or — in the form of cost sharing or full payment of services — from middle-income recipient countries.

☐ *Achieving visible impact when dealing with the 'most difficult' cases.* Focusing on the least developed countries, as called for by the Business Plan, posed a major challenge: how to achieve a stronger and more visible impact, as demanded by major donors, when dealing mainly with 'most difficult cases'. As with other types of aid, impact is easier to bring about where the basic preconditions for development are in place. When this is not the case, the difficulties have to be openly acknowledged. This problem is further compounded by donors not providing the required funding for comprehensive programmes of assistance — especially those who demanded a stronger and more visible impact. UNIDO has been trying its best to make headway in bridging these gaps.

☐ *Insufficient funding by donors and their own priorities:* According to the Business Plan, UNIDO should give emphasis to delivering integrated packages of services — for which purpose it developed the integrated programmes. The big difficulty here was that the donors, with very few exceptions, refused to fund programmes as a whole. Instead, they selected for funding only particular components in keeping with their own priorities. This left UNIDO with several programmes where the funding did not reflect the composite needs for support in the recipient countries, and where the complementarity aimed at in the original integrated programmes could not be fully achieved. It is unfortunate that very few donors have adapted their financial support to the new modes of operating that they themselves have demanded from UNIDO.

☐ *Difficulty in shaping UNIDO's actual functioning to the demands of its global forum role and normative functions:* The Business Plan re-emphasized these roles, such as: producing industrial statistics; exchanging experience gained from promoting sustainable industrialization through innovative approaches; providing services in relation to international conventions, norms and standards; and establishing international networks and partnerships that can stimulate economic cooperation among developing countries at different levels of industrialization. However, lack of funding has forced UNIDO to limit its interventions to selected upstream areas.

No other organization has a specific mandate for doing the above in relation to sustainable industrial development in the non-OECD countries. At the same time, there is a need for strengthening the organization's capacity for combining the experience from technical cooperation at country and regional levels with global forum and normative activities such as disseminating knowledge about, and setting standards for, best practices. No other (non-commercial) organization has the same potential for extracting and documenting lessons learnt from industry-related operational activities in developing and transition countries.

☐ *Obstacles to getting closer to clients:* Although the Business Plan called for UNIDO to get closer to its clients, it did not ask member states to provide any additional funding and staffing to achieve this. A number of proposals were submitted by UNIDO to its governing bodies to address this problem, which involved provision of additional resources or the redeployment of headquarters staff to the field. The decision was to follow a gradual and cautious approach. The organization, therefore, was unable to get closer to many clients despite its efforts and good intentions.

☐ *Obstacles to achieving effective system-wide cooperation:* UNIDO has, over time, accrued significant experience in collaboration and entered into a number of agreements with other organizations. It encountered a number of constraints, however, in achieving cooperation with other organizations, despite the supportive spirit that generally prevails. One reason is the far-reaching agenda implied by some agreements. Another is the insufficiency of financial resources.

# CONCLUSIONS

The year 1998 was the one in which many of the measures required to implement the transformation under the Business Plan were introduced. Among them were those taken to: improve the financial and cash-flow situation; reduce over 20 percent of its staff force because of the budgetary cuts; improve staff morale; introduce administrative, management and programmatic reforms and other actions. Many actions were also taken in the subsequent years to further refine the quality control for programmes and activities introduced in the early years. The main objective of these measures was to achieve stability in all aspects and make the organization more efficient, effective, credible, and relevant to meet the challenges set by the Business Plan.

As a result of the above, 1999 was a turning point in UNIDO's history. Not only did it witness the successful implementation of many measures introduced under the transformation drive, but also it saw UNIDO embark on a new, more direct path towards the industrialization of developing countries and economies in transition with a renewed commitment by its staff and member states.

That year also saw the first implementation of the new integrated packages of services based on the service modules. These integrated programmes and other aspects of the transformation of the organization received enthusiastic approval and support of member states expressed in unambiguous terms during sessions of the governing bodies.

The integrated approach to industrial development was founded on the conviction of all stakeholders — governing bodies, donor countries, clients and management — that this was the way to make optimum use of UNIDO's comparative advantage. It is a long-term approach that does not seek or even welcome short-lived 'here today, gone tomorrow' solutions. Rather, in partnership with developing countries and economies in transition, UNIDO designs integrated programmes that will make a lasting difference to their economic and social well-being. It sows the seeds for a strong and stable future.

The stabilization period also saw fundamental changes in the way the organization works. A strict distribution of work by division or branch gave way to interdisciplinary cross-organizational teamwork that involved not only headquarters staff, but also those posted to the field offices. A greater emphasis on cooperation and collaboration introduced flexibility to a previously rigid organizational structure, leading to greater efficiency and synergies. The vision of the staff was broadened beyond their particular field of expertise to envelope the whole gamut of UNIDO's activities.

It takes time to build up a reputation for excellence. UNIDO's service to the cause of industrial development has been buffeted by a chronic shortage of funding and a fundamental change in the perception of its role both by donor and recipient countries. UNIDO has not only weathered the storm but also turned itself inside out to adjust to a new set of global priorities, emerging as a strong, relevant and capable entity, whose reforms were emulated by other larger organizations and whose client orientation was a direct response to the wishes of its member states. Its credentials both as a global forum for a range of issues pertaining to industrial development and a champion of industrialization in the developing countries have never been finer. Whilst striving for continuous improvement, UNIDO draws on lessons learned from the past in order to offer a better future for men, women and children in the developing world and countries with economies in transition.

It takes time and also patience for concrete results to materialize, and those who are anxious for an early harvest may not be fully satisfied. The activities showed a foretaste of future success and that the seeds of industrial development were planted on fertile soil. UNIDO's work has also consisted in laying the foundations for a carefully structured sustainable development process, whilst continuing to improve the management of the organization and its services.

The achievements of the stabilization phase were well summarized by the External Auditor of UNIDO[6] in his final concluding report[7]. He said:

> During my term of office of eight years, I have witnessed the severe difficulties faced by the organization as to its raison d'etre, as well as the resulting uncertainty faced by its staff until the end of 1997. Since then, member states, management and organization's staff have jointly worked hard to reverse this trend and regain the confidence of the international community. I am now pleased to report that the organization has achieved relevance, financial stability, improved technical cooperation delivery and quality of services offered through more focused activities. The future looks promising for UNIDO. My staff and I would like to take this opportunity to extend our good wishes for the future to the organization and its staff.

---

6  The President of the Federal Court of Audit of Germany, appointed directly by member states, who during his tenure witnessed the most critical period in UNIDO's history.

7  PBC.18/3; IDB.26/2, 3 June 2002—Report of the External Auditor on the 2000–2001 biennium.

# CHAPTER 8

# REVITALIZATION AND THE WAY AHEAD

The first phase of the transformation of UNIDO (1998–2000) brought about stability in all aspects required to implement the Business Plan adopted by member states in 1997. The activities carried out during the stabilization phase showed a foretaste of future success. They also laid the foundations for a carefully structured sustainable development process, whilst continuing to improve the management of the organization and its services.

After having reached a state of comparative stability, UNIDO did not rest on its laurels. On the contrary, the very raison d'etre of the organization was examined more deeply than ever before in a whole variety of forums both within and without the organization. This was necessary to obtain a clear sense of where industrial development needs to go in the 21st century and what UNIDO's role should be. UNIDO started to re-specialize and professionalize to ensure further sharpening of the focus of its activities, clarify further its integrated programmes (IPs) to better meet client demands and to ensure that UNIDO plays an important role in fulfilling the new architecture of the international economic system. As a dynamic organization, UNIDO is constantly on the lookout for new opportunities and areas that will enable it to better serve its stakeholders.

All these changes contributed to the birth of a new organization — one that is financially stable to meet the future challenges; increasing technical cooperation delivery; seeing voluntary contributions double; earning increasing commitment and trust by donors and recipient countries; and achieving a high collection rate of assessed contributions. More importantly, it is an organization that is relevant, more client-oriented, modern, flexible, decentralized to the extent possible, and trusted by all stakeholders to meet the challenges envisaged under the Business Plan.

These achievements have not only been acknowledged by the governing bodies and member states of UNIDO, but also been independently confirmed by a comprehensive assessment carried out by a major donor in 2004. More information on this assessment, the first in-depth evaluation of UNIDO since the Danish Assessment of 1997[1], is provided later in this chapter.

The medium-term outlook for the organization therefore looks good. For the Director-General and his senior team, however, this is not sufficient: they consider that a further series of actions and initiatives are required to be taken to sustain the achievements of the past and guarantee UNIDO's long-term future, thus securing its place as a leading specialized agency of the UN system. There is, however, a limit to the productivity one organization can achieve in isolation. In the area of UNIDO's specialization, that limit is imposed by the collective efficiency of the UN system in the field of economic development. For this to be addressed, the UN will have to play a major leadership role in shaping the current economic development agenda.

# REVITALIZATION (2001–2004)

The years 2001–2004 can be characterized as a period of revitalization of the organization — a reward for the hard work and sacrifices made by all associated with UNIDO over the previous years in overcoming the critical situation the Organization had reached. The revitalization of UNIDO offers the opportunity to work together to defeat poverty, inequality and backwardness. The major actions taken during this period in this regard are listed below.

## PROGRAMMATIC ADVANCES

While fully respecting the Business Plan, the re-specialization to further sharpen the focus of UNIDO was carried out in various phases, the purposes of which were to better meet the demands of recipient countries and ensure that activities carried out by the organization were contributing to the MDGs, the UNDAF and CCAs. A number of initiatives were launched to enhance UNIDO's contribution to the achievement of these objectives:

☐ UNIDO's Strategic Guidelines — Towards improved programme delivery (adopted by the IDB in November 2002).
☐ UNIDO's Corporate Strategy (published in August 2003).
☐ Operationalizing UNIDO's Corporate Strategy (published in February 2004).

### UNIDO'S STRATEGIC GUIDELINES[2]

These strategic guidelines, initiated by Japan — the largest contributor of assessed contributions — were adopted by the IDB in November 2002 and set out how UNIDO should implement its medium-term programme framework. The overall

---

1  Assessment of UNIDO — Capacity Development for Sustainable Industrial Development under Changed Conditions, Danida, May 1997.
2  Strategic Guidelines: towards improved UNIDO programme delivery, adopted by the IDB in November 2002 and formally published in March 2003.

aim was to focus and further improve UNIDO's technical cooperation activities in line with the available resources. The planning of activities is required to be within the themes and priorities laid down in the Business Plan and in line with the funds that UNIDO can mobilize for their implementation through existing resources and increased efforts to raise additional funds from new and innovative sources. The Plan stresses that UNIDO's technical cooperation activities should be demand-led and focus on areas where the organization has a comparative advantage. It is also necessary to ensure that activities are developed where appropriate within the context of UNDAF and in such a way that they contribute to the achievement of the MDGs.

These strategic guidelines also encourage the sustainability of the results of development assistance from UNIDO. The transition from aid to self-sustained growth occurs through the promotion of national and local ownership of UNIDO's programmes and by utilizing systems, equipment and facilities that reflect the maintenance and management capabilities of the countries in question. Additionally, UNIDO, wherever possible, recruits experts locally with a view to facilitating the growth and development of indigenous knowledge and capabilities.

The Strategic Guidelines group UNIDO's activities into three areas of focus:

☐ *Strengthening industrial capacities:* To assist developing countries and interested countries with economies in transition to strengthen their institutional capacities to benefit from improvements in market access, and promote the rapid and full integration of these countries into the multilateral trading system. This is to be achieved by: developing programmes for strengthening productive capacities; providing support in the field of standardization, quality control and conformity assessment procedures; and promoting the transfer of technology with a view to enhancing the productivity, competitiveness and quality of the industrial base of all developing regions of the world.

☐ *Cleaner and sustainable industrial development:* To be provided through cooperation with the Global Environment Facility (GEF) in those focal areas where UNIDO has a comparative advantage; to further develop cleaner production activities centered around the UNIDO/UNEP National Cleaner Production Centers (NCPCs), focusing on specific subsectors, including industrial waste and pollution control activities; as well as to help to assess and overcome the negative environmental consequences of industry and mining on water degradation.

☐ *Global Forum activities:* To improve the understanding of how best to use sustainable industrial development to reduce poverty and ensure that the poor benefit from the process of globalization. This should involve both strategic and action-oriented, project-related research to strengthen the systematic promotion of industrial development through UNIDO's technical cooperation programmes in developing countries and countries with economies in transition.

## UNIDO'S CORPORATE STRATEGY[3]

The Corporate Strategy is a conceptual complement to the decisions taken by UNIDO's governing bodies in recent years, particularly the Business Plan adopted in 1997 and the Strategic Guidelines adopted in 2002. The purpose of this document introduced in 2003 is to assist in the further focusing of UNIDO's specialized competences and services in fulfillment of its mandate to promote industrial development and growth in developing countries and countries with economies in transition.

A corporate strategy aims at creating a unique and valuable position for an organization, involving the definition of its priorities and a set of activities tailored to those priorities. The strategic positioning of any organization involves performing activities that are different from those of its competitors or performing similar activities in different ways. A fit among the activities is essential not only for competitive advantage, but also for the sustainability of that advantage. Sustainability comes from the activity system as a whole, not from its isolated parts, and is the key to operational effectiveness.

Given the dynamics of the development process, UNIDO's corporate strategy focuses on productivity growth and the organization's activities are built around this central theme to achieve optimal effectiveness. Productivity enhancement provides the necessary strategic fit across all the activities and interventions.

In order to achieve its dual role of global forum and provider of technical cooperation, UNIDO must focus on the key elements that contribute to productivity enhancement in the development process, and that eventually result in economic, social and environmental wealth. In the context of a market-oriented, globalizing, international economic environment, the provision of global public goods provides the justification and rationale for the operations of multilateral organizations. In the case of UNIDO, these relate to the area of industrial development. More specifically, the creation, transformation and management of knowledge about industry can be considered a global public good, which is the legitimate concern of UNIDO.

This covers areas such as the transfer and upgrading of technology, learning, innovation and the building of skills and capabilities that have a direct bearing on productivity growth. The global forum function also involves: benchmarking industrial performance and identifying international best practices for dissemination; organizing sector- and theme-specific information exchange of experts and decision-makers from different countries and regions; and disseminating knowledge on current and emerging trends, challenges and opportunities to inform policy makers. In doing so, UNIDO draws on in-house and collaborative research as well as the rich pool of experience generated by its technical cooperation programmes.

In this way, the global forum and technical cooperation functions reinforce each other in the quest for relevance, effectiveness and impact. The results of the

---

3  Developing Industry: Productivity Enhancement for Social Advance, August 2003.

global forum function help UNIDO to improve the whole range of its services, while the experiences and insights gained from the technical cooperation activities are factored into the global forum function.

## OPERATIONALIZING UNIDO'S CORPORATE STRATEGY[4]

The Strategic Guidelines and the Corporate Strategy were taken a step further with the issuance in 2004 of a policy paper on how to put them into operation. This document was based on a comprehensive review of the organization's programmatic activities as the foundation of a considered and coherent response to the revised international development objectives, in which the corporate strategy forms the core of the response. This rests on the premise, derived from empirical research and experience, that productivity enhancement, driven by improved skills, increased knowledge and upgraded technology, plays a crucial role in promoting faster growth.

A new approach is proposed that focuses on the promotion of productivity growth as the central theme for its activities, both to optimize their effectiveness and provide the needed strategic fit between them. This approach is aimed at promoting sustainable industrial development by reinforcing the multiple links between entrepreneurship, technology, productivity enhancement and growth, and at facilitating a better conceptual and operational design of the organization's support services.

Based on the underlying strategy of productivity enhancement for social advance, UNIDO is seeking an effective integration between its global forum function — the conceptualization of the current policy challenges facing developing countries and countries with economies in transition — and its approach to technical cooperation on the ground. Here, the strategy provides for UNIDO's intervention to be clustered at two key areas of the organization's comparative advantage: technology diffusion; and capacity-building for market access and development.

## ADJUSTING AND SHARPENING THE SERVICE MODULES TO NEW REALITIES

It may be recalled that at the time of the preparation of the Business Plan, UNIDO had some 250 different types of activities, which during the stabilization phase had been grouped into 16 service modules to ensure better and more focused delivery of UNIDO's services in accordance with the Business Plan. Based on the experience with the implementation of these 16 service modules and to carry out more effectively the mandate given by the governing bodies, the organization undertook a thorough review of its service modules in the latter half of 2001. These services were then reduced to eight service modules in 2002 to make them more consistent with the global development priorities, and the MDGs in particular.

---

4  Operationalizing UNIDO's Corporate Strategy: Services and Priorities for the Medium Term 2004–2007, February 2004.

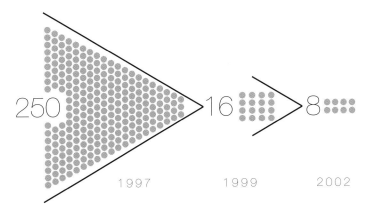

SHARPENING OF SERVICES

250 → 16 → 8

1997          1999          2002

Their modus operandi were also adjusted so as to ensure that their outputs are more closely aligned to the central theme of productivity enhancement enunciated in the document, thus enhancing the synergy and strategic fit between the services. These eight areas are:

- ☐ Industrial governance and statistics;
- ☐ Investment and technology promotion;
- ☐ Industrial competitiveness and trade;
- ☐ Private-sector development;
- ☐ Agro-industries;
- ☐ Sustainable energy and climate change;
- ☐ Montreal Protocol (MP);
- ☐ Environmental management.

This sharpening of UNIDO's services has brought about a number of specific areas of emphasis in the medium term, which has, in turn, led to the identification of a number of priority services within the eight service modules. In order to better define and ensure the effective integration of various disciplines, as well as to bring UNIDO's activities further in line with global priorities, four thematic areas were introduced in 2004. Each programme developed by UNIDO should now fall within one of these themes:

☐ *Poverty reduction through productive activities:* To stem the prevailing trends towards growing inequalities and to fight poverty at its root cause, economic opportunities and productive employment need to be generated in a balanced manner, in which the transition from agricultural to industrial economies is crucial. Entrepreneurship needs to be actively promoted so as to stimulate economic diversification, initially in relation to agro-processing and other areas of adding value to natural resources.

☐ *Trade capacity-building:* Identifying growth-oriented companies and enterprises that have the motivation and ability to enter international markets, and catering to their specific requirements by designing a package of services involving investment, technology, conformity assessment, etc.

☐ *Assistance to countries emerging from crisis situations:* UNIDO specifically contributes to furthering human security with its activities of post-crisis industrial rehabilitation and reconstruction. Revitalizing the industrial sector is one of the major driving forces to achieve socio-economic stabilization after a crisis situation.

☐ *Energy and environment:* Energy is necessary for economic growth. UNIDO's approach to reducing or removing obstacles that hinder access to affordable and sustainable energy in rural areas includes three essential elements: facilitation of access; creation of employment; and technology transfer. Similarly, environmental management is needed for sustainable development. In addition, the impacts of industrial pollution and energy production and use are increasingly being recognized as global issues, climate change being a prime example. Within the framework of UNIDO's corporate strategy and in line with the MDGs, UNIDO's programmes in energy and environment aim at removing the barriers to sustainable development. They emphasize the importance and the need for transfer and diffusion of sustainable technologies to developing countries.

## MEETING THE GLOBAL FORUM CHALLENGES

As mandated by the Business Plan, UNIDO has been actively engaged in a number of global forum activities. These involve both strategic and action-oriented project-related research, which focuses on creating awareness of how sustainable industrial development can contribute to reducing poverty and ensuring that the poor benefit from the process of globalization. Based on the two key areas of UNIDO's comparative advantage identified in the UNIDO corporate strategy — technology diffusion and capacity-building for market access and development — the organization has taken a number of initiatives to meet the challenges. Two principal lines of research selected are the establishment of a database on productivity and economic indicators, and an assessment of the contribution of productivity performance and structural change to poverty reduction. As stated earlier, there is very close synergy between global forum and technical cooperation activities.

During 2003, the *Industrial Development Report*[5] was re-launched as UNIDO's flagship publication, offering a tool to assess the state of world industry. The report focused on the roles of innovation and learning as engines of industrial development and the part played in this by global value chains. There was great appreciation for UNIDO's efforts to develop the Industrial Development Scoreboard, an indicator to benchmark industrial performance, as it is a vital aid to competing in a global economy. UNIDO's call to prioritize innovation and learning for wealth creation and

---

5 Industrial Development Report 2002/2003: Competing through innovation and learning, 2003.

growth promotion was also appreciated. In addition, member states demanded to know what recommendations UNIDO could make both to the poorer countries and to the international community to further their efforts to eradicate poverty.

For these reasons, the second issue of the Report[6] focused on the dynamic processes of productivity growth, wealth creation and social advance in Sub-Saharan Africa (SSA), analyzed in the context of the internationally agreed development goals and targets of the Millennium Declaration and the national poverty-reduction strategies. It pinpointed opportunities and policy options available for the SSA countries to reduce poverty through structural change, productivity growth and diversification, and by building up the institutional and social capabilities essential to overcome adverse initial conditions. The report also updated and expanded the Scoreboard and the advances towards specifying policy initiatives — regarding investment, trade, technology and entrepreneurship — that could be adopted at the country level to achieve effective and profitable integration into the global trading system, taking full advantage of the opportunities offered to the least developed countries by the multilateral rules. An analysis is also made of forward-looking approaches to industrial development that take advantage of environmentally sound and advanced technologies.

These reports are also intended to meet another key demand: that of spelling out, for the benefit of the rest of the multilateral system, the recommendations stemming from UNIDO's work on how to adapt policies so that they can provide better opportunities to the poor countries. It is part of the broader effort to design a concrete proposal to improve the working of the multilateral system. At its core is the adoption of a common Business Plan articulating the efforts of the whole system around the provision of the public goods necessary to defeat poverty, relying on the competencies of the UN specialized agencies, funds and programmes. The reports reflect the progress UNIDO has made along these lines.

## RESULTS OF PROGRAMMES DEVELOPED UNDER THE BUSINESS PLAN

Most of the IPs launched as of 1999–2000 and other activities were evaluated on the basis of a participatory approach by all stakeholders and focusing on the views and needs from the beneficiary countries' perspective. Evaluations provided governments and counterparts, donors, member states and UNIDO management with an in-depth analysis of the relevance, efficiency and results (effectiveness) of these activities, included recommendations for their extension and reorientation as well as lessons learned for an improvement of the approach.

These evaluations have concluded that the IPs have made an impact in terms of raising UNIDO's profile and visibility in the countries in which they are undertaken

---

6  Industrial Development Report 2004: Industrialization, Environment and the Millennium Development Goals in Sub-Saharan Africa, 2004.

and have contributed to a better coordination and consistency of country-level activities, thus confirming that they represent the correct approach to take. This approach is a necessity for the new modalities of multilateral field cooperation, which require stronger cooperation, and harmonization of all UN programmes within the context of PRSPs, CCAs and UNDAFs.

UNIDO's IPs teach that in selecting the industrial objectives to be supported, there is a need to focus. Such an approach is more likely to result in measurable impact within a reasonable time. Given its limited resources, UNIDO can only expect to comprehensively support a few out of the many development objectives that a country may have. The same is true of many other agencies, particularly UN organizations.

The three levels of programme integration — country efforts, external aid and within UNIDO — have increased the efficiency of assistance, produced a multiplier effect, and led to greater impact. While individual components and outputs of a programme may be perfectly viable on their own, it is their integration that provides much of the value added and the catalytic effect. Disintegration of a programme not only negates the effort invested in its preparation but also, most importantly, reduces its potential impact.

Working in teams producing IPs has also provided both an opportunity to develop comprehensive solutions to identified problems and a challenge to established methods of work at UNIDO.

These evaluations, however, noted that in most cases, donors have not yet changed their project-related funding approach and allocate funding for projects and components within the IPs based on their bilateral requirements and priorities. This has been to the detriment of the very nature of integration and resulted in cases where fundamental components could not be implemented due to a lack of funding, while other components that were less central to the programme objectives were implemented because of funds made available by donors. The organization anticipates that new donor funding mechanisms, particularly those developed in response to national poverty reduction strategy processes will have beneficial implications for programme design and funds mobilization activities of the organization.

The evaluations also list the results achieved in terms of outputs and outcomes at the policy, institutional and enterprise level. In many instances, UNIDO has provided high-quality and innovative services leading to excellent results and in some cases even to landmark achievements. In particular, activities aimed at institution building and strengthening led to the best results, underlining the fact that UNIDO's main and most successful line of intervention is institutional capacity-building. The evaluations also showed a strong demand for advice and information on the new role of government in general and the ministries of industry specifically on required policy interventions to enhance competitiveness and productivity growth.

# MANAGEMENT

## RESTRUCTURING UNIDO'S SECRETARIAT

In 2002, a major organizational restructuring was implemented, with the aim of reconfiguring UNIDO's two substantive divisions in a manner to promote coherence of efforts, strengthen a strategic approach and improve UNIDO's delivery and technical capacity. The broader objective was to align the functions, activities and priorities of the organization with the new realities of a changing global economic landscape and to meet the sharpened focus mandated by the member states[7].

The structural change was completed with the appointments of three new managing directors to head the new divisions, who were selected following an open competitive process, which was noted by some observers in the UN system as a 'best practice'. UNIDO now has three divisions with clear terms of reference, responsibility, authority and accountability to fulfill their mandates: the Programme Development and Technical Cooperation Division (PTC); the Programme Coordination and Field Operations Division (PCF); and the Division of Administration (ADM). The results of this change are evident from the improved quality of programmes and projects being developed to meet client needs as well as increased technical cooperation delivery achieved in recent years.

## STRENGTHENING OF INTERNAL CONTROLS

While it was recognized that important steps had been taken by the organization to strengthen its control functions, its governing bodies recommended in late 2002 that further strengthening of the oversight and control functions should be achieved. As a result, the Office of the Comptroller General (OCG) was established in June 2003 to help improve performance and assure accountability. As with the appointment of the managing directors, the position of comptroller general was also filled through open competitive recruitment. As requested by the governing bodies, a charter for OCG was also issued in 2004[8], which, inter alia, provides authority, responsibility and functions of the office and the measures to ensure the independence of the Comptroller General.

This office has overall responsibility for the functions of internal oversight, programme and project evaluation, programme policy monitoring, financial controls, information and communication management, and other relevant areas with a view to, inter alia, promoting improvements in a coordinated manner to ensure the optimal use of the resources available to UNIDO. The office has been conducting proactive systematic reviews and evaluations of all operations of the organization and has been providing independent and objective assessments of the rationale, adequacy, efficiency, effectiveness and impact of these operations and services and on the man-

---

7  Restructuring UNIDO Secretariat (DGB(M).91, 14 Nov 2002.
8  DG Bulletin: Office of the Comptroller General Charter, UNIDO/DGB/(M).93, 6 September 2004.

agement control systems. The office has also been providing independent upstream advice on financial, managerial and programmatic matters, as well as working on strengthening controls in all areas, including information systems, to ensure the integrity of the organization's operations. The office is also taking the initiative of providing advice on results-based management to further improve the organization's accountability.

## IMPROVING THE PROGRAMME/PROJECT CYCLE AND ACCOUNTABILITY

A number of enhancements were introduced in 2004 in order to:

- ☐ Improve the quality control in all phases of the technical cooperation cycle;
- ☐ Enhance effectiveness and efficiency in the management of the technical cooperation cycle;
- ☐ Improve the level of compliance with procedures;
- ☐ Define clear responsibility of staff and managers for the various actions relating to the programme or project cycle and utilization of the resources entrusted to them thus contributing to improved accountability;
- ☐ Improve the relationship between global forum and technical cooperation activities and vice versa, by requiring the strategy to be realigned under the four "thematic areas" and applying the same level of quality control to all activities;
- ☐ Strengthen UNIDO's results-based management processes and management culture.

Four Programme and Project Approval Committees (PACs) comprising most of the senior staff were also established in 2004 as subsidiary bodies of the Executive Board with the mandate to: approve programmes and projects; integrate programmes and global forum activities under their thematic areas of responsibility; and ensure compliance with UNIDO policies, priorities, guidelines, quality standards (e.g. relevance, efficiency, effectiveness, impact, sustainability), regulations, rules and decisions of the governing bodies, as well as to advise the Director-General and the Executive Board on policy, programmatic and funds mobilization matters relating to their areas of responsibility. With these measures, all senior managers from the two substantive divisions, PTC and PCF, are actively involved in the decision-making process of the organization.

In order to achieve the above, in March 2004 an "Interim Management Control Framework for Programmes/Projects" was issued, which shows the required processes and responsibilities in the form of an activity checklist for each stage of the programme/project cycle, as well as the role, responsibility and accountability of the various stakeholders and PACs. A comprehensive set of updated guidelines based on the interim framework, and after consultation with all stakeholders, has been finalized. For the first time in UNIDO's history, this provided detailed consolidated information on all phases of the programme/project cycle, responsibility, authority, accountability and other relevant aspects of all stakeholders relating to the technical cooperation cycle. These comprehensive guidelines replaced all other guidelines and instructions on this subject, thus contributing to the performance and accountability of all involved in the process. Staff will be trained in the application of the guidelines and procedures to further improve the overall performance of the organization.

## IMPROVING STAFF PERFORMANCE

A series of extensive consultations was held by the Director-General with the senior management to further focus UNIDO's technical interventions and to confirm the role, responsibility and accountability of managers. Achieving strategic goals and objectives depends greatly on how well the staff at all levels perform — in particular at the managerial level. In order to pursue managerial excellence, a competency model for managers was promulgated, which established professionalism as one of the core values of the organization. A senior management development programme focusing on strengthening professional excellence was also launched. In addition, a new staff performance appraisal system was introduced. Now, managers have to use these tools to demonstrate the technical and managerial competencies required to fully realize the potential of staff.

In PTC and PCF, managing directors and branch directors are now required to present, on an annual basis, high-quality thematic papers relating to their field of responsibility, which are reviewed by experts and published in relevant technical journals. The quality of these thematic papers is an integral part of the annual assessment of the performance of the staff member. Senior managers have also been tasked with implementing good management practices to enhance the individual performance of staff members as well as enhancing overall organizational capacity. As such, these senior managers are fully accountable for ensuring the sound management of the human and financial resources entrusted to them, and their performance in this regard is assessed. Performance awards have been introduced for high performers, such as managers, support staff and team leaders, in order to recognize their outstanding contributions.

## ENHANCED ROLE OF MEMBER STATES

As a means to facilitate the pro-active participation of member states on issues of major concern to the organization, and to encourage more interaction between the organization and member states, the Director-General and governing bodies introduced a system of informal consultative groups of member states. These groups are chaired by one or two permanent representatives (ambassadors) to the organization; voluntary membership is open to all other interested member states. Their work is supported as and when required by the Secretariat.

Recent consultative groups have included:

☐ *Intersessional working group on proposed amendments to the financial regulations:* This group was established to review the financial regulations of the organization and other financial matters, which required adjustments in view of the many major developments that have taken place in the organization since 1997. Their work greatly contributed to the amendments required to the financial regulations and to improve budget presentations.

☐    *Informal consultative group on voluntary contributions and* UNIDO *membership:* This group was established to assist the organization in improving its ability to meet development challenges by assuring a more stable inflow of financial resources from voluntary contributions, thereby increasing accessibility to development and thus augmenting the predictability of available resources for development purposes. Other issues included the recovery of arrears in assessed contributions and enlarging UNIDO's membership. Their work has contributed to widening the membership of the organization.

☐    *Informal consultative group on trade capacity-building:* The purpose of this group was to assist the Director-General in implementing the UNIDO initiative on trade and market access facilitation. Their work has helped to increase the support of member states for UNIDO's trade capacity-building activities and cooperation with other international organizations, notably WTO.

☐    *Informal advisory group on decentralization (field representation):* The group was established to assist the Director-General in making an informed and transparent decision on carrying forward the process of decentralization in the most cost-effective manner as mandated by the 10th session of the General Conference in December 2003. This group has been instrumental in assisting the organization to proceed with the strategic alliance with UNDP at the field level, which was signed in September 2004.

All groups provide regular reports on their work to the IDB, as well as periodic informal progress reports to all member states during the course of the year. These groups have greatly contributed to enhancing the trust and confidence amongst the organization and member states.

## PROMOTING DIALOGUE THROUGH INDUSTRIAL DEVELOPMENT FORUMS

In order to provide strategic direction for the activities to be carried out and encourage more dialogue on the substantive issues between the organization and member states, a system of industrial development forums or side events to the governing bodies' sessions was introduced. These forums have been regularly held since 1999. As a result, the tradition of such forums has become well established and the discussions on substantive subjects of industrial development held during these events have become an integral and much-respected component of the governing bodies' sessions.

The Industrial Development Forum and the six round tables held during the 10th session of the General Conference in December 2003 was the most ambitious to date, reflecting the importance and complexity of its theme: The Role of Industrial

Development in the Achievement of the MDGs.[9] This topic is considered as critical to ensuring that UNIDO's contributions to international development are firmly embedded in the international development agenda and that the organization remains at the forefront of the development debate. For this reason, UNIDO was able to draw on a wide range of experts including national leaders and senior policy decision makers, as well as leading representatives of multinational organizations, national administrations, academic research institutions and the business community as keynote speakers, panelists and contributors.

Within the six round tables held following the Industrial Development Forum in 2003, discussions highlighted the various aspects of how industrial development has a significant role to play in the achievement of the MDGs. UNIDO believes that it can make a critical direct contribution, through its various technical cooperation and global forum activities to the achievement of four of the eight MDGs:

☐ MDG 1: Eradicate extreme poverty and hunger.
☐ MDG 3: Promote gender equality and empower women.
☐ MDG 7: Ensure environmental sustainability.
☐ MDG 8: Develop a global partnership for development.

## MEASURING PERFORMANCE

The measurement of performance is considered essential to assess the impact of UNIDO's services — whether their intended results are being achieved — and to measure changes brought about by its technical cooperation programme in order to show donors and recipients the validity of the approach used to deal with development problems, as well as its impact.

UNIDO has identified three levels of indicators: *milestones*, which are the results or products delivered by UNIDO; *success indicators*, which measure the changes at the level of the direct beneficiaries (UNIDO's counterparts) usually at the institutional level, but sometimes at the level of pilot enterprises; and *impact*, or changes, at the level of the target beneficiaries (the universe of enterprises in a particular sector or geographic location) in accordance with a country's objectives. UNIDO is continuously improving its programme performance measurement system in cooperation with the other organizations in the UN system.

UNIDO has also made considerable progress in implementing *results-based management*[10], which calls for a holistic management system used by an

---

9 The Role of Industrial Development in the Achievement of the Millennium Development Goals: Proceedings of the Industrial Development Forum and Associated Round Tables, Vienna 1–3 December 2003.

10 UNIDO Annual Report 2003, Chapter VI: Performance Management, 2004; and CRP(GC.10/CRP.5) dated 24 November 2003.

organization to ensure that all its activities contribute towards the achievement of its strategic objectives and that the results of activities are systematically assessed against objectives and targets as a means of continually improving strategy, performance and productivity (the development of the RBM project was partially funded by the UK's Department for International Development, DFID). The experience shows that RBM systems not only improve overall performance, but also increase staff motivation through a better appreciation of the important contribution everyone has to make towards achieving the organization's strategic objectives.

As shown below in the strategy map, UNIDO's RBM system views and measures performance from four perspectives: meeting customer needs by focus on impact and the MDGs; innovation, learning and the development of UNIDO's human resources; the efficiency of UNIDO's internal processes; and funding. This use of RBM is known generically as the 'Balanced Scorecard' approach and UNIDO is amongst a group of forward-thinking aid agencies and organizations that have adopted this type of approach.

UNIDO Strategy Map

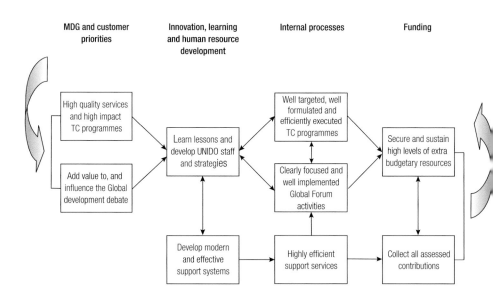

"Taking account of customers priority needs and learning lessons from Technical Cooperation and Global Forum programmes helps UNIDO to innovate, develop its human resources and efficiently deliver the high impact and MDG focused programmes demanded by its customers that are necessary to sustain high levels of extra budgetary resources, and so the cycle continues…"

During the last few years, UNIDO has developed a number of indicators and has been reporting performance improvements in the Annual Reports across each of the four perspectives shown in the above strategy map. These include performance indicators addressing:

☐ Customer satisfaction
☐ Technical cooperation approval and activity analysis
☐ UNIDO staff training
☐ Administrative efficiency and resource use
☐ Funds mobilization

Increased emphasis is being placed on technical cooperation performance reporting, i.e. the 'MDG and customer priority' perspective shown in the UNIDO strategy map. To facilitate improved reporting from this perspective, a systematic and improved method of assessing performance against UNIDO's Business Plan, the Strategic Guidelines, the Corporate Strategy, the Medium-Term Programme Framework, the Programme and Budgets and the MDGs is being developed.

The latter is a challenge faced by all aid agencies. UNIDO's methodology to assess technical cooperation results uses core indicators (quantitative and qualitative) to assess the contribution of UNIDO services at the levels of industrial governance and industrial institutions and support systems that lead to improved industrial capabilities. The methodology shows indirect linkages with aggregate national industrial performance and the MDGs. The framework focuses on five key structural influences on industrial performance — called 'drivers' for convenience. The diagram below describes the framework.

UNIDO's methodology for assessing results

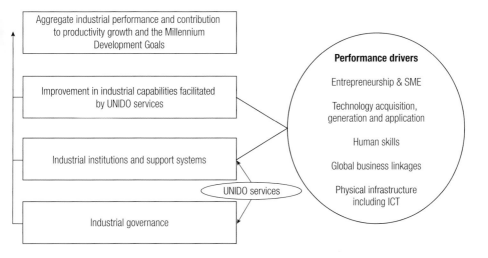

# ADMINISTRATIVE AND FINANCIAL

After achieving financial stability, during the revitalization phase the organization continued to further improve the financial and administrative areas to enhance efficiency and effectiveness and to ensure its financial integrity. Some of these issues, though known, could not be implemented earlier due to priority accorded to achieving stability in all aspects. Some of the notable major measures taken during this period within the available limited budgetary resources (i.e. without requiring additional resources from member states) are the following, which have significantly changed the working methods of the organization and have long-term implications on its operations.

## INTRODUCTION OF THE EURO

As mentioned in Chapter 4, one of the immediate problems faced by UNIDO when it became a specialized agency was caused by the currency it used for budgeting, accounting and reporting — the US dollar — and the currency of its expenditures — the Austrian Schilling (now Euro). At that time, the problems emerged when the US dollar depreciated by about 34% against the Austrian Schilling (ATS). To avoid a recurrence of such a situation and to reduce the impact of exchange-rate fluctuations, the governing bodies of UNIDO then approved a split-currency system of assessment and budgeting. In this arrangement, about 18% of the budget was assessed in dollars and 82% in ATS. The accounting and reporting, however, continued to be in US dollars. This arrangement continued until the end of the biennium 2000–2001 and although it did address the issue of the organization's purchasing power, it also created a number of other problems related to accounting and reporting in US dollars. For instance, in accordance with the financial regulations and rules, different exchange rates had to be used for preparing financial statements and budgetary performance reports, complicating any comparison and analysis between the various financial reports. This also contributed to such problems as significant unrealized gains or losses, poor accountability for resources, etc.

In order to address the above and improve the organization's financial performance and accountability, a single currency system of budgeting, assessment, accounting and reporting based on the Euro was proposed to member states, who after extensive discussions and analysis approved it. This mechanism became effective on 1 January 2002. With this, UNIDO became the first organization in the UN system in Europe to move to such a system. Since then, a number of other organizations, after consultation with UNIDO, have followed suit or are taking actions to do so.

The introduction of the Euro-based single-currency system, combined with the introduction of the new financial computer system, as mentioned below, created a synergy that significantly improved the financial management and controls and enhanced the efficiency and transparency of UNIDO's entire operations for all stakeholders.

# INTRODUCTION OF A NEW FINANCIAL SYSTEM

UNIDO had in place an archaic mainframe computerized system, which was developed more than twenty years ago and no longer met the requirements of the organization. For instance, financial status reports could only be run once a month after a complex monthly closure procedure, then printed and distributed to all concerned one to two weeks after the month-end. Until the next reports were available, programme and project mangers and other users had to keep informal records of their own or rely on memory to carry out the business. This not only caused difficulties in carrying out efficient and effective project management, controls and accountability, but also considerable printing, distribution and other administrative costs.

The organization therefore decided to implement a new state-of-the-art financial performance and control system during 2001. This system was implemented in less than a year and became operational on 1 January 2002 when the Euro was adopted. This major undertaking was carried out without the provision of additional staff or financial resources. The total implementation costs amounted to only US$ 1.7 million, as confirmed by the then External Auditor.

The present and previous external auditors have remarked very positively on this: 'UNIDO [...] has recently seen the introduction of a comprehensive new accounting package. This, by all accounts, including the comments of my predecessor, was carried out particularly successfully with regard to timing and cost.'[11]

The above total cost includes: software, hardware, installation, consultancy, training, project management, travel, acceptance testing and bespoke work. It is estimated that a further US$ 1–1.5 million will be required to complete the migration of all other mainframe systems to modern interactive systems, thus a total estimated cost of about US$ 3.0 million to have modern systems in place.

Although the scopes of the system implementations may differ from organization to organization, and each organization computes IT project costs differently, a comparison with the other organizations in the UN system of the cost of replacing their existing systems[12] is enlightening (all figures are in US dollars):

|  | US$ millions |  |
|---|---|---|
| FAO | 34* |  |
| UNHCR | 30–40 |  |
| WFP | 29** |  |
| ILO | 25 |  |
| UNDP | 23* |  |
| UNESCO | 14.5 |  |
| UNIDO | 3* | *Estimated.  ** Includes global connectivity, hardware, etc. |

---

11   Comment made in the first interim report of the new South African External Auditor, March 2003.
12   Taken from a recent JIU report (JIU/REP/2002/9, Geneva, 2002, Managing Information in the United Nations System Organizations: Management Information Systems) and from the UN ICT Managers forum on the UN System CEB and HLCM site.

As stated above, the system came into effect on 1 January 2002, as planned, and was then rolled out successfully to all in-house staff following intensive internal training. Several field offices also have direct access to the system; it is thus providing all staff with online information on the status of activities for which they are responsible. This has led to greater efficiency in the management of programmes and projects, financial discipline and accountability, as well as improving the organization's ability to better report on various activities at a considerably lower cost to all stakeholders. This has contributed tremendously to the transparency of all operations of the organization. Paper reports are no longer generated on a monthly basis as all required information is available online.

## IMPROVING PROGRAMME AND BUDGET TRANSPARENCY

The formulation of UNIDO's programme and budgets has been guided by the Business Plan, providing the basic programmatic framework and focus of UNIDO activities, which have also taken fully into account the subsequent guidelines approved by the governing bodies to further sharpen the focus of UNIDO activities.

UNIDO's budget is now presented in a programmatic format to better articulate its priorities, objectives, services and costs. Programmes are equated and budgets prepared around the eight service modules as opposed to organizational units, thus greatly improving the transparency of the budget and ensuring accountability for results against the allocated resources.

The Director-General also introduced strict criteria to select programmes and to reject proposals that did not meet the criteria. Programmes are now demand- and not supply-driven, closely tied to the organization's mandate and objectives and avoid internal and external duplication.

For the biennium 2004–2005, the organization for the first time also introduced performance indicators for each programme to assess the results achieved and enhance accountability of the programme managers.

# CLOSENESS TO CLIENTS

The Business Plan called for getting closer to clients through a more decentralized approach that would address their diversified needs and demands at regional and country level. However, as mentioned earlier, no additional funding and staffing was provided to achieve this. During the stabilization phase, a number of proposals were submitted to UNIDO's governing bodies to address the issue, which involved provision of additional resources or the redeployment of headquarters staff to the field. The decision of the governing bodies was, however, to follow a gradual and cautious approach within the available resources. This prevented the organization from getting closer to many clients despite its efforts and good intentions.

While recognizing and taking note of the efforts made by the organization to achieve decentralization within the available resources, UNIDO's General Conference in December 2003 requested the Director-General to carry forward the process of decentralization to the field and further strengthen and rationalize the field operations of the organization. The Conference also requested the Director-General to present additional recommendations on decentralization to the IDB in 2004, following a review of the field operations.

As mandated by the General Conference, OCG carried out an extensive review of the field operations, and concluded that the structure in place was no longer adequate for the prevailing circumstances and did not provide the desired value for money in view of the need for relevance, effectiveness and promptness of action in a fast-evolving environment[13]. The review recommended fundamental changes both in the field and at headquarters, and proposed a number of innovative options to achieve the objectives of decentralization in an efficient and cost-effective manner within the available resources. One of the options proposed was to pursue a strategic alliance with UNDP at the field level, subject to reaching a mutually beneficial agreement, as this would allow a large presence in the field at a much lower cost, enhancing the quality of country-level assessment, in particular its analytical aspects, and strengthen the operational impact of UNDAF. Such a move would also be in line with the UN Secretary-General's initiative to improve the effectiveness of the UN system to ensure that its combined resources are put to the best use, as well as to set a pioneering example to contribute to system-wide collaboration and coherence in the UN.

This proposal was extensively discussed internally, with UNDP and member states. In order to ensure full transparency of the process and participation by all interested member states during the negotiation process, the Director-General established an informal advisory group on decentralization (field representation) of member states under the co-chairmanship of the ambassadors of China and Germany. This group worked closely with the Secretariat. After extensive discussions by the group and the governing bodies of UNIDO, the organization was given the green light to enter into an agreement with UNDP, which was concluded in September 2004[14].

The purpose of this strategic alliance is to develop a joint programme of technical cooperation in the area of PSD, aimed at implementing the recommendations contained in the report of the United Nations Commission on Private Sector and Development[15] and the Corporate Strategy of UNIDO, as well as the development of joint programmes and projects in the other fields of UNIDO expertise. Both organizations will also explore the possibility of joint funds mobilization. UNIDO will provide expertise on issues of sustainable industrial development covering areas like trade capacity-building; investment promotion; agro-industries; energy; cleaner and sustainable industrial development; entrepreneurship; and SME development.

The agreement also defines the scope of cooperation between UNIDO and UNDP at the country level keeping in mind the MDGs and CCA/UNDAF priorities. It defines

---

13   Report on the Assessment/Evaluation of UNIDO's Field Representation, OCG/04/01, 2004.

14   Info Note to Permanent Missions to UNIDO on Cooperation Agreement with UNDP, September 2004.

15   Unleashing Entrepreneurship, http://www.undp.org/cpsd/fullreport.pdf

further the cooperation modalities between UNIDO and UNDP within the parameters of national ownership, as well as how UNIDO expertise will be utilized by UNDP both in the design and implementation of programmes and projects in areas of UNIDO's core competences, funded by various sources including UNDP, MP and GEF.

The new approach will allow UNIDO ultimately to expand its field presence to some 80 countries — at the end of 2004 UNIDO had 29 field offices, and 8 focal points with a limited role; some of these offices were not staffed, as envisaged, due to resource constraints. A roughly threefold increase in field presence will be achieved following a phased approach that will focus on:

☐ The establishment of UNIDO Desks (national/country Offices) in UNDP country offices at locations where UNIDO does not have an office;

☐ The conversion of UNIDO field offices into UNIDO Desks (national/country offices); and

☐ The establishment of UNIDO regional technical centers, and where feasible, joint UNIDO/UNDP regional technical centers.

The phased approach will be implemented by first opening 15 UNIDO Desks (national/country offices) at locations where UNIDO does not have a field presence or at locations where UNIDO activities do not call for maintaining UNIDO field offices. These Desks (offices) will be opened for a pilot phase of two years with financing shared by the two organizations. The value of this agreement will be reviewed within the first 12 months of operation — by November 2005 — which will determine whether the UNIDO Desks have been effective and whether they should continue or be expanded or closed.

This strategic alliance thus fits in with the Secretary-General's plan of reform for the UN, as well as meeting one of the objectives of UNIDO's Business Plan, which called for being closer to the clients to address their diversified needs and demands at regional and country level.

## LESSONS OF UNIDO'S TRANSFORMATION PROCESS

Many lessons can be learned from UNIDO's transformation process. These can be divided into general lessons and those specific to the IPs, the key instrument through which the programmatic transformation was carried out. The general lessons fall into the following — not always mutually exclusive cross-cutting issues:

☐ Leadership
☐ Organizational structure and personnel
☐ Financial, budgetary management and controls
☐ Governance

☐     Coordination and cooperation with other UN organizations, multilateral organizations, and civil society

☐     Public image and public relations

## CROSS-CUTTING ISSUES

Some key factors are:

☐     Transformation needs to be driven and owned by the organization's stakeholders, who must all participate actively in the entire process with full commitment.

☐     Transformation is not a one-off event, but a process.

☐     Recipients of services must be involved from the very beginning in the design and implementation of their programmes.

☐     Tacit values, the intangibles of an organization, need to be considered — these include culture, values, leadership, current and past practices and incentives.

☐     Transformation requires a long-term commitment and sustained political and financial support from all stakeholders — donor and recipient countries alike. There are no quick fixes for successful transformation.

☐     Transformation requires a spirit of shared responsibility and common purpose, a complete re-thinking of priorities, approaches and procedures. It must focus on the positive and must preserve what was good about an organization and abandon what was not relevant.

☐     A new culture of learning and teamwork has to be inculcated so all stakeholders fully understand and share the objectives, and thereby accept ownership of the transformation process.

☐     All stakeholders should be involved in the process to define major focuses, services, and priorities and in their adjustments to keep the transformation on track. All stakeholders, including staff at all levels, need to understand their role and function in a transformation process.

☐     The required structural adjustments should take place at an early stage, and proactive adjustments must be made to meet changing requirements. In UNIDO's case, the empowered Executive Board, the Board of Directors, multi-disciplinary, cross-organizational teams and team leaders played a critical role.

☐     Transformation must be designed and implemented by the management and staff themselves rather than relying on external expertise.

☐     It should be stressed and understood that transformation is not about cutting budgets or staff. It is essentially about *making an organization more responsive to the needs of its clients.*

### LEADERSHIP

High-quality leadership with a clear strategy, vision, management skills, good business knowledge and commitment to the organization's cause is a prerequisite for successful transformation. The leadership must emphasize partnership with staff, donors, recipient countries, member states, other UN, multilateral and bilateral agencies, and the private sector and civil society. The leadership must be decisive and unafraid of taking tough or unpopular decisions.

Priority broad direction setting can, and must, be undertaken by member states, but the organizations themselves, particularly their leaders, must add a strong and easily communicable policy and strategic vision to refine these priorities. This lesson is clearly shown in the experience of the Business Plan, which could not have been implemented without the further refinement given by the Director-General's personal stamp, or his vision of how he wanted the organization to develop.

Leaders need to have at least an appreciation, and should preferably have some experience, of 'change management'; if they do not have such experience themselves, then their senior team must. A capable and complementary senior team is therefore vital.

## ORGANIZATIONAL STRUCTURE AND PERSONNEL

UNIDO's experience shows the necessity of fitting organizational structures to its pro-grammes. The new organizational structure of UNIDO is fully aligned with its programmatic priorities as given in the Business Plan and the further refinements provided by governing bodies. Responsibilities are clearly delineated by terms of reference for organizational units. A new career development system and staff appraisal system is in place. Teamwork is recognized and rewarded. Promotion is based on objective assessment, and first and foremost on merit. Staff and teams need to be given clear and feasible targets to ensure a shared vision and strategy and effective implementation. Recruitment should not be subject to political pressures and external or internal interference.

## FINANCIAL, BUDGETARY MANAGEMENT AND CONTROLS

To ensure an organization's financial integrity, stability and viability, it is critical that a strong financial discipline be maintained. The organization must carefully look into the actual resources expected to be at its disposal and then enter into commitments; these commitments should not merely be based on the budgetary provisions, which experience shows do not always materialize due to member states not paying their obligations in a timely manner or not paying in full.

The Programme and Budget documents must be clearly written and concise. Programmes should be demand-driven with clear indicators to assess performance; they should follow the Business Plan priorities and should not be linked to the organizational structure; they should have definite time limits or 'sunset' provisions so that they remain focused on clearly defined but limited objectives. Member states cannot be expected to support budget priorities and requests for programme funding if they are not clearly communicated.

To improve the organization's performance and assure accountability, it is critical that strong control and monitoring functions be in place, which on a proactive basis should, inter alia: monitor the organization's operations and send early warning signals to management to enable them to take corrective measures in a timely manner; promote organization-wide improvements in a coordinated manner; ensure the optimal use of resources; carry out systematic assessments, reviews and evaluations to provide independent and objective assessments of the rationale, adequacy, efficiency, effectiveness and impact of programmes, services and operations. In the case of UNIDO, such functions are performed centrally in OCG. This has proved an efficient and effective way of carrying out control and monitoring.

## GOVERNANCE

The experience of UNIDO has shown that transformation could be achieved quickly and effectively with clear guidance from member states and direction from governing bodies or 'boards of management' (comprising high-level representatives of member states).

The governing bodies' sessions should be short, businesslike and focused on substantive, rather than political and procedural, issues. UNIDO and its member states have been quite successful in achieving these objectives. However, there is a need to have so-called 'expert boards of management', in which more technical experts attend meetings. UNIDO's approach of addressing this by having the side-events (industrial forums) to the governing bodies' sessions to help guide its policies and strategic direction has been very successful and may also be of interest to other organizations.

On an operational level, UNIDO's experience demonstrates conclusively the need for widespread changes in an organization's strategic and internal management structure and style. Hierarchies must be flattened, transparency increased and effective rules of the game introduced quickly for successful transformation. This is especially required for decentralization and delegation at headquarters and in the field, but also in relations with member states.

Openness and transparency, re-adjustment and improvements — especially by heads of the organizations and senior management — based on real and continuous consultation are the hallmarks of successful transformation.

However, transformation cannot be done in a mechanistic way. It must take into account the characteristics and idiosyncrasies of a particular organization's staff, policies and structures. Each transformation process must therefore be tailormade.

## COORDINATION AND COOPERATION WITH OTHER ORGANIZATIONS

Merely signing declarations of intent and memorandums of understanding is not enough: programmes of cooperation at the working level based on clear delineation of areas of focus are needed. UNIDO's approach was to redesign its services into a few core areas and withdraw from other areas. Practical cooperation between organizations would be facilitated if each organization knew clearly what its comparative advantages were.

UNIDO's increasing reliance on networking with the private sector (for example its Public–Private Partnership programme), research institutes and universities, has maximized the value of resources and improved impact. CSOs should not be forgotten, and innovative strategies and cooperative mechanisms could better integrate CSOs into the work of UN organizations. Recognizing the role of civil society in the current global context should be a priority in any transformation.

## PUBLIC IMAGE AND PUBLIC RELATIONS

To improve image and reputation, a clear and well-targeted communications strategy is required to disseminate best practices and success stories, particularly the impact of the programmes. One difficulty is that development is a long-term phenomenon. It is often hard to demonstrate enough short-term impact to satisfy the demands of some donors and, less often, recipient countries.

A strategy of improving public relations built on success, strengthens the resolve behind an organization and its mandated priorities and programmes, builds up a critical mass of external support, and sets an example for others.

UNIDO established in 2004 a Goodwill Ambassadors programme to improve its visibility, profile and global reach, both with governments and business circles. A number of eminent business leaders and public figures from various regions of the world were appointed in 2004 with the purpose of collaborating in the implementation of UNIDO's activities.

## GENERAL COMMENTS

It would be wrong to assume that UNIDO's transformation was a smooth, painless exercise. That it was not. At the beginning there was considerable 'text book' resistance from some management, staff and organizational units. Morale was low and fell even lower in the early stages of the transformation process due to a number of measures that had to be introduced to bring the financial situation under control and achieve stability.

There was resistance to working in teams or with other specializations. Generalists had initial difficulties in appreciating the concerns of specialists, and vice versa. Branch directors felt their importance and authority compromised by IP teams and team leaders. Technical branches felt their critical mass seriously threatened when their lead specialists were continually called upon to take part in IPs, which necessitated frequent field trips. UNIDO's personnel services felt challenged by the requirement to evaluate and reward teamwork and to overhaul procedures. The organization's financial and IT services were challenged with developing and adjusting procedures and systems to meet the new accounting and reporting requirements. The continual work in retreats, working groups, seminars and other forums in the context of meetings with various stakeholders, also stretched resources; some claimed they were an obstacle to fast and effective programme implementation.

The emphasis on IPs meant that many smaller projects were discontinued, many of them 'pet projects' of individual branches and staff members. It also caused resentment among those whose projects could not fit into this new framework, although on the positive side it intensified competition to get into IPs.

The priority given in the early stages of the transformation process to technical cooperation activities, and cuts in resource allocation to global forum activities such as research, also caused disquiet and dislocations.

Despite these difficulties, UNIDO, with clear direction and sustained commitment, came through its transformation process successfully. This is the major lesson for others: transformation can be achieved through effort and long-term commitment and by working together.

## CHALLENGES FOR THE FUTURE AND THE WAY AHEAD

Although UNIDO's transformation process has been remarkably successful and its results are very encouraging and repeatedly commended by all stakeholders, to continue its pace of change and consolidate the achievements that help sustain it, the organization will have to work on the following fronts:

☐ Ensuring the success of the strategic alliance with UNDP.
☐ Addressing the imbalance between environmental-related projects and other core services.
☐ UNIDO's relationship with the other UN programmes, funds and agencies working in the economic development field.

## ENSURING THE SUCCESS OF THE STRATEGIC ALLIANCE WITH UNDP

UNIDO, as a relatively small organization, does not have the resources to establish an extensive field network of its own. However, the increasing decentralization of development planning and coordination activities by the international development community makes it critically important for UNIDO also to have a corresponding degree of representation in the field if it is to make an effective contribution to the formulation and implementation of such national development frameworks as PRSPs, CCAs and UNDAFs.

After having been caught on the horns of this dilemma for much of its existence as an independent specialized agency, UNIDO in 2004 found an innovative solution to it by entering into a strategic cooperation agreement with UNDP at the field level, which will allow UNIDO to place national or international staff members in UNDP field offices. As mentioned earlier, this agreement provides for the initial establishment of UNIDO Desks (national/country offices) within UNDP premises in 15 pilot countries, with the expectation that this number, in time, will rise as high as 80. In addition, UNDP will support the inclusion of areas of UNIDO expertise in the country-level frameworks referred to above, assist UNIDO in presenting its areas of expertise to national counterparts in order to increase the scope of its programming and make every effort to utilize the services of UNIDO for the design or implementation of programmes and projects related to industrial activities funded by UNDP and associated international protocols.

The signing of an agreement is the first step in addressing the issue, but the major challenge lies in a full commitment at all levels by the two organizations to make this strategic alliance a true success and a model to be followed by the other UN organizations to achieve system-wide synergies, taking into account the comparative advantages of each organization.

## THE IMBALANCE WITH ENVIRONMENT-RELATED PROJECTS

The share of UNIDO's technical cooperation delivery dedicated to the implementation of international environmental protocols and support institutions amounts to about 70 percent of the organization's total technical cooperation portfolio. There is thus an urgent need to redress this imbalance by increasing technical cooperation delivery associated with other areas of its core competencies, such as investment promotion, technology transfer, trade capacity-building, private sector and agro-industrial development, and energy.

Redressing of this imbalance is a challenge of critical importance for UNIDO's future contribution to the achievement of the MDGs, since it is precisely these services that will help developing countries and economies in transition to enhance their productivity levels and generate the growth required to meet the MDGs. There will thus be an urgent need for UNIDO, in close cooperation with its member states, donors and other interested parties, to increase the development and funding of projects in fields other than those related to the environmental protocols. The organization has already begun to take steps in this direction, inter alia, by drawing the attention of its staff, donors, governing bodies, and member states to this issue and encouraging them to promote such programmes and projects. The agreement with UNDP is also expected to contribute to addressing this issue.

## RELATIONSHIP WITH OTHER UN ACTIVITY

As seen in chapter 1, there is a limit to the productivity one organization can reach in isolation. Therefore, the further progress of UNIDO depends on a blueprint on the way forward for the UN system as whole. This is abundantly clear with regard to field coverage and, as stated above, the organization has taken steps to integrate into the UN Resident Coordinator system. For this, however, a clear roadmap needs to be made available for the substantive interventions in the fields listed for UN programmes, funds and specialized agencies. This is the idea behind the reform proposal submitted in this book.

# INDEPENDENT CONFIRMATION OF TRANSFORMATION

Member states have repeatedly acknowledged the organization's commitment to continuously improve its efficiency and effectiveness, and its transformation. These acknowledgments are well documented in various decisions and resolutions adopted by the governing bodies of UNIDO as well as in the statements made by the member states to various sessions of the governing bodies. Furthermore, in May/June 2004, DFID of the UK undertook an independent assessment of UNIDO (see below).

## DECISIONS AND RESOLUTIONS OF THE GENERAL CONFERENCE

The decisions and resolutions taken at the 10th session of the General Conference, the supreme governing organ of UNIDO, in December 2003[16], demonstrate the continued involvement of the governing bodies in the decision-making and monitoring process, as well as recognition of the achievements made by the Director-General and the organization with regard to its transformation. These include:

☐ Confirmation of the Business Plan as the basis for UNIDO's programmatic activities.

☐ Recognition of UNIDO's extensive experience and expertise in promoting industrial development, and especially the success achieved in the delivery of its technical cooperation services during the past six years through such mechanisms as IPs and country service frameworks, individual projects and thematic initiatives.

☐ Acknowledgement of UNIDO's substantive contribution to the achievement of the MDGs through the effective implementation of its Business Plan, the medium-term programme framework and the Strategic Guidelines.

☐ Noting with interest the corporate strategy aimed principally at promoting productivity growth as a means of supporting the achievement of sustainable industrial development and the measures being taken to operationalize the strategy.

☐ Approving the organization's proposal to focus its services on a selected number of priority areas, thus enhancing the impact of UNIDO's services in the field.

☐ Supporting UNIDO's efforts for a greater synergy between its global forum and technical cooperation activities.

☐ Recognizing the ongoing efforts and the significant achievements of the organization to reform and strengthen its administration and implementation capacity for the benefit of developing countries and countries with economies in transition, and to help attain the MDGs.

☐ Noting the significant reforms of the organization and of the achievements of the Director-General in driving through a major organizational and programmatic transformation.

---

16  GC.10/INF.4—Decisions and Resolutions of the 10th General Conference.

☐    Noting the transparent and open process used to appoint senior managers in the organization, as well as of the accomplishments in improving the gender balance in UNIDO.

☐    Requesting the Director-General to continue the good practice of consultations both within the house as well as with member states on important matters to further improve the work of UNIDO.

## STATEMENTS BY MEMBER STATES AT THE INDUSTRIAL DEVELOPMENT BOARD

When reviewing the activities carried out by the organization during 2003 and the first few months of 2004 at the May 2004 session of the Industrial Development Board (which consists of 53 member states elected by the General Conference)[17], member states again noted with satisfaction the developments that had taken place and commended both the Director-General and the Secretariat for the actions taken to successfully transform UNIDO. A synopsis of some of the statements made is provided below:

☐    Noted that UNIDO has managed to strengthen its status as an eminent development organization and has regained the confidence of the international community as the result of a continuing reform process that has brought forth redefined service modules, financial stability, a results-based management approach and the establishment of the Office of the Comptroller General.

☐    Noted that the reform process of UNIDO over the last six years has led to the transformation of UNIDO into an organization that is making a significant contribution to the industrial development of developing countries.

☐    Noted UNIDO's holistic and strategic system of results-based management, which aims to ensure that all its activities contribute towards the achievement of its strategic objectives and that results are systematically assessed against objectives and targets as a means of continually improving strategy and performance.

☐    Supported the focus of UNIDO activities on selected priority areas as agreed at the General Conference while continuing to be of the firm view that UNIDO should consolidate its expertise in specialized niches where it has a clearly recognized comparative advantage.

☐    Acknowledged with satisfaction the fact that, in 2003, various technical cooperation projects of UNIDO received prizes of excellence in specialized international events.

☐    Commended UNIDO, and particularly the efforts made by the Director-General, for active participation in conferences related to South–South Cooperation and to enlarging PSD.

☐    Commended UNIDO for its tireless efforts to improve the socio-economic conditions of developing nations by introducing new technologies, like biotechnology.

---

17  Industrial Development Board, 28th session, 25–27 May 2004; these are excerpts from speeches made by various delegations.

☐    Commended the Director-General on his continued efforts in promoting sustainable industrial development in the developing countries and countries with economies in transition.

☐    Thanked the courageous leadership of the dynamic Director-General, the strong commitment of his team, as well as the unflinching support of the member states, which has allowed UNIDO to stand as an example of stability, credibility and performance among UN's specialized agencies. Now that positive trends have started setting in, the time is ripe for consolidation of gains and capitalizing on strengths.

The above synopsis clearly demonstrates the continued commitment by member states to the work of the organization, their full satisfaction with the results achieved and the high degree of interest placed on ensuring that the focus of its work is further sharpened whenever an opportunity arises.

# INDEPENDENT ASSESSMENT BY A MAJOR DONOR

In May/June 2004, DFID of the UK undertook an independent assessment of UNIDO as part of its assessment on the effectiveness of the 26 multilateral institutions with which DFID has an institutional partnership. In order to achieve this, DFID developed an objective, evidence-based system for assessing and monitoring multilateral effectiveness, which it applied to all 26 multilateral institutions.

Several key principles guided DFID in their development of a multilateral effectiveness framework: the importance of dialogue with the multilaterals concerned; the identification of comprehensive, generic criteria that are applicable despite differences in mandate and structure; reducing subjectivity and using the agency's own information as far as possible; and focusing on strengths and weaknesses and recognizing recent progress. This framework aims to provide a diagnostic tool for analyzing effectiveness in a consistent and objective manner for all of DFID's multilateral partners.

DFID intends to use these assessments for diagnostic and monitoring purposes and to: (a) increase their understanding of the effectiveness of multilateral organizations; (b) provide a basis for dialogue with the organizations concerned within the framework of DFID's institutional strategies; (c) provide an input into DFID's financing decisions; (d) provide inputs into the monitoring of multilateral effectiveness; and (e) participate in a more informed way in discussions with bilateral and other partners on multilateral effectiveness.

The approach followed by DFID covered organizational systems that enable multilaterals to achieve results on the ground. These included: corporate governance, strategic planning, resource management, operational management, quality assurance, management of staff quality, monitoring and evaluation, and reporting. Each of these systems were assessed in terms of internal performance, focus on country-level results and inter-agency partnerships and were carried out using a checklist of indicators for each component, using an adapted Balance Scorecard format. This assessment included 72 indicators at the above three levels.

Out of the 72 indicators used by DFID to assess internal performance, country-level results and inter-agency partnership, 70 were applicable to UNIDO. The following is a summary of DFID's assessment ratings of UNIDO:

| Rating | Description | Number achieved | Percentage |
|---|---|---|---|
| Green | All the assessments are positive | 51 | 73 |
| Amber | There are concerns about some issues, but improvements being put in place | 18 | 26 |
| Red | The assessments are negative, and no plans for improvement yet | 1 | 1 |
| Blue | No information | 0 | – |
| White | Not relevant | 2 | – |

Of those indicators given an 'amber' assessment, mostly at the country level, five are fully or partially addressed to UNIDO's member states and donors; the remaining 13 are addressed to the Secretariat and relate to decentralization (at the time of assessment the agreement with UNDP had not been concluded), risk strategy paper, results-based management/performance indicators, internal oversight and evaluation. Some of these indicators are considered as more important than others and the achievements and actions already taken by the organization are acknowledged. The indicator given a red rating relates to monitoring by the governing bodies as to how the organization supports national PRSPs.

This assessment report by DFID confirms the following: the reform process of the last seven years has greatly increased the cost-effectiveness and relevance of UNIDO and consequently the confidence in the organization by member states; increasing technical cooperation delivery; growing consensus on the strategic direction of the organization; a good integrated approach to programming; increasing demand for services due to a growing recognition of its contribution to the achievement of the MDGs; strong commitment by the Director-General to establish close innovative partnerships with relevant UN and other organizations, as well as his proposal on *The Future of Multilateralism: the way forward in the economic development field*.

This independent assessment again confirms the relevance of the organization, and the turnaround it has made in the last seven years during its transformation by achieving stability in all aspects, at the same time becoming efficient, effective and a credible player with high performance in the international arena.

# CONCLUSIONS

As confirmed by member states, the governing bodies, and the independent assessment, the programmatic, financial, administrative and management reforms introduced since 1998 have resulted in a comprehensive transformation of UNIDO and the restoration of the organization to a position of respect in the development community. This is underlined by a steady increase in voluntary contributions, which have grown from about US$ 50 million in 1998 to some US$ 103 million in 2004. This rise in resource availability is being reflected in a corresponding increase in UNIDO's technical cooperation delivery, which has also rebounded from some US$ 69 million to about US$ 100 million in 2004. These indicators highlight the effectiveness of the programmatic and administrative reforms carried out over the last seven years as well as the renewed commitment by donors and member states to the goals of the organization.

The process of re-specializing UNIDO's services helped the organization to achieve a real concentration on low-income countries in general and sub-Saharan Africa and the least developed countries in particular. By 2004, UNIDO's technical cooperation services to low-income countries accounted for over 73 percent of its portfolio, while in 1996 it amounted to only 48 percent.

The enhanced public perception of UNIDO is also underlined by the relatively high collection rate of assessed contributions, which now amounts to some 92–93 percent in recent years; in the past these percentages varied from 57 to 83 percent. This has allowed the organization to implement a similar percentage of the resources approved in the programme and budgets in the last few biennia. In appreciation of the increased relevance and effectiveness of UNIDO, moreover, a number of new countries have joined the organization in recent years, and many existing member states have expressed their strengthened commitment to it, *inter alia*, by paying their assessed contributions on time and making larger voluntary contributions for UNIDO's technical cooperation programme. In stark contrast to the mid-1990s, even the international media are reporting favorably on the increased significance of UNIDO's developmental contributions following its transformation.

UNIDO plays an important dual role of providing global public goods and directly supporting sustainable industrial development in many countries. The Organization can continue to play a role with the present level of funding and staffing. It could, however, create more impact if additional resources were made available, and by working closer together with other organizations, building on its expertise and particular strengths.

As stated in Chapter 1, it is increasingly evident that the UN system organizations will have to work together if they are to meet international development objectives and achieve the MDGs. This holds particularly true for UNIDO. After almost 7 years UNIDO has reached a point where any future efficiency gains will depend on similar gains throughout the common system and the capacity of UNIDO to both benefit from and contribute to them. UNIDO believes that its reform efforts cannot proceed in isolation. There is a critical need to increase the degree of operational interaction and coordination between the relevant UN programmes, funds and specialized agencies, and the BWIs.

It was against this background that the Director-General of UNIDO, Mr. Carlos Magariños, submitted the proposal outlined in Chapter 1 to the Secretary-General of the United Nations, Mr. Kofi Annan, and the CEB of the UN. He suggested that a "Business Plan to Reorganize and Reinvigorate the UN Economic Development Functions" be set up, on a voluntary basis for the UN system as a whole. Were it to be adopted, the plan, to which the Secretary-General and the CEB concurred, would enhance the supply of development-related public goods throughout the UN system, thus enhancing the ability of the common system to achieve the MDGs.

# ANNEXES

# BUSINESS PLAN ON THE FUTURE ROLE AND FUNCTIONS OF UNIDO

# THE BUSINESS PLAN AS KEY PLAYERS SAW IT

# BUSINESS PLAN ON THE FUTURE ROLE AND FUNCTIONS OF UNIDO [1]

*Adopted by the Industrial Development Board on 27 June 1997 (decision IDB.17/Dec.2)*
*Endorsed by the General Conference on 4 December 1997 (resolution GC.7/Res.1)*

In the context of the ongoing reform process, the present business plan provides the basis for enabling UNIDO to adapt its functions and priorities and orient its activities to the new realities of the changing global economic environment and ensure its viability and efficiency.

UNIDO will concentrate on those support functions in which the Organization has a comparative advantage over other multilateral development organizations and bilateral assistance. Activities will be directed primarily to support institutions rather than to individual enterprises, thus emphasizing upstream activities such as policy advisory services and institutional capacity-building. Support will be provided for the development of SMEs as the principal means for achieving equitable and sustainable industrial development. Emphasis will be given by UNIDO to the integration of women in industrial development.

UNIDO will provide its support primarily in comprehensive packages of integrated services and will further strengthen its existing capacity in this regard through interdisciplinary team-building.

While sharpening its focus in accordance with the above direction, UNIDO should continue to pursue the implementation of its mandates to support and promote the sustainable industrial development of developing countries and countries with economies in transition. Preserving the universal character of the Organization, UNIDO will give special emphasis to least developed countries, in particular in Africa.

Throughout its programmes, UNIDO will promote international industrial cooperation: between developed and developing countries, among developing countries and between developing countries and countries with economies in transition.

---

1 The present text was originally contained in the annex to Industrial Development Board decision IDB.17/Dec.2.

## FUTURE ACTIVITIES OF UNIDO

The activities of UNIDO will be regrouped in two areas:

### A    STRENGTHENING OF INDUSTRIAL CAPACITIES

**1**    Promotion of investment and related technologies;

**2**    Programmes in support of the global forum function and policy advice, including those relating to:

**a**    Industrial policy advice based on action-oriented research;

**b**    Institutional capacity-building at the country and sectoral levels;

**c**    Quality, standardization and metrology;

**d**    Industrial information through networking, including information on the transfer of technology;

**e**    Industrial statistics.

### B    CLEANER AND SUSTAINABLE INDUSTRIAL DEVELOPMENT

**1**    Support programmes on environmentally sustainable industrial development strategies and technologies, including on transfer of environmental technologies within industrial subsectors assigned high priority;

**2**    Development of specific norms and standards relating to environmentally sustainable industrial development strategies and technologies, and implementation of international protocols, agreements and conventions.

The above implies discontinuation of a number of activities:

**a**    Activities in the field of privatization;

**b**    Separate enterprise-level interventions not linked to the institutional or policy level;

**c**    The preparation of project-specific feasibility studies within investment promotion activities, while maintaining a basic training capacity on relevant methodologies;

**d**    Promotion of advanced technologies without proven industrial use;

**e**    Research and industrial studies which are not clearly target-oriented;

**f**    Activities in the field of energy, except those related to improvement of energy-efficiency of industries and to cleaner production;

**g**    Activities in non-agro-based industries (engineering, metallurgical and chemical industries), unless related primarily to environmental issues or to agro-based industries;

**h**    Services in relation to industrial subsectors which have already been assigned low priority;

**i**    General activities related to country-level programming at Headquarters, in light of the future changes in field representation;

**j**    Human resources development activities not integrated in a specific project or programme;

**k**      Emergency relief activities with no industrial development aspect.

The discontinuation of activities will apply to new projects only. It is understood that approved projects will be implemented in accordance with the relevant project documents.

## CONCENTRATION OF ACTIVITIES

While maintaining its universal character and vocation, a geographical, sectoral and thematic concentration of the activities of UNIDO will be pursued by giving added emphasis to the following:

**a**      Services to LDCs, in particular in Africa, with special attention to the regional and subregional level;

**b**      Services in support of agro-based industries and their integration through subsectoral linkages into national industrial structures;

**c**      Services in support of SMEs and their integration into national industrial structures.

## FINANCING AND BUDGET

The format and presentation of the programme and budget document is to be revised to reflect a programmatic approach, in particular by grouping the substantive activities of the Organization into two major programme areas covering (a) the strengthening of industrial capacities and (b) cleaner and sustainable industrial development.

The preparation of the proposed 1998–1999 programme and budgets should be based on the programmes as elaborated in the business plan, reflecting a number of issues, i.e. changes in membership, discontinuation of activities, streamlining the organizational structures and introducing efficiency-enhancing measures. In this respect, an indicative level of 20 percent and 10 percent reduction of the budget is proposed for the preparation of the budget proposals.

Budgetary adjustments are to be achieved by:

**a**      The introduction of efficiency-enhancing measures, including, *inter alia*, outsourcing of some administrative activities, reduction in the number and/or length of policy-making organs meetings, and reduction in non-staff expenditure items, including travel, publications, consultants and meetings;

**b**      The discontinuation of activities;

**c**      The streamlining of organizational structures.

It is understood that the implementation of budgetary adjustments could result in costs for staff separations in the programmes affected.

New approaches to (a) enhance funds mobilization, including cost-sharing arrangements for programmes and (b) promote the timely payment of assessed contributions by Member states are to be pursued.

# NEW ORGANIZATIONAL STRUCTURE

The structure of UNIDO will emanate from the business plan and, based on the two clusters, will include the following substantive divisions: (a) Investment promotion and institutional capacity-building; and (b) Sectoral support and environmental sustainability. A third component will comprise functions related to administration, operational support and coordination of field representation. The Office of the Director-General will include a small organizational unit dealing with functions related to policy coordination, external relations, legal advice and internal audit.

In the interest of ensuring a flat organizational structure, the head of one of the three organizational components will be designated, on a continuing basis, to act as deputy to the Director-General, whose responsibilities shall include coordination within UNIDO and acting on behalf of the Director-General, in the case of the latter's absence from Vienna. Also in keeping with the leaner hierarchical structure, authority will be delegated to the maximum extent possible to the middle-management levels of the Organization, whose role would be accordingly strengthened.

In defining the organizational structure of the Organization, an effective decentralization of activities and strengthened field representation has to be secured. This implies, *inter alia*:

**a**    Redeployment of resources and professional staff with required level of expertise from Headquarters to the field;

**b**    Appropriate delegation of authority;

**c**    Formulation of key functions and responsibilities of field offices.

In this context, subregional offices will be established wherever functionally justified. Contributions from host countries, through cost-sharing or other arrangements, as well as the particular situation of the least developed countries, will be important elements to be taken into account when determining the location of individual field offices.

Functional and programmatic coordination between UNIDO field representation and that of other UN bodies have to be improved. UNIDO country offices will be integrated in a unified UN representation whenever feasible and cost-effective.

# THE BUSINESS PLAN AS KEY PLAYERS SAW IT

The following are extracts of personal reflections from five ambassadors who were intimately involved in the development of the Business Plan: Istvan Posta of Hungary, Hans Förster of the Netherlands, John Freeman of the United Kingdom, Yuji Ikeda of Japan and Yogesh Tiwari of India.[1]

## ISTVAN POSTA

As I recall, the initiators of the proposal did not have a clear vision about how to carry out this work but their intention was to secure the continuous control of the member states between the two sessions of the IDB over the steps to define the organizational structure, aiming at furthering the Common Ground Paper. In decision IDB/S.7/Dec.3., I was requested to establish and chair an Intersessional Working Group to further advance the process of definition of the future role and functions of UNIDO. The adopted mandate was clear but flexible: the Board decided 'to establish an Intersessional Working Group with equitable geographical representation', 'invited member states to continue to contribute to the formulation of basic parameters to guide the work in adapting the organization to new economic realities', and finally requested the Chairman 'to establish a timetable for negotiations and to submit a progress report to the Board not later than its seventeenth session'.

On the very first informal gathering of the diplomats in charge of UNIDO's activity, we agreed not to continue working on the Common Ground Paper, which would involve us in a political or linguistic type of drafting exercise. Rather, we agreed to elaborate a paper giving very practical answers to define the mutually acceptable future role and functions of UNIDO. As an aside let me mention — if I am not misled by my memory — that our Dutch colleague Neline Koornneef proposed the name 'Business Plan' as a temporary title of the document to be elaborated. We all under-

---

1   Istvan Posta, *'Reflections on the importance and role of the consensual solution of the Business Plan to the successful transformation of UNIDO'*, 2000; Hans A. Förster, *'Personal thoughts on UNIDO's reform process as a contribution to UNIDO's study on its reform'*, 2000; John Freeman, *'A United Kingdom perception of UNIDO's Situation'*; Yuji Ikeda, *'In Search of Comparative Advantage'*, 2000; Yogesh Tiwari, *'Solving a Crisis through Consensus and Partnerships'*, 2000. All five Ambassadors have written in their personal capacities. The views expressed in this chapter do not necessarily represent the policies of their governments.

stood what kind of paper it might be, although we thought we would later find a better title. Then during our meetings we concentrated more on substantial issues and finally we got used to this title. At the end of the exercise nobody proposed to change it. The other important agreement was to try to draft one single document with the participation of a limited, but geographically balanced group of countries. Though it might seem very obvious today, I should mention that earlier the usual way of elaboration of any document in UNIDO was to have a draft from the G-77 and a draft from the donor countries, followed by the merging of the two documents through various political compromises. Using the prevailing recognition of the urgency of the situation and the strong determination to find a solution in a short time frame, I encouraged a common drafting procedure, with the participation of all parties concerned. I do believe that our agreement on these two basic starting points played an essential role in the success of this exercise.

...

A very difficult period in the life of UNIDO was over with the adoption of the Business Plan. The Business Plan was a response to a concrete crisis situation when the very existence of the organization was at stake. The response was successful; the member states could elaborate a programme acceptable as a minimum compromise for the developing countries as well as for the donor community to continue the activity of UNIDO through providing services in accordance with the changed economic and political environment. I consider the Business Plan as a political response to the challenges posed by a given political economic situation. It is a compromise the developing countries were ready to accept and the major donor countries were willing to go along with. Obviously, as any compromise, the Business Plan also contains questionable formulations, it is not free from internal contradictions and certainly some of its concrete proposals were not proven by the practice. However, it was not the intention of the authors to elaborate a perfect document but to provide the possibility for UNIDO to continue its activity for the benefit of the member states. And in that sense the Business Plan was a successful and useful tool.

...

Two and a half years later in December 1999, I was invited to attend the General Conference of UNIDO where the Director-General reported on the results and experiences of the implementation of the Business Plan. I could see that while the new management put UNIDO on a new track outlined in the Business Plan, the organization was not free from difficulties either. However, the problems raised are of different nature and in no way connected with the question of survival of the organization. The elaboration and adoption of the Business Plan contributed to this qualitatively new situation.

HANS FÖRSTER

Having gone through a considerable amount of reform efforts and reorganizations in the preceding years, UNIDO faced the worst crisis of its existence in late 1996. At the December session of the Industrial Development Board (IDB), the United Kingdom announced its intention to withdraw from the organization and the Federal Republic of Germany indicated that, unless very drastic budgetary cuts would be effectuated, it would take Britain's (and Australia's and the United States's) example and follow suit. Both countries left their EU partners feeling uncomfortable, as little previous consultation had taken place. Matters such as adherence to international organizations are – and were already then – considered to be subjects on which EU member states should preferably speak with one voice.

It was with no other ambition than to harmonize apparently diverging views within the EU that the incoming EU presidency, the Netherlands, took the initiative of organizing a number of meetings as from January 1997. It soon became clear, however, that these divergences were based on very different appreciations of the work UNIDO had delivered so far. Thus it was decided, after consultation of the EU working group on UN matters, the 'Conun', to try and draft a common 'preliminary assessment' of UNIDO's relevance for past and future development efforts.

EU Permanent Missions rapidly discovered that such an assessment was no easy task and additional expertise was needed. So it was decided to hear the Director-General, then Mr. Mauricio Maria y Campos, his staff members, representatives of the Staff Council, and, particularly, other Permanent Representatives. Thirty to forty interviews later — it is difficult to select just a small number of representatives, the Presidency decided to rather hear as many as possible — we thought we had a fairly clear idea of what the organization meant to the countries directly concerned, what its shortcomings were, what its future could be. Although some EU partners remained more critical than others, all of them helped without reservation in the drafting of the 'assessment' asked by Conun, and the Presidency was indeed able to produce a common paper within the — incidentally, very short — deadline set by the working group. The Assessment opened the way for further support to UNIDO, provided the organization would be able to transform itself.

It took some time to convince UNIDO member states of the necessity of reform considered by the EU to be a condition for continued support. Several Missions voiced concern that this was yet another example of 'donor fatigue' and served no other purpose than the reduction of developed countries' contributions. Fortunately, in the process leading to the conclusion of the 'assessment', Missions had been able to create a climate of mutual trust, overcoming traditional and political cleavages. Ambassadors of important countries, such as India, Pakistan, Sudan, Brazil, Tunisia and many others, helped persuade their colleagues that a revitalization of UNIDO would be in the interest of all, not in the last place of developing countries themselves.

...

Now, more than two years later, the organization has changed beyond recognition. Having borne for so many years the stigma of a 'difficult' organization within the UN family, it has now become one of its most dynamic and rejuvenated members. Shock therapy seems to have worked. All the same, some problems remain, the most important of which is finances. Its budget shrunk, UNIDO depends more than ever on voluntary contributions, which are still slow to come. Developed countries should realize that their commitment to reform must be matched by adequate funding without which the life span of UNIDO will just have been prolonged for a mere couple of years. After all the efforts invested in the revitalization of the organization this would represent a true catastrophe: much of the confidence so painstakingly created would be lost. Moreover, the failure of this example of autonomous reform of a UN specialized organization would no doubt have its repercussions on the reform process of the UN as a whole. UNIDO faces a vicious circle: it needs financial resources to create success stories, but it needs success stories to mobilize financial resources. Donor countries should show more audacity and more confidence in the organization, and give it the chance it deserves.

...

Looking back at the process as it took place in 1997 and 1998, two factors seem to have been of crucial importance.

First, the role of the EU. Although the Union was divided internally, with Denmark on one side, and the FRG on the other side of the spectrum, the others being somewhere in between, it has on the whole been able to speak with one voice, all through the crucial years 1997 and 1998. Perhaps that voice did not always carry a totally transparent message for everyone. But the fact that the subsequent Presidencies (Netherlands, Luxembourg, United Kingdom and Austria) were always able to speak for 15 member states made it one of the key players during this exercise. Without it, no 'rescue operation' of UNIDO would have succeeded. Without the Union, both the FRG and the United Kingdom would almost certainly, and many others most likely, have left the Organization, thus almost certainly condemning it to irrelevance, or even death.

Second, the unprecedented efforts of all Permanent Missions in Vienna. No doubt it was a rare and fortunate coincidence that at this critical juncture in UNIDO's existence so many constructive, patient and dedicated Representatives served in Vienna. They showed that true reform of an international organization need not always come from its management or from New York: it can just as well be 'bottom up' once traditional dividing lines are crossed. In this sense the UNIDO experience is no doubt an interesting case in point for many other international organizations, and in particular those which are in difficulty themselves.

JOHN FREEMAN

UN reform matters. If the multilateral system is to respond to the challenges of the new century, it needs to continue to modernize. And for modernization to succeed, member states need to work in new ways, focused on specific outcomes best achieved through the multilateral system. The modernization of UNIDO is an example of what can be achieved by member states working together.

In 1996/7 UNIDO had to face up to an uncertain future. If the Organization had failed to reform itself, it is doubtful if it could have survived as a separate UN body. The process by which it was reformed is also instructive, not least the ways in which member states in Vienna have worked together with the Secretariat to determine UNIDO's future.

The UNIDO Business Plan grew out of an extended process of consensus building. It was a time-consuming and demanding process based on the realization that UNIDO could not survive without change. But there was a more positive aspect also: there was a chance together to focus UNIDO on the objectives and specific geographies of the greatest importance to donors and recipients alike. Sterile debates, reiterating regional group positions, were largely avoided. There was a focus and a seriousness to the discussions among member states.

Exchanges often cut across customary groupings and positions. There was a common effort to produce practical outcomes and to define the areas in which UNIDO could make a distinctive contribution, reflecting its comparative advantages as a multilateral organization, to sustainable industrial development.

…

The process of change in UNIDO did not come to an end, however, once the Business Plan had been approved and an associated 20 percent budget cut achieved. Member states have a continuing role to ensure that the organization adheres to the Business Plan prescription in both programmatic and managerial terms, including appropriate decentralization to the field.

UNIDO is a small organization that needs to be aware of its limitations and cut its cloth accordingly. It cannot do everything; it cannot operate everywhere. In the next stage of its evolution UNIDO needs to clarify further its new integrated programmes, limit their number (because if there are too many the Secretariat will not be able to implement them) and ensure they work effectively. That is the real test of reform: is UNIDO contributing to the international development targets, is it making a difference? If it is, the process of change on which member states have been engaged with the Secretariat will have been worthwhile and may have lessons for other parts of the multilateral family. For reform needs champions and UNIDO can be one such.

…

The result of these discussions in the form of the Business Plan is well known. But there is an ongoing lesson also: member states are capable of working together on key common objectives which cut across divisions between the North and the South in ways that are beneficial to developing countries.

## YUJI IKEDA

In January 1997, a bilateral meeting between the EU and Japan was held at the Netherlands Mission where an exchange of views on the reform of UNIDO took place and where I presented the Japanese view of the Business Plan. In retrospect, the meeting turned out to be pivotal as almost all the key elements of the Business Plan emerged from the participating donor country ambassadors. The ensuing consultation that the EU and Japan conducted respectively with developing countries, such as the African group in the case of Japan, was characterized by constructive spirit. This same spirit was maintained throughout the period leading to the final substantive agreement on the Business Plan at the IDB in June of that year. This amicable and productive spirit among the players, created throughout the UNIDO process, seemed to have an infectious effect at the meetings of other organs in Vienna, such as IAEA.

...

Given this situation, the donor and recipient countries working together did, in my view, produce a reasonable and respectable set of working programmes, something more than a *modus vivendi*. At the sme time, however, we should not be too complacent about what we have produced. For the continued success of UNIDO, it will be crucial for the Secretariat and member states to implement the Business Plan in a flexible manner so that UNIDO be attuned to the needs of the time.

...

Additionally, I would like to emphasize the importance of the political will of member states, both donors and recipients, to make the Business Plan meaningful by working together with the Secretariat. We look forward to witnessing UNIDO's success stories, which in turn will broaden the basis of support for UNIDO from the governments and business circles of member states.

## YOGESH TIWARI

My basic conviction was to save UNIDO even though I was not clear on how it could be done. As I got involved, I realized that for UNIDO to survive it was imperative that confidence be re-established between the donor countries and the recipient countries. At the same time, UNIDO would have to be restructured and would have to operate with funding at a lower level than previously. I therefore interacted with all major donor countries and gradually convinced the most sceptical among them to look from the perspective of the acutely necessary industrial development of the developing countries. Without the cooperation of the major donors it was not possible. At the same time, the alternative of clear-cut polarization and conflict with the developing countries was not in their own interest, as indeed evidenced by the fact that most donor countries were actually giving aid bilaterally. Therefore, any attempt by the major donors to weaken international cooperation would be understood by developing countries as something against their own interest. Two colleagues who played a role in acceptance of this thinking were the Permanent Representatives of Holland

and of Denmark, and later also the Permanent Representative of the United Kingdom. They also helped to persuade major donors like Germany and Japan to take a more moderate approach.

…

We all agreed that reforming and restructuring UNIDO was necessary to respond to the changing global environment dominated by globalization, privatization and the need for competitiveness. With the developing countries, my first task was to persuade them to accept that UNIDO could not survive without the donor countries' active and willing cooperation. Secondly, there were many developing countries, which had benefited from the services of UNIDO, some of which were not paying their contributions and therefore were not in any moral position to demand earlier levels of contributions from developed countries and the maintenance of the status quo. Over the next months these trends converged and with the exception of a few countries in either camp, the majority of countries were willing and ready to have a consensus solution through a cooperative approach.

…

I think the lesson of UNIDO's case for other UN organizations is to realize that bureaucratic structures can be made leaner and at the same time can become more efficient. All this can be achieved in a relatively short period of time if all partners, developing and developed countries, work in concert along with a strong leadership within the secretariat.

# AUTHOR AND SUBJECT INDEX